Power, Politics and
Performance

Power, Politics and Performance

A Partnership Approach
for Development

by
Winston Dookeran

with contributions from
Manfred D. Jantzen and Avinash Persaud

IAN RANDLE PUBLISHERS
Kingston • Miami

First published in Jamaica, 2012
by Ian Randle Publishers
11 Cunningham Avenue
Box 686
Kingston 6
www.ianrandlepublishers.com

© 2012 Winston Dookeran

ISBN 978-976-637-529-4

National Library of Jamaica Cataloguing-in-Publication Data

Power, Politics and Performance: A Partnership Approach for Development
Winston Dookeran and Manfred D. Jantzen

      p. : ill. ; cm
Includes bibliographical references and index.

ISBN 978-976-637-529-4 (hbk)

1. Economic development – Political aspects
2. Political science – Economic aspects
3. Caribbean Area – Politics and government
4. Political leadership - Developing countries – Economic conditions
5. Sovereignty
I. Jantzen, Manfred   II. Title

330.9   dc 22

Cover and Book Design by Ian Randle Publishers
Printed and Bound in United States of America

Dedicated to the Memories of
Lloyd Algernon Best
and
Desmond Allum SC

CONTENTS

LIST OF ILLUSTRATIONS

FOREWORD

Both inside and outside the Caribbean, the challenge to improve governance as a link to political development and sustainable economic growth, has, over the ages, engaged the acute interest of persons in the academic and political fields alike.

In a fascinating collection of Essays of ideas which span the gamut from Thomas Hobbes to Mahatma Ghandi and against the background of writings from Machiavelli to Marx, the diligent authors of *Power, Politics and Performance* have outlined a convincing case that the best route for the optimum development of Small States requires the dynamics of a Partnership Approach – with its citizens, regional institutions and the global community.

The book clearly identifies the myriad problems which face all Caribbean States: size, the building of human capital, the paucity of natural resources, the vulnerability to natural disasters, and the legacy of our shared history. To these, one may add a number of the dominant concerns facing all mankind in the world today: climate change and global warming; terrorism; trafficking of illegal drugs and illicit arms; the spread of infectious diseases with the dangers of a health pandemic; insecurity within the financial markets; volatility in the terms of trade and investment; and inadequate access to finance and technology. While this publication places the focus on Caribbean nations, it is hardly surprising that the insights and the prescriptions which it provides are in large measure also valid for universal application. The existence of the global village demonstrates that 'No man is an island.'

Everywhere, there is a growing acceptance that the old and traditional style of governance is obsolete. But even though the old order is no longer extant, that new order for which we yearn has yet to be established as a result of constant and cataclysmic changes virtually with each passing day. Consequently, there is still an ongoing search to create a brand new paradigm for the exercise of political power and the management of national economies. To pass the final litmus test, any replacement must be accountable, responsible, inclusive, open and transparent or it will not survive.

Power, Politics and Performance identifies the critical issues which have long been the subject of intellectual discourse and which now require urgent action if we are to chart a course for a safe and prosperous destination. The future prospects for the economic growth and social development of our Caribbean society must be guided by the compass of good governance. It must permit each citizen and broader elements of society to become fully engaged as we strengthen our democratic systems, to ensure the due observance of basic rights and fundamental freedoms for all; as we foster the fulfilment of individual potential and promotion of social well-being for the people.

While this welcome and penetrative work of scholarship is both timely and refreshing, it has yet to pass the exacting test of the political crucible. The joint authors, Winston Dookeran and Manfred Jantzen are no neophytes to the political scene. History does not afford them the unique opportunity of demonstrating how sound theories can be validated by resolute political action and, thereby, effectively secure the transformation which they so ably articulate.

It is high time that the perception of politics as an obstacle to the advancement of the Caribbean be removed. To become the catalyst for meaningful change, politics must be visionary but, yet, pursued through positive activism and principled purpose.

As we completed the first decade of the 21st Millennium, this is indeed the moment to espouse bold concepts which extend the frontiers of our knowledge, that also reflect a full appreciation of what is essential to fashion new political models, engender change and deepen the democratic process.

May this publication serve as an intellectual bridge to span the gap 'between expectations and performance'; to stem the 'rising tension between intention and reality' and most importantly, to make the true art of politics synonymous with good governance.

Most Hon. P. J. Patterson, ON, OCC, PC, QC
Former Prime Minister of Jamaica

PREFACE

This book deals with three interconnected notions or concepts: power, politics, and performance. The work draws upon the experience of the development of political economy with special reference to how performance is influenced by the interaction between power and politics. It represents a collection of essays done over time, but has been brought together by a unifying thread of how to effect policy performance in the world of development. It promotes the idea of a partnership approach in the context of the new politics of coalition experienced in many countries, most recently in the United Kingdom and in Trinidad and Tobago.

We argue for a partnership approach, expressing a philosophy of collaboration and a consensus-based political economy for small states. We identify the imperatives for development challenges for financial stability and the structures required for building a knowledge-based economy through regionalism; and we explore issues facing small developing states and their sovereignty. We also focus on key issues of leadership and the political processes suggesting that in the end, leadership is about finding solutions and such solutions require radical transformation of political parties and political institutions. Leaders must understand the global information environment. We examine and analyse specific problems and distortions in small states and deal with the challenge of building effective leadership.

I have benefited enormously from my political involvement in the politics of Trinidad and Tobago over the years, but more specifically since the formation of the new political party, the Congress of the People, in 2006. It is my search to get the politics right in a society in which politics had imprisoned my people that lead to my political activities, which culminated in a change in government in Trinidad and Tobago.

This change represents a point of departure and promise on how power should be exercised; these challenges have intensified as issues of nation building and sovereignty come to the fore. Working with Manfred Jantzen, we have together developed some distinct insights into the practice of leadership which we believe may be applicable to many small states that have emerged in search of a new paradigm for politics and economy.

Winston Dookeran

ACKNOWLEDGEMENTS

We would first like to thank the Foundation for Politics and Leadership which facilitated our collaboration and provided a mechanism through which some of our ideas were developed; and the Congress of the People and the People's Partnership which are the practical expression of our political philosophy and our vehicle to realign the politics in this small island state of Trinidad and Tobago. The Lawrence Duprey Research Grant to The University of the West Indies has generously contributed to making parts of this project a reality, especially those dealing with executive leadership and the Ministry of Finance of Trinidad and Tobago kindly offered its hospitality in facilitating our project in the summer of 2010.

Senator the Honourable Timothy Hamel-Smith, President of the Senate of Trinidad and Tobago, and a leading lawyer and partner at M. Hamel-Smith and Co., through the *Foundation for Politics and Leadership*, provided valuable insight in chapter six 'Coalition Politics and Good Governance' in realigning the politics of Trinidad and Tobago. Alvin Curling, Senior Fellow at the Centre for International Governance Innovation (CIGI) and former Speaker of the Ontario Legislature in Canada, in many fruitful discussions proposed and shaped the reforms outlined in chapter four, 'Foundation for Politics and Leadership'. We would also like to thank Dr Ricardo Hausmann, who is the Director of the Center for International Development and the Professor of the Practice of Economic Development of Harvard University, for his workshop given at the Finance Ministry in July 2010. His ideas contribute to a section in chapter two 'Getting Development Right'. Professor Avinash Persaud authored chapter nine; and Dr Manfred Jantzen authored chapters one and five and contributed to other chapters as indicated in the footnotes.

We would like to thank Chateram Rambally, Vashti Guyadeen, Charlene Hanooman, Lisa Henzell, Krystle Mahase and Darryl Dean who provided valuable assistance with earlier drafts and publications from which this book emerged, and Kiran Mathur, who assisted in researching and editing. Pia Reinert helped us in the final effort to get the manuscript ready for publication and we thank Dr Halima-Sa'adia Kassim for final editing.

Last but not least, we thank our wives Shirley and Ruth for their unwavering support in hectic times.

INTRODUCTION
A PARTNERSHIP APPROACH TO DEVELOPMENT

Mahatma Gandhi's 'Seven Blunders of the World' include: wealth without work, pleasure without conscience, knowledge without character, commerce (business) without morality (ethics), science without humanity, worship without sacrifice, and politics without principle.[1]

A Historical Perspective

The *Partnership Approach* to distributing power, and entrenching good governance and development in small states, is rooted in political philosophy. Throughout history, political theorists have examined two core questions: By what right or need do people form states? What is the best form for a state? A consensus eventually emerged that 'the state' would refer to a set of enduring institutions through which power is distributed and its use justified. 'Government' would refer to those who manage state institutions and create the laws by which the people, including the governors, would be bound according to the social compact.

Sovereignty is a foundational idea of politics and law and rests on two concepts, supreme authority in the state and on political and legal independence of geographically separate states. It is a modern notion of political authority and the state is the political institution in which sovereignty is embodied. It focuses on independence and justice. Stephen Krasner outlines four ways in which sovereignty has traditionally been understood in the literature. These are: interdependency sovereignty; domestic sovereignty; international legal sovereignty; and *Westphalian* sovereignty.[2]

Thomas Hobbes articulated how a social contract, that justifies rulers' actions (even when contrary to the individual desires of the governed), can be reconciled with sovereignty. John Locke, like Hobbes, described a social contract theory based on citizens' fundamental rights in the state of nature. Unlike Hobbes, he believed that in a natural state, man would form a society in which moral values are independent of government authority and widely shared to general benefit.

Immanuel Kant argued that participation in civil society is not merely for self-preservation, as Hobbes believed, but a moral duty.

He was the first modern thinker who fully analysed the structure and meaning of obligation; arguing that an international organisation was needed to preserve world peace. Far more pragmatic and somewhat consequentialist, Machiavelli's politics held good and evil as the mere means to an end of a secure and powerful state.

The Indian philosopher Chanakya, (c.350–283 BCE) described four ways to achieve that power and stability; namely, acting with equality, enticement, punishment or war, and the sowing of dissent. In the development context, these ideas, whilst sometimes sound for preserving stability and sovereignty, must be tempered by a code of conduct for the leader, so that the dangerous possibility and hubris of absolute personal power is averted, and the futile, circular nature of seeking power for its own sake is avoided.

In the 20th century, long after the 1648 *Westphalian* consensus establishing the modern state, Friedrich Hayek argued the inefficiency of central planning in response to the overwhelming state role in Marxist states, and the dominance of Keynesian economics. Members of central bodies could not know enough to match consumers' and workers' preferences with existing conditions.

Hayek further argued that central economic planning – a mainstay of socialism – would lead to a 'total' state with tyrannical power. He advocated free market capitalism in which the main role of the state is to maintain the rule of law. Development in small states must move away from outdated and restricted quasi-socialist notions to recognise the power of markets in driving economic growth, whilst recognising the special need for pragmatic regulation and inclusiveness in the developing world.[3]

According to Matthew L. Bishop and Anthony Payne,[4] the Caribbean construction of sovereignty and statehood rests on the peculiar attachment of these island states to national sovereignty in spite of the pressing need to create more effective regional institutions. The apparent strength of insular identities, directly derived from the distinctive West Indian experience of statehood, continues to sustain an enduring conceptualisation of sovereignty which is both narrow and considered to be the sole preserve of national leadership. Furthermore, this concept has been reinforced by political leadership reflecting a highly personal style which makes compromise difficult.

Figure A: Partnership Approach Model

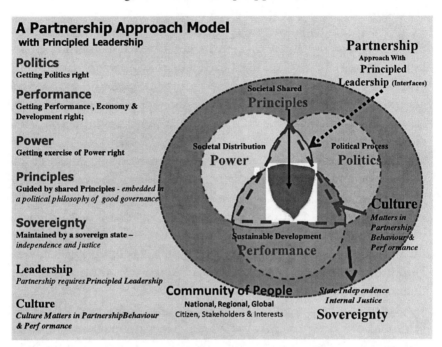

Change and development requires the interaction and expression of power as politics – with the latter's definition the foundation to our philosophy of political collaboration. This naturally leads to the concept and imperatives of sovereignty and regionalism – vital for small, recently independent states, which must be able to compete. Yet political power is quickly distorted and maligned. To combat this, we propose principled politics built into the system at ground level by a flexible and action-oriented leadership.

The Partnership Approach

The concept of partnership has evolved and cannot continue to be concerned with only its narrower personal application. Partnership must now refer to broad social and political applications in local, regional, and global contexts. This includes international economic partnership and the building of social and political contracts on local and international scales. Indeed, one of the United Nations

Millennium Development Goals is to develop a global partnership for development.

We expand the concept of partnership to describe a new style of political leadership, focused on bringing together communities and interest groups to further the development of a small nation state. Our concept of partnership will also embrace coalition politics and government. The *Partnership Approach* outlined in Figure A represents synergies of politics, power, performance, and principles at the core, all in the development context.

The *Partnership Approach* applies on four distinct levels to co-ordinate a network of participating stakeholders. The first is on the global stage and is particularly concerned with regional communities of interest. The second is at the societal level and involves a social compact, with community and citizen participation. Then there is partnership on the organisational level, involving both public and private stakeholders. Finally, there is the individual level, where partnership involves leadership, teams and small self-organising groups.

Together, these dimensions continuously evolve and reflect the behaviour of a complex-dynamic system. The nature of society's drivers and entities is less important than the connections between them; the relations between the economy, social interest groups and international influences should be the target for analysis and development. Solutions grow out of interaction between these entities and any institutions emplaced should foster collaboration. This system throws out unintended consequences which, in order to be addressed, require enlightened leadership and a working partnership with critical segments of society. Our approach is the most inclusive and effective one to foster small states' development.

A Sustainable Performance Framework

We define sustainable development as development that meets the needs of the present without compromising the ability of future generations to meet their own needs. For small states, getting sustainable development and performance right is a critical dimension of the *Partnership Approach*. The sustainable development and performance challenge can be conceptually expressed in several ways.

Figure B: Sustainable Performance Framework

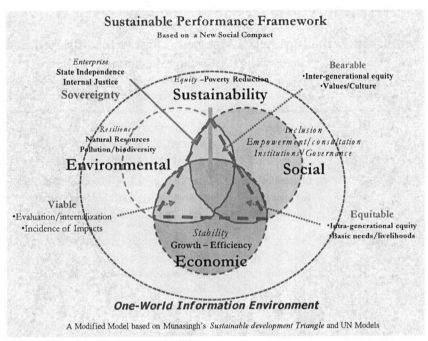

A Modified Model based on Munasinghe's *Sustainable development Triangle* and UN Models

Figure B shows a perspective on sustainable development based on 'Munasinghe's Sustainable Development Triangle'[5] and a UN model illustrating the key elements and connections between environmental, economic and social concerns. Our Sustainability Model also includes the sovereignty of the state and the *One-World Information Environment*.

Another perspective views sustainable development and performance as a national process with critical components in which each component not only represents a complex adaptive system itself but also is an interconnected, interrelated, interactive, and integrated element of the whole. Here, sustainable development is a function of people, resources, wealth, infrastructure, state, and leadership. This conceptual formula can serve as an approach to evaluate the contribution of each component to the overall national development. Each component can be assessed as driver and/or obstacle to sustainable development. This assessment should initiate strategic thinking or more precisely, complex system thinking, to develop a strategic plan with relevant actions and measurable impact results.

This book is guided by the *Partnership Approach*, and the interdependent dimensions with strategies and goals outlined in Figure C:

Figure C: The Partnership Approach: Dimensions with Strategies, Goals with Measurable Outcomes

Dimensions	Goals	Strategies and Measurable Outcomes
1. Politics	Getting the Politics Right	By Achieving Good Governance through Community based-Government and Citizen Participation
2. Power	Getting the Exercise of Power Right	By Achieving a 'just' Distribution of Power among Societal Stakeholders, Communities and Citizens (Including Political Parties)
3. Performance	Getting Development Economy Right	By Achieving Sustainable Performance through Equity, Inclusion, Stability, Resilience in a Knowledge-based Innovation driven Entrepreneurial Economy
4. Principles	Guided by Core Principles	Achieving a lasting Social Compact through Country First and People-Centred Shared Values
5. Sovereignty	Maintaining a Sovereign State	By Achieving 'real' Sovereignty through claiming a 'Rightful Place' among Nations and 'enforcing' Internal Justice
6. Leadership	Led by Principled Leadership Programme	By Developing 'Principled Leaders' through a 'Competency'-driven, Professional Behaviour and Role Modelling
7. Culture	Building an Entrepreneurial Culture	By Shifting from 'Survival Culture' to 'Growth Entrepreneurial Culture'

Power Politics and Performance presents a model for enhanced growth and development in small developing states and sets the tone for a shift in political culture in the Commonwealth Caribbean.

Notes

1. Mahatma Ghandi gave a written note, listing these seven blunders of the world, to his grandson Arun, just before he was assassinated on the final day. A list closing an article in *Young India* (22 October 1925); *Collected Works of Mahatma Gandhi* Vol. 33 (PDF) 135.

2. Discussed in more detail in Chapter 3, Politics, Development and Sovereignty.

3. This obvious historical perspective on sovereignty from Hobbs et al. is selected from Westphalian sovereignty from Wikipedia

4. Matthew L. Bishop and Anthony Payne. Caribbean Regional Governance and the Sovereignty/Statehood Problem. Waterloo: The Centre for International Governance Innovation, Caribbean Papers, January 2010.

5. Mohan Munasinghe is a Sri Lankan physicist and economist. With a focus on energy, sustainable development and climate change, he is the Chairman of the Munasinghe Institute for Development, the Director-General of the Sustainable Consumption Institute at the University of Manchester, UK, and the Vice Chairman of the Intergovernmental Panel on Climate Change (IPCC-AR4), that shared the 2007 Nobel Peace Prize with former Vice President of the United States, Al Gore.

ACRONYMNS AND ABBREVIATIONS

ACS	Association of Caribbean States
AML	Anti-Money Laundering
AOSIS	Alliance of Small Island States
APEC	Asia-Pacific Economic Cooperation
CARICOM	Caribbean Community
CARTAC	Caribbean Regional Technical Assistance
CCJ	Caribbean Court of Justice
CDB	Caribbean Development Bank
CIGI	Centre for International Governance Innovation
COFAP	Council of Finance and Planning
COMECON	Council for Mutual Economic Assistance
COP	Congress of the People
COTED	Council of Trade and Economic Development
CSME	CARICOM Single Market and Economy
ECLAC	Economic Commission of Latin America and the Caribbean
EPA	Economic Partnership Agreement
EU	European Union
FSA	Financial Services Authority
FTAA	Free Trade Area of the Americas
G20	Group of 20 Finance Ministers and Central Bank Governors
GATT	General Agreement on Tariffs and Trade
GDP	Gross Domestic Product
ICT	Information Communication Technology
ICTA	Imperial College of Tropical Agriculture
IFCs	International Finance Institutions

IMF-WB	International Monetary Fund-World Bank
IOSCO	International Organisation of Securities Commissions
NGO	Non-governmental Organisation
NJAC	National Joint Action Committee
OECS	Organisation of Eastern Caribbean States
OECD	Organisation for Economic Co-operation and Development
PNM	People's National Movement
PSIP	Public Sector Investment Programme
R&D	Research and Development
RRC	Regional Research Centre
SEC	Securities and Exchange Commission
SLDP	Solution Leadership Development Programme
SME	Small and Medium Enterprises
TOP	Tobago Organisation of the People
TOT	Total Organisational Transformation
UK	United Kingdom
UN	United Nations
UNC	United National Congress
UNCAC	United Nations Convention against Corruption
UNU-WILDER	United Nations University World Institute for Development Economics Research
US	United States
USSR	Union of Soviet Socialist Republics
UWI	University of the West Indies
VAT	Value Added Tax
WEI	World Education Indicators
WTO	World Trade Organization
WWW	World Wide Web

CHAPTER 1

Paradigm Power: One-World Information Dynamics*

The Frontier World

We are living in a turbulent opportunity-rich Frontier World in which nearly everything is possible (at least so it seems). The new *Frontier Space* is the space created by information. This global information and communication platform opened up a new frontier space to be explored and claimed by a new breed of individuals willing to take risks as explorers, discoverers, and entrepreneurs. These frontier individuals and their organisations make up the new rules of the game and lay claim to territories in the form of markets.

It is in this turbulent frontier environment, where fierce competition for market territories and unbridled greed for accumulation of wealth by individuals, organisations, and nation states prevails; the traditional Third World countries and small nation states have to navigate a path for development. The information driven *Frontier World* changes the relationship between the state, citizen, and private enterprises. The emergence of the *Entrepreneurial Economy* as the driver of national growth and sustainable development depends on this new breed of information and knowledge entrepreneurs. These risk-taking entrepreneurs are the first wave explorers, innovators, and discoverers that a society must encourage and support to actively participate and claim a share of the *Frontier Economic Space*.

The role of the state and government must shift from owner and controller of resources to genuine facilitator and catalyst of this frontier economy. It is this new information and knowledge-driven entrepreneurial economy that will be the driver of growth and sustainable long-term development.

Leaders must constantly adapt alongside change in a new environment where information is the dominant resource and technology has enabled instantaneous information transfer. This chapter investigates the global environment, within which the society, the organisation, and the leader must act. Global changes are now immediate and local. However, there is also a strong assertion of local cultures and processes which relates to, and impact on global changes in a force known as *glocalization*.

History records waves of development which carry sweeping, fundamental changes. Curiosity drives science, technology applies it, the market distributes it and builds on it, and the mind adapts and profits from the results. In this age, individuals are far more empowered than before. As information is gathered and filtered into knowledge through networks, partnerships and systems which foster collaboration, become necessary. This is usually reflected in the consolidation of firms, as transaction costs fall with organisational partnership. This is especially important in the face of the clash between archaic and slow-to-adapt systems and rapidly changing populations and mindsets. Regulations, the environment, and human issues encompass the general challenges we face.

The flow of information creates a virtual market for ideas, driven by greed and fear. This must still be regulated to prevent instability. Given the challenge of smelting the raw information into productive and actionable knowledge, we must ensure that a network of partners exists to build the information into useful solutions.

Understanding Paradigm Power: One-World Change
Solution Leadership Challenge[1]

In the 21st century, information has become the dominant resource creating a one-world information space. Solving problems in this one-world information environment demands complex adaptive thinking.[2] Leaders seeking solutions must gain an understanding of complex adaptive systems, their behaviour, and their information environment in order to survive and thrive. The challenge for leaders and their enterprises is to find globalised solutions, as they face the one-world economy with its powerful information dynamics. Global-local solutions require a multi-disciplinary integrated system approach grounded in complex adaptive system behaviour.

Reality is shifting because the traditional human world has become unstable and is no longer sustainable. This reality revolution causes immense stress with ill consequences. Yet, it also holds unique opportunities to create a new and viable human environment. Whilst this global tectonic change poses further challenges to sustainable development for all organisations in society, we are interested in the special challenges facing the leadership of public and private enterprises in developing nations.[3]

What solutions must be executed to achieve sustainable growth and organisational development, particularly in developing nations? How can solution leaders be developed and what risks must they take to create a future that they can proudly pass on to their children? Today's unfolding global change is concurrent with local change. This synergistic and dialectical process is creating a new one-world order: an emerging one-world civilisation that impacts all human enterprises. This phenomenon unfolds global change through globalisation of information and knowledge; it enfolds local change through creativity, innovation, and transformative community development.

Together, these global centrifugal forces and local centripetal forces are shaping the context and direction of an emerging global human enterprise. This enterprise is synergising human energy, using the freed energy released from the old order to build the new one. In dialectical dynamics, out of the old and its opposing forces is emerging a new worldwide civilisation. We are already experiencing a one-world information environment.

Figure 1.1 Frontier Information Space

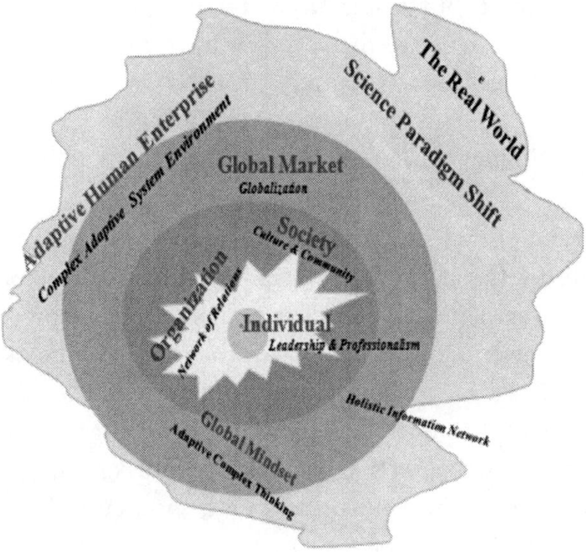

Solution leaders must revolutionise their thinking and learning, leading and managing. In today's interdependent one-world information environment, for an organised human system to survive, thrive and sustain performance, growth and development requires adaptation and significant change. Such paradigm shifting change requires a realignment of our perception of reality.

Glocalization

In today's world, we are recognising that mankind's main problems are global and local, complex and nonlinear. Both global and local change in this environment feed on each other. Global change affects local human activities, conversely, local change impacts global change in the planetary environment. This complex adaptive interactive process we will refer to as *glocalization*.[4]

Glocalization runs at the speed of light. In this new information environment, the distinctions between global and local are blurred and at times indistinguishable. Actions and consequences are frequently the result of distant events. In the traditional environment, all actions were local, in a literal physical sense. In today's one-world information environment, actions are frequently executed at a distance, and the consequences reverberate and felt at a distance. Actions and their consequences are not locally confined, but occur anywhere and at any time. After all, information flows at close to the speed of light and is only limited by its need for a physical infrastructure.[5]

Global Paradigm Shifting

Paradigms are applicable to societies, organisations, and individuals.[6] Paradigms are useful as models of reality and filters for perception; they provide us with the hidden operational rules and practices; they are embedded patterns of behaviour and habits. If we think seriously about the world and act effectively in it, some simplified map of reality, some theory, concept, model, and paradigm is necessary. Without such intellectual constructs, there would be a state of confusion. People think and act on patterns. Over time, individual events, no matter how great, will fall within a pattern. Such simplified paradigms or maps are indispensable

Figure 1.2 Human Enterprise Waves

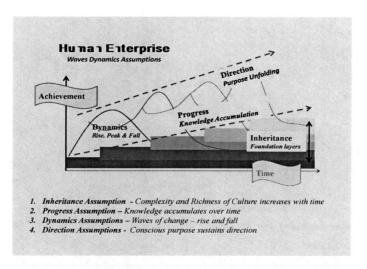

1. **Inheritance Assumption** - *Complexity and Richness of Culture increases with time*
2. **Progress Assumption** – *Knowledge accumulates over time*
3. **Dynamics Assumptions** – *Waves of change – rise and fall*
4. **Direction Assumptions** - *Conscious purpose sustains direction*

to human thoughts and actions. The most powerful paradigms are our mindsets, our organisational culture, and societal culture.

Human history is the history of civilisations

We consider a paradigm shift a deeply transformative change in a civilisation, society or organisation. Each paradigm shift demands a new way of thinking and acting. Shifting paradigms is 'riding waves of change'. Historically, paradigm shifts represent waves of human progress.[7]

Throughout history, there has been constant change in social structures because of changes in environment and technology. Potential polarisation of people may result. The greatest threat to global civilisation is that political power resides with jealous nations, with deep cultural divides produced by thousands of years of clashing religious beliefs and related ideologies. These deep cultural divides could cause a clash of civilisations spurred through religion.[8]

Globalisation has its promises and opportunities, but it also has its risks. The new world is quickly giving many citizens much to fear, especially the uprooting of many previously stable sources of identity and security. Where change is most rapid, widening gaps in the distribution of income swiftly become cause for alarm.[9] Yet, the reality is that globalising forces will tend toward an increasingly one-world information environment.

Figure 1.3 Waves of Civilization

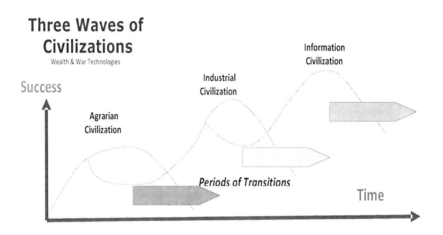

Historically, global waves have fundamentally transformed societies. These global waves destroy old paradigms and alter human civilisation. Globalisation is part of the latest wave that is shifting our perspective of reality. These waves powerfully change the way people in a society create value or make a living.

After the hunter and gatherer wave, the agricultural wave was one of the early paradigm shifting waves. It shifted nomadic and tribal life to permanent settlements powered by physical animal and human power. It gave rise to the agrarian societies that still exist. With the leisure and bounty of agricultural surplus came commerce. The commercial wave brought long distance trade by land; and in parts of Western Europe and Asia commerce became driven by sea travel. This gave rise to great commercial trading centres and seaport cities. By the last quarter of the 18th century, a new wave emerged in England. The Industrial Revolution started in the textile industry and spread throughout Western Europe and North America. By the mid-20th-century, it had engulfed most of the globe. Machines drove industrialisation and gave rise to industrial organisation and the now great cities of the world.

A new wave then emerged. The computer and the electronic revolution drove this information wave. Information became a resource through the computer, which allowed storage and access to information over long distances. This information wave has transformed most 'advanced nations' into information and service based societies. Satellites, global positioning, and the end of the cold war made satellite technology available to business in the late 1980s, and leading societies moved into the knowledge age. This knowledge wave, for the first time in human history, was driven by the mind. It put a premium on the individual human mind and its capability to transform information into value or useful knowledge.

The human mind, supported by the most sophisticated technology, is now able to roam and extend itself into the new information space. This virtual, global information space opens up new human potentials that force the mind and communities into a new evolutionary spiral. It may foreshadow the birth of a truly 'one-world' civilisation. The next wave is already on the horizon, enabled by 20th century science and technological revolution. This imagination wave, driven by virtual reality simulation, will allow human beings to actualise their imagination. The only limit appears to be the human mind and its capacity to dream and to be creative.

Science-Technology Paradigm Shift

Global Change Framework

There has always been a search by man to understand 'reality'. In Western civilisation, this search gradually separated itself into a three pronged approach of philosophy, theology (religion) and science. Philosophy demands reason. Even empiricists defended their arguments with appeals to reason. Theology (religion) demands faith; and science demands research.

Figure 1.4 Types of Waves

Wave Type	Wave Power	Time
1. *Nomadic Wave*	Physical/Animal/Human Powered	
2. *Agricultural Wave*	Physical/Animal/Human Powered	
3. *Commercial Wave*	Trade/Ship Powered	1100
4. *Industrialisation Wave*	Machine /Factory Powered	1780
5. *Information Wave*	Electronics/ Computer Powered	1940
6. *Knowledge Wave*	Mind /Satellite Powered	1980
7. *Imagination Wave*	Creativity/Artificial Intelligence Powered	2000

Human curiosity drives science; technology is developed to claim ownership; the market is used to communicate and transfer value; the human (business) enterprise facilitates the accumulation of wealth; and the mind is used to adapt and benefit from the changing environments.

Science-Technology Paradigm

A science driven paradigm shift is changing the world as we know it; its technological applications affect all human systems. Systems are forced to adapt to significant changes in their environments just to stay healthy. It is rapidly changing the very fabric of human existence and it is the major force in the emerging global network of communities - the basis for an emerging one-world civilisation.

Whilst change has always been part of the universal process as viewed by older Newtonian science; the result of the understanding and application of newer Einsteinian science has been to increase this rate of change. Transportation technology, governed as it was by Newtonian laws, limited change. The speed of transport was directly related to improvements and innovation in transport technology. In modern times, the railroad, the boat, the car, the airplane, and the telephone, all affected the speed of transport; and communication was limited to the speed of sound and physical sight. Even the speed of satellites moving in orbit, and airplanes several times the speed of sound, are nothing compared to the achievements of the new technology driven quantum rate of change.

For most of human history, we could only watch the beautiful dance of nature as bystanders. Yet, we are today on the cusp of an epochal transition, from being passive observers to being active choreographers of nature. In these turbulent times, we, as individuals, organisations, even as societies, are looking for more than just survival. We know that the world is changing almost faster than we can keep up. Sometimes the change is heady and invigorating, sometimes bewildering and exhausting. Sometimes we fail, sometimes we succeed, but most of us sense that we must adapt and learn to deal with the turbulent environment.

Whilst there has always been change, the rate of change that speeded up in late 20th century is continuing to do so well into the 21st century. During the last century, a paradigm shift occurred from the traditional Newtonian understanding of a well-ordered physical universe to a new quantum-physical understanding of a complex and dynamic energy based universe.

Each new understanding of the universe has generated laws successfully dealing with the nature of the universe on the material level. The practical application of quantum energy based science has been expressed in the development of nano-technologies, the computer revolution affecting human intelligence and learning, and the development of artificial life.

Quantum physics-based technologies dramatically increased the rate of change in the last decades of the 20th century. Quantum-physical sciences allow us to study the universe at the energy level of reality. This quantum rate of change, driven by the science paradigm shift, has produced revolutionary social, economic, and political changes worldwide.

These new technological applications affect all human systems, because we now can operate at the speed of thought. It forces human systems to adapt to significant changes in their environment just to stay healthy. This marked shift in understanding the universe and changes in science and technology affect the global market economy, society, organisations, and individuals everywhere. It is rapidly changing the very fabric of human existence.

Global Science-Technology Revolutions

A science paradigm shift is changing civilisation and is driven by three global revolutions with their synergies. These technologies drive the rate of change that affect every aspect of our lives. This science paradigm shift is driven by a quantum revolution, affecting how we deal with and understand matter; the computer revolution, affecting intelligence; and a bio-molecular revolution, impacting life.

Science is a primary factor affecting how the human being discerns and grasps the nature and properties of the universe. What is recognisable throughout history is the rippling effect of transformations and revolutions throughout the world due to scientific progression.

The forces of the science and technology revolution drive global change now and to 2025, their impact can be summarised.[10] By 2025 the quantum revolution will have produced new materials, new energy, new forms of matter, and the power and materials to build a planetary society. The computer revolution will have created a computer that is virtually free and unlimited, artificial sources, ability to create intelligence within reach, a link for all people with a powerful global technology, and telecommunications and economic networks. The bio-molecular revolution will have given us a complete genetic description of all living things, the knowledge to cure diseases, feed the expanding population, and the possibility of becoming choreographers of life on earth.

The evolution of science and its approaches, methods and research, has largely been responsible for advances in technology. It is these same technologies, developed out of new scientific findings, which are used to upgrade scientific processes. The powerful driving forces generated by revolutionary changes in science and technology include a quantum revolution creating new matter; a bio-molecular revolution impacting life and human health. 'Natural laws' and 'quantum physics laws' each work in their own realm and have successfully provided fertile grounds for new technologies.

For example, a scientific breakthrough can be converted into a competitive product or service. It becomes the asset of an organisation or business enterprise, which most often has to redesign every aspect of its existence: its value-creating processes, production and operational processes, supply value-chain, marketing, human and work relations, leadership; the entire system.

The Adaptation Challenge

Adaptation Formula

In today's turbulent information environment, civilisation must adapt or suffer the consequences of dysfunctional performance and behaviour. To stay healthy, we must adapt to the changing environment; we must steer and successfully operate external and internal information driven processes according to changes. Adaptation is an information rich process.

This conceptual formula can serve as a guide for assessing a system's adaptability. For a healthy individual or professional, organisation or society, the rate of learning tends to match the rate of change and there is only a relatively small tension gap. For an 'unhealthy' human system, the rate of change continuously exceeds the rate of learning and as a result, there is an adaptation gap. The system becomes ill. Clearly one of the primary challenges of all human systems is to keep the adaptability gap as narrow as possible. This requires matching the usually faster rate of change in the one-world information environment and information driven market economy with the system's own rate of learning. The human system must adapt by speeding up the learning rate. Whilst the rate of change drives or forces the growth of the system, the rate of learning must attempt to match in order to maintain the system in a healthy state of disequilibrium. Increasing the rate of learning will keep the system healthy.

Developing countries have a dual challenge. They must not only catch-up, but must also match the continuous rate of change and learning of developed countries and their powerful globally competitive enterprises. A 'quantum rate of change' must be followed by a 'quantum rate of learning'. *N.B* As a result, this may require a revolution in how, what, when and where we learn. Education must undergo a revolutionary change to match the 21st century information environment. For developing countries, the solution to the above questions may mean deep society wide social, economic and political change.

Figure 1.5 Adaptability Gap

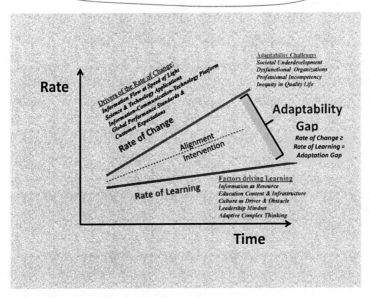

One-World Change Drivers

With the dramatic spread of global information technology, information has become the new resource. There is no place on earth where information cannot penetrate. The globe is girded with a hyperactive pulsating communications network that affects us all. Satellites, wireless technology and fibre-optic cables bind us together into a global village and create an emerging global workspace.

Global knowledge, global enterprise, a global information market, as well as a global mindset are emerging phenomena in the real time of a one-world information environment. Each of these global phenomena contributes to the general dynamics of the global environment and quality of life. We will consider them the key drivers of the complex dynamics of one-world global change. They unleash powerful forces that pose adaptation, alignment and adjustment challenges for individuals, organisations, and societies in the context of an emerging global civilisation. They require a profound response, a shift in the prevailing mindset. Global knowledge, particularly the shifting paradigms of science and technology, drives global change. Whilst historical waves and contemporary trends underpin global change, global knowledge drives global change.

Economic and Technological Laws

Some key change drivers originate from the combination of several technological and economic forces expressed as 'laws'. Moore's law asserts that for the foreseeable future, computer chip density (computing power) will double every 18 months whilst the cost remain constant. Computing devices will become more powerful, faster, and smaller without increasing in price. Robert Metcalfe, 3Com founder,[11] stated that a network's value increases exponentially with each additional node or user. The utility of a network is equal to the square of the number of users. This law applies to cellular phones and the Internet.

Economist Ronald Coase's 1937 assessment of market efficiency[12] explained that firms organise to reduce the transaction costs of repeated and complicated activities involved in creating, selling and distributing their goods and services. He argued that firms exist because the cost of organising and maintaining them is cheaper than the transaction costs involved with working in an open market. He lists six transaction costs: search, information, bargaining, decision, policing, and enforcement. As the market becomes more efficient, the size and organisational complexity of the modern industrial firm become uneconomic, since they exist only to the extent that they reduce transaction costs more effectively.

Combining Moore's Law and Metcalfe's observation causes an effect called the 'Law of Disruption' or social unrest. As technology rapidly becomes more powerful and affordable, more people will use it, increasing its value exponentially. However, social systems such as the legal and justice systems evolve at a slow and incremental pace.

The gap arising from these different rates of change causes sudden and dramatic disruption of political, social, and economic systems. Figure 1.6 illustrates the potential gap that can cause severe disruption in society. Whilst social systems improve incrementally, technological systems improve exponentially. As a result, a gap is created. As this gap increases, so does the potential for non-continuous, disruptive and revolutionary change.

Figure 1.6 Law of Disruption

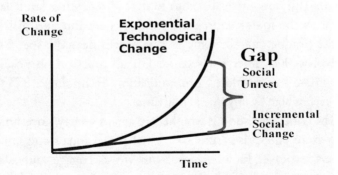

Law of Disruption
Social Unrest –Adaptation Gap

Rate of Change

Exponential Technological Change

Gap
Social Unrest

Incremental Social Change

Time

One-World Issues

Global issues produce both stresses and opportunities. These issues demand a one-world solution approach.[13] Issues with sharing our humanity require a global environment solution. These issues include: the fight against poverty, peacekeeping, conflict prevention, combating terrorism, universal education, global infectious diseases, the digital divide, and natural disaster prevention and mitigation.

Regulation issues need a one-world global regulatory approach. These issues include: reinventing taxation for the 21st century, biotechnology rules, global financial architecture, illegal drugs, trade, investment, and competition rules, intellectual property rights, e-commerce rules, and international labour and migration rules. Sharing our planet involves the global commons. These issues include: global climate change, biodiversity and ecosystem losses, fisheries depletion, deforestation, the water deficit, and maritime safety and pollution.

Information Dynamics:
Information Resource, Speed, Space and Value

Information is the dominant value and wealth-generating resource. It flows at the speed of light, at nearly 186,000 miles per second. In the process, it redefines human space.

We live in a time of profound transition, in an age of disorienting change more intense than we have ever experienced. Information has become the new critical resource that is replacing land, labour, and capital as the major source of wealth generation and distribution. It has the unique characteristic that it moves near the speed of light, at nearly 186,000 miles per second. For all practical purposes, with the appropriate Information Communication Technology (ICT), it can be used everywhere by any one at any time.

The critical question is whether we are, as society, government, public and private enterprises, and individual professionals and citizens, ready for this resource. How prepared are we to engage and adapt to this new information reality? Do we have the appropriate 'global mindset' that allows us to think and learn, lead, and manage in a one-world environment? Do we understand the dynamics of the new information driven global economy? What is the impact of this one-world information flow on the adaptive complex enterprise, on organisations? Do we have the appropriate competencies to manage information as the dominant wealth-generating resource that allows us to compete in the one-world economy?

One-World Information Space and Exchange

The rest of this section briefly discusses these four critical dimensions of information dynamics: Information is a critical *resource*; it flows at near light *speed*, defining its own *space* and creating *value*. Information as a resource is redefining the boundaries of the society, organisation, and individual within an emerging one-world civilisation. It has created a one-world information space, allowing the operation exchange of a one-world market. The flow of information respects no physical border, knows no boundaries, it is instantaneously everywhere worldwide. The flow of information creates an interrelated, interconnected, interactive, and integrated worldwide information exchange – a virtual market space accessible to anyone. This new market powerfully affects global customers' networked expectations.

The one-world information exchange is located in the material world and in cyberspace where machines communicate with machines. Both are a part of the ICT infrastructure that we now use for global information transactions. One reason the market is even being conceived of as a 'one-world environment' is that technology is integrating the world of information. The internet, for example, is creating a universal cyberspace market. Technological development begets global electronic links on a scale unparalleled in human history, tearing down parochial interests, whilst creating a one-world business culture. Developments such as email, e-money, virtual online transactions, cyber cash, smart cards, digital money, and electronic commerce and banking are opening up this one-world marketplace.

As a result, this exchange is creating a collective one-world consciousness that promotes an emergent one-world civilisation. Such a global civilisation consists of global communities of stakeholders, each with their own interests, but collectively, if at times indirectly, seeking

Figure 1.7 System Interdependency

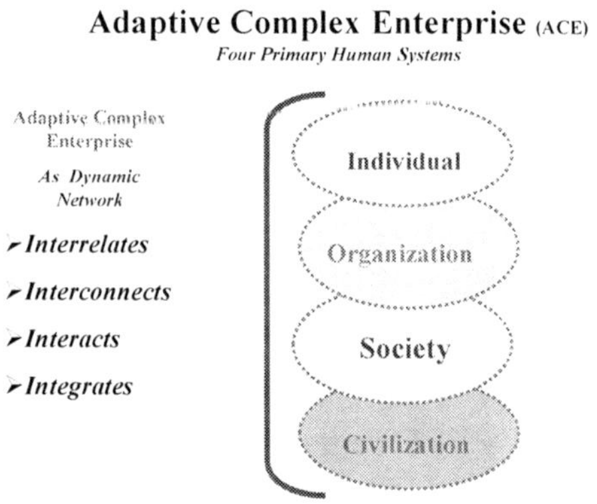

Adaptive Complex Enterprise (ACE)
Four Primary Human Systems

Adaptive Complex
Enterprise

*As Dynamic
Network*

➤ *Interrelates*

➤ *Interconnects*

➤ *Interacts*

➤ *Integrates*

Individual

Organization

Society

Civilization

the improvement of humanity and nature. The one-world information exchange can be viewed as an information superhighway, as a global information web, as a global network of relations, and as an information platform where the global community of stakeholders conducts its information business.

This one-world information exchange is a mental market that thrives on the exchange of mental goods and services in an information-driven space that serves the global community of stakeholders. The one-world community of stakeholders consists of the individual, the organisation, society, and the emergent one-world civilisation itself. Each has its own local and one-world network of relationships that define the information space they inhabit. In this new environment, relationships and the use of information now define global and local communities of interest.

Information Dimensions

How does this new marketplace affect local organisations' boundaries and space? One-world information connects stakeholders, whose relationships define the space that particular networks and communities inhabit. It is individual, organisational, societal, and global relationships that define the boundaries of stakeholder communities and their unique information space, not traditional physical factors or proximity.

One-world information connects the various global communities and their stakeholders through the information communication technology infrastructure. ICT, through its local and global systems and processes, can physically connect stakeholder communities both externally and internally. Potentially, a person can be connected to any other on earth, creating an entirely interconnected network. One-world information is also interactive as it facilitates communication and value creation. For information to be of value it must be accessible and acted upon. It requires dialogue, discussion, and teamwork. Teamwork is the most valuable form of information activity. Interaction between people fosters creativity more than isolated thought.

One-world information integrates; bringing and holding together the community of stakeholders. It integrates various systems and processes into a meaningful whole. It allows the human system to change, learn, and adapt to changing environments. Global information as a resource, continually builds value for its stakeholder communities. It does so by channelling the needs, wants, demands, and values of its stakeholders who act and work together through the one-world information exchange. These stakeholders have global, not local expectations, demand global performance standards, increasingly market their competencies globally and finally seek a global, not local, quality of life. The one-world information exchange market is transforming local citizens, customers, stakeholders, organisations, and even societies into global entities.

Local changes continuously affect all global activities, because this one-world information exchange exists with its physical and virtual network. We have all experienced the effects of local changes in ecological, economic, or political systems, causing major turbulence in the global information environment, including the global financial and economic markets. Local political changes have global repercussions; local crime, disease, and terrorists have impact everywhere. We can no longer escape from the power of the one-world market.

The Invisible Hand of One-World Information Exchange

A planet-wide information platform allows information and communication to flow almost magically in the World Wide Web (WWW) activated by human systems satisfying a near insatiable thirst for information and voracious appetite for self-empowerment. Out of these apparently chaotic activities is emerging a new powerful one-world information exchange. This new information-exchange-market concept returns us to Adam Smith's notions: the invisible hand of the information market guides all information transactions and collectively assures that the common good eventually prevails.

The one-world information exchange is driven by greed and fear. The powerful assumption is that while greed and fear may drive individuals and communities, their collective market transactions will allow a common good to emerge. In addition, at least in theory, it is that common good, altruism, the love and respect for life, all life; that will dominate the core values of the global institutions serving the emerging one-world civilisation.

At times, swings between fear and greed are extreme. Greed is linked to the accumulation of wealth; with the fear of losing wealth linked to the protection of wealth through the institutionalisation of law and order. Clearly, unbridled greed will be destructive and reasonable regulations and enlightened leadership are required. Global institutions are needed to regulate this new one-world information market exchange.

We are experiencing a shift from a local market exchange of goods and services to a one-world market. This new market is a network of relations in information space where value is created, exchanged, and maintained. Similarly, there is shift from the physical local workplace to a virtual global workspace. The global information network and its physical infrastructure allow locally empowered human systems, including individuals, to become 'super-empowered.' Individuals employing global technology that allows access to the one-world information network can and do cause havoc and destruction globally and indeed, locally.

Such super-empowered individuals can deliberately influence and dramatically affect global change. A political leader, a terrorist, a disease-carrying individual, as well as the noble individual can be enormously influential. Conversely, an enlightened leadership or a few people with a noble purpose can also leverage their intention and do much good on a regional or even global scale.

Information Resource Value.

Information is a resource. It is the flow of information that aggravates the current global fault lines. Information is what actually brings change. Information is the creative energy of the universe; it gives all matter meaning. The flow of information provides the energy to a reality-altering information paradigm. Information is the universal resource that flows in cyberspace and mind space. Information becomes a product that modifies human consciousness and when altered by the human mind, brings change. When we interact with information, we are challenged to change in some way.

Information is by its very nature an unlimited and renewable resource. Creating its own space without boundaries, information is the lifeblood of any human enterprise. Information is ubiquitous – it is transferable and transmittable over long distance. Information can be destroyed, mutilated, changed, and created, renewed, managed, energised, and quantified. Information as a resource is collected, stored, contented, and directed. It is through the ICT infrastructure that information is used as a resource and is communicated, transferred, and dispersed allowing interaction between the systems.

Information (the unlimited and unlimiting resource) comes from the mind (the source), transforms through the mind (the value creating core process), is created for the mind (as a mental product), goes through a network of relations (the community of participating stakeholders), supported by technology (information systems), and operating in the one-world information exchange (in cyberspace and mind space).

Figure 1.8 Information Resource Management Wheel

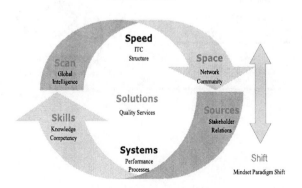

Information as a resource demands organisational systems that allow human interaction to create value. It is the sharing of information as a resource that engenders both individual and collective learning. Information requires leadership with a global mindset capable of adaptive complex thinking[14] to manage it.

There are at least four phases of value: data, information, knowledge, and understanding (power). Data collection and processing is the phase of moulding the raw resource; as is information manipulation and analysis with sophisticated software. Knowledge is a value creating process that requires information as well as human competencies. Finally, the exercise of power gives direction to the other three processes. Power creates value by giving purpose to knowledge, information and data. There is a gap challenge between each phase as illustrated in Figure 1.10: the technology gap in collecting data and transforming it into information; the competency gap in the transformation of information into knowledge, and the strategic direction gap in providing meaning to knowledge by giving direction and purpose. These gaps, if not addressed, become fatal disconnects.

Figure 1.9 Defining Information Value

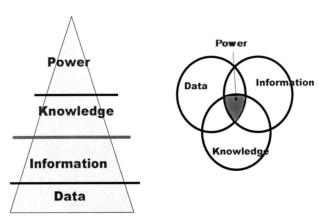

Defining *Information*

Figure 1.10 Information Value Gaps

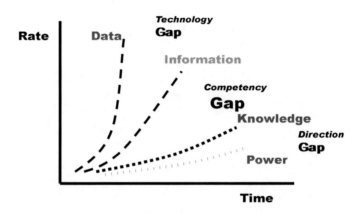

The Gap Challenge

Scarcity of Knowledge and Meaning Gap.

Today, whilst we have an abundance of information, we have a scarcity of actionable knowledge, that is, information transformed into value and meaning. Information is abundant but meaning and knowledge are scarce. Information as a resource only becomes value or wealth generating when we have capable and developed minds that can act upon the flow of information delivered by the powerful ICT platform. To create current and future wealth requires a long-term investment in intellectual capital. Education becomes the critical component of wealth and value generation to improve everyone's quality of life.

Knowledge for Service.

The challenge of a knowledge-based economy demands that information must be transformed into knowledge, as the most critical component of service. The knowledge for service framework illustrates the knowledge dynamics within the larger global change framework (previously outlined). This dynamic consists of four realms of influence: ideas, theory, application, and knowledge. These four spheres are inter-related, inter-connected, inter-active, and integrated as illustrated in Figure 1.11.

Figure 1. 11 Knowledge Service Framework

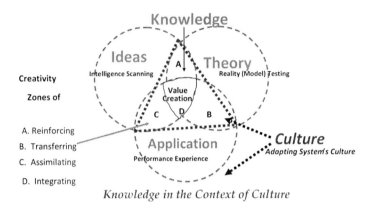

Knowledge in the Context of Culture

Ideas and theory reinforce each other. Generating ideas involves intelligence scanning from the real world. Theory transfers to application, and application transfers to, and further enriches theory. Effective theories always require testing models in reality. Application is assimilated as part of ideas and vice versa. Application must always include real world experience. Finally, knowledge is the integration of ideas, theories, and applications into a body of knowledge or expertise. How can we apply this framework to a strategic change intervention? In chapter four, we develop a leadership programme that uses the knowledge for service framework as the underpinnings for knowledge transfer intervention.

The Cutting Edge Thinkers

Who are the cutting-edge thinkers of today?

The scientists are the philosophers of the 21st century. They are thinkers in complexity. Their thinking challenges us in the same way that the philosophers of the old did. They deal with the ultimate questions about the universal reality – matter, energy, life and consciousness – as well as the quality of life on this planet.

In *The New Humanists*,[15] John Brockman and his contributors discuss an emerging third culture. The first two cultures were that of the literary intellectual and that of the scientist. This new culture, consists of scientists and other thinkers in the empirical world replacing the traditional intellectualism exploring and rendering visible the deeper meanings of our lives, redefining who and what we are. This new culture deals with critical scientific issues that impact all of us. These include revolutionary developments in molecular biology, genetic engineering, nanotechnology, artificial intelligence, artificial life, chaos theory, massive parallelism, neural nets, the inflationary universe, fractals, complex adaptive systems, linguistics, superstrings, biodiversity, the human genome, expert systems, punctuated equilibrium, cellular automata, fuzzy logic, virtual reality, cyberspace, and teraflop machines among others.

Unfortunately, despite all the recent advances, the dominant 'intellectual mindset' was neither science-based nor science influenced. Brockman claims that while the 20th century was a period of great scientific advancement, but instead of having science and technology at the centre of the intellectual world and having a unity in which scholarship included science and technology along with literature and art, the official and formal culture kicked them out. Traditional humanities scholars were powerful enough to maintain the old by looking at science and technology as some sort of technical special product. Brockman asserts that elite universities nudged science out of the liberal arts undergraduate curriculum and out of the minds of many young people, who, as the new academic establishment, so marginalised themselves, that they are no longer within shouting distance of the action.

However, Brockman now sees encouraging signs that the *third culture* is spreading, which includes scholars in the humanities who think the way scientists do. Like their colleagues in the sciences, they believe there is a real world and their job is to understand it and explain it.

In short, something radically new is in the air: New ways of understanding physical systems, new ways of thinking about thinking that call into question many of our basic assumptions. A realistic biology of the mind, advances in physics, information technology, genetics, neurobiology, engineering, the chemistry of materials – all are challenging basic assumptions of who and what we are, of what it means to be human. The arts and the sciences are again joining as one culture - the third culture.

Those involved in this effort on either side of the old divide are at the centre of today's intellectual action. They are the new humanists who see the world through new paradigm shifting lenses. The new frontier world has emerged.

Notes
*Contributed by Manfred D. Jantzen
1. Adapted from Manfred D. Jantzen, Ph.D. Solution Leadership, A Guide to Strategic Change. Unpublished Manuscript, University of the West Indies 2010. Solution Leadership provides a guide to strategic change and execution management. It identifies and attempts to understand critical organisational problems in the context of the powerful one-world information dynamics. It provides a solution execution approach with action guides to solve these problems both on global and local levels. Developing competent Solution Leaders is critical to this problem solving and action driven undertaking and is a leitmotif throughout. Solution Leadership employs a solution execution approach and methodology grounded in understanding of the dynamics of Complex Adaptive System Environment. Solution Leaders engage in adaptive and complex thinking to lead and manage the Adaptive Complex Enterprise, grow and maintain it in the turbulent one-world information environment.
2. The following books are required readings for those who want to understand basic concepts of the Science of Complexity and Complex Adaptive Systems as the basis for learning Adaptive Complex Thinking:
    (1) F. David Peat and John Briggs, *Turbulent Mirror: An illustrated Guide to Chaos Theory and the Science of Wholeness*. (New York: Harper & Row, 1989). This illustrated guide to chaos theory and the science of wholeness (complexity) is necessary reading for the first time student of science of complexity.
    (2) James Gleick, *Chaos: Making a New Science*. (New York: Penguin)1988. This book is a must read for beginning students of science of complexity. Gleick helped popularise the concept of chaos theory with this book. The concept had largely been the province of mathematicians, but Gleick showed broader applications for the idea that systems behave in orderly ways in spite of seemingly random and chaotic individual events. And, indeed, investors, meteorologists,

economists, astronomers, and biologists have all incorporated chaos theory into the models they construct.

(3) Murray Gell-Mann, *The Quark and the Jaguar: Adventures into the Simple and the Complex.* (New York: W.H. Freeman 1994). He is the Nobel Prize winning physicist on whose outline of complex behaviour this author began to build the CASE model.

(4) Ralph D. Stacey, *Strategic Management & Organisational Dynamics*, 2nd edn. (London: Pitman Publishing, 1996). This work is still the best that explains and applies in a clear manner the difficult concepts of complex system behaviour. Chapter 9, 'System dynamics far from equilibrium'(309-351), discusses complex feedback systems coevolving into open-ended Evolutionary space.

(5) Ian Marshall and Danah Zohar. *Who's Afraid of Schrödinger's Cat? An A-to-Z Guide to All the New Science Ideas You Need to Keep Up with the New Thinking.* (New York: William Morrow and Company, 1997).

(6) Klaus. Mainzer, *Thinking in Complexity: The Complex Dynamics of Matter, Mind and Mankind,* 4th edn. (Berlin: Springer, 2007).

(7) Margaret J. Wheatley. *Leadership and the New Science: Discovering Order in a Chaotic World.* (San Francisco, CA: Berrett-Koehler Publishers, 1992.

(8) Peter M. Senge. *The Fifth Discipline: The Art & Practice of The Learning Organization.* (New York: Doubleday, 2006).

(9) T. Irene Sanders. *Strategic Thinking and the New Science: Planning in the Midst of Chaos, Complexity and Change.* (New York: Free Press, 1998). Sanders developed a new model of strategic thinking, based on chaos and complexity that breaks down the process into two components: insight about the present and foresight about the future. Both of these require 'visual thinking,' and she has developed a tool called 'FutureScape' that facilitates such thinking.

(10) Tyler Volk. *Gaia's Body: Toward a Physiology of Earth.* (New York: Copernicus, 1998). This book treats planet earth as a living complex adaptive system. Gaia, the name for this system, is viewed as the largest entity in the nested system of life on Earth. While earth is not an organism, it nevertheless shows a kind of physiology with a fascinating internal dynamics that resembles a 'living system'.

3. Ervin Laszlo, *Quantum Shift in the Global Brain: How the New Scientific Reality Can Change Us and Our World.* (Rochester, VT: Inner Traditions, 2008). Laszlo discusses how the new scientific reality can change us and our world.

He discusses the 'Reality Revolution' in terms of: (1) Macro-shift in society, (2) Paradigm Shift in Science, (3) Global Shift in Action.
4. The term Glocalization comes from merging global and local indicating that we live in an interactive world, in such a complex world action at a distance that is becoming the norm in our global information environment. Changes in information on the New York Stock Exchange can and do have real consequences in the operation of a factory in China.
5. Don Tapscott and Anthony D. Williams, *Wikinomics: How Mass Collaboration Changes Everything.* (New York: Portfolio, 2010). The authors explain how mass collaboration is happening not just at websites like Wikipedia and You Tube, but also at traditional companies that have embraced technology and breathe new life into their enterprises.
6. Thomas S. Kuhn, *The Structure of Scientific Revolutions* (Chicago: University of Chicago Press, 1986). The originator of the paradigm concept, in *The Structure of Scientific Revolutions*, discusses the power of paradigms in science. Kuhn wrote, 'Successive transition from one paradigm to another via revolution is the usual developmental pattern of mature science.' (p.12) Kuhn's idea was itself revolutionary in its time, as it caused a major change in the way that academics talk about science. Thus, it could be argued, it caused or was itself part of a 'paradigm shift' in the history and sociology of science. The Merriam-Webster Online Dictionary defines paradigm as 'a philosophical and theoretical framework of a scientific school or discipline within which theories, laws, and generalisations and the experiments performed in support of them are formulated; broadly: A philosophical or theoretical framework of any kind.' This is the concept we will use.
7. Alvin Toffler and Heidi Toffler, *War and Anti-War: Survival at the Dawn of the 21st Century* (New York: Little, Brown and Company, 1993), 18–24. The Tofflers discuss the dynamics of the three waves of human civilisation.
8. Samuel P. Huntington, *Clash of Civilization and the Remaking of World Order*, (New York: Simon & Schuster, 1998). Huntington argues that we should view the world not as a collection of states, but as a set of seven or eight cultural 'civilisations,' one in the West, several outside it and fated to link and conflict in terms of that civilisation's identity. Furthermore, modernisation does not mean Westernisation; economic progress has come with a revival of religion; post-cold war politics emphasise ethnic nationalism over ideology; the lack of leading 'core states' hampers the growth of Latin America and the world of Islam. Most controversial is his view of Islam. Not only does he point out that Muslim countries are involved in far more inter-group violence than others, he argues that the West should worry not about Islamic fundamentalism but about Islam itself, 'a different

civilization whose people are convinced of the superiority of their culture and are obsessed with the inferiority of their power.'

9. Alan Greenspan, *The Age of Turbulence, Adventures in a New World*. (New York: Penguin, 2007), 18. Greenspan, the former chair of the Federal Reserve Board, USA, summarises the challenges that individuals and societies are facing:

> In the face of the increasing integration of the global economy, the world's citizens face a profound choice: to embrace the worldwide benefits of open markets and open societies that pull people out of poverty and up the ladder of skills to better, more meaningful lives, while bearing in mind fundamental issues of justice; or to reject that opportunity and embrace nativism, tribalism, populism, indeed all of the 'isms' into which communities retreat when their identities are under siege and they cannot perceive better options.

10. Michio Kaku, *Physics of the Impossible: A Scientific Exploration into the World of Phasers, Force Fields, Teleportation, and Time Travel* (New York: Anchor, 2009). Kaku examines the technologies of invisibility, teleportation, precognition, star ships, antimatter engines, time travel and more – all regarded as things that are not possible today but that might be possible in the future. He ranks these subjects according to when, if ever, these technologies become reality.

11. 3Com was a pioneering digital electronics manufacturer best known for its computer network infrastructure products. It was acquired by Hewlett-Packard in 2010.

12. Ronald Coase. 'The Nature of the Firm', *Economica* 4 (16) (1937): 386–405.

13. Jeffrey E. Garten, ed. *World View: Global Strategies for the New Economy* . (Boston, MA: Harvard Business Press, 2000).

14. See note 2, above.

15. John Brockman, ed. *The New Humanists: Science at the Edge*. (Sterling Publishing, 2003).

CHAPTER 2
GETTING DEVELOPMENT RIGHT:
LEADERSHIP AND GOVERNANCE IN SMALL STATES[1]

The Challenge for Small States

Principled leadership must rest on consensus building structures. Democracy is the vehicle, but the Western liberal model often ignores the roles of inequality; liberty; human and property rights; and capabilities in the developing world. There is a new definition of development which centres on the diversity of products and competitiveness based on capabilities, as suggested by Dr Ricardo Hausmann.[2] Successful leaders of the information age are undivided in either ignoring all interest groups or integrating them all in a focused partnership. Small states have the potential to play a critical role in shaping governance in the democratic order of our times. From a global perspective, there are approximately 200 nation states: 134 classified as small developing states, 105 with less than 5 million people, 45 with less than 1.5 million people and 34 island states, including those in the Caribbean and the Pacific. It was always questioned whether small states would survive. As small states passed that hurdle, the issue then became whether they could build the resilience to cope with internal and external risks. This continues to remain a key challenge. The question now is whether small states can be sustainable with the new shifts in global politics and economics.

Societies in small states are caught in a profound wave of change as they respond to a different globalised order. The political and economic paradigms of yesterday have lost their legitimacy to promote workable solutions for an impatient generation with higher expectations. It could be argued that the realignment of the political culture towards the citizens' interests and rights or entitlements for higher standards of living should have been achieved with Independence. However, two generations have failed in this task. The stage is therefore set for exploring new approaches.

Politics has emerged as a formidable obstacle to the process of economic change in almost all Caribbean societies. The premise of the old Caribbean politics as the sustaining culture supporting integrity, equity, and political rights in the workings of the political process is constantly under scrutiny, and undermined by a new oligarchy of corruption that dominates the present power structure. Societies rooted in pluralistic divisions retreat, rather than advance, when confronted with the challenge of embracing a new political and social belief system.

Economic growth is the engine of development, but development is about people, about expanding their possibilities, improving their quality of life, and enhancing their capabilities. Nation-states are in a constant search for justice and for identity in striving for character and a purpose to economic and social advancement. For almost half a century, scholars sought to respond to the desire of independent people to live their lives, to give expression to independent thought, and to advance the cause of a critical tradition.

In the immediate post-colonial period, the focus was on development of the political economy. Today, after several decades, the focus is on the political economy of development. What is the difference? Put briefly, development of the political economy relates to the tasks of state and nation building. It is about designing and devising political and economic systems compatible with national realities and aspirations. In contrast, the political economy of development relates to the changes in the balance between winners and losers in the process of advancement, defined to include sustained growth and inclusiveness. The political economy of development must not only be sensitive and responsive to vital national and regional interests, but also take cognisance of shifts in a changing world order.

The first reform wave was about 'getting the macroeconomics right'. The second wave was 'getting the institutions right'. If development is the goal, 'getting the governance right' is the current wave, which acquires a special meaning as it can influence sustained growth and inclusive development. Politics and economics must be treated as inseparable in the analysis of development. In the final analysis, 'right policies will yield right outcomes'.

The issue of the 'crisis economy'

While the analysis is rooted in the experience of Trinidad and Tobago, the economy with the largest Gross Domestic Product (GDP) in the Caribbean community, its application is relevant to a wider regional economy. Tracing the context of the economic debate from the first wave of macroeconomic stability –the Washington Consensus –to the second wave, i.e., institutions matter, the question may be asked: what next? The answer to that question lies in the risks faced by Caribbean economies due to current global economic imbalances and the political dynamics of resource-rich countries falling into a downward spiral. It is apparent that once this trend begins, it is hard to stop. The local risk factors of emerging fiscal deficits, falling competitive advantage, and secular decline in productivity in the Caribbean economy cannot be mitigated through short-time cyclical capital inflows.

What is required is a radical reform of a development strategy to construct a knowledge-based economy, which challenges leadership to a better macroeconomic management approach. It has been argued that development today is elusive as economic linkages are missing and growth is limited by cycles in world prices.

The structural issues of inequality and poverty will not be solved easily in a context of a political economy where those controlling natural resource wealth use that wealth to maintain their economic and political power or in a currency reserve system where the international dollar reserves are equivalent to the United States (US) borrowing from the rest of the world.

Politics and Development
A strategic conversation on the missing politics in development

As we move forward in the 21st century, development has come face to face with politics, one of the key factors in the advancement of growth and development. Previous attention on this link focused on politics in policymaking and the conferring of benefits on parts of the society that will enhance the whole society's well-being and national interest. Specifying national interest is the work of the political process that is usually conducted in a competitive democratic system. This brings out large differences in the choice of the national interest, differences that at times may manifest in competing ideologies. Today, the debate has shifted towards the right policies that will yield the right outcomes.[3]

The polity of a society strives to work out the best balance between political and economic goals (i.e. reconciling the political and economic logic), while reflecting the national values of the society. Often, this equilibrium is unstable and constrained by the powers of the institutions in the society and the state. The application of the calculus of political economy allows the society to find the right balance that will promote sustained growth and development. Politics is about the distribution of power in a society, while political economy is about compensation to the 'winners' and 'losers' in any given distribution of power.

Development is about closing the gaps in social equity and the growth potential of the society. How to acquire and consolidate power depends on the nature and the outcome of the mechanisms of the political system. How to compensate the losers is part of the process of reshaping the society's social welfare. The politics of development is often viewed in narrow terms of the distribution of income and opportunities. Looking at inequality and injustice in our global economy, higher weights should be assigned to these goals in the policy paradigm of development. The market works by rewarding countries and individuals with the most productive assets; it fails by generating negative externalities for the vulnerable and by increasing the risks faced by the weak.

The market also has power – rules and regimes – which systematically favour already rich countries and people. To address these inequities, a global social contract is needed to deal with unequal endowments and to build sound institutions that will supply global public goods, construct global regulations to address market failures, and provide better representation of developing countries in world bodies.[4]

These elements in the global social contract raise critical issues of politics which cannot be overlooked. The idea of conditionality has dominated policy dialogue; but processing conditionality as 'making it happen' is the more pertinent development challenge. The argument will shift in a generic sense from 'what' to 'how', opening up a plethora of political matters.

Politics in development is likely to get deeper, as each political choice will have different development outcomes. As such, analysis of the political choices becomes an essential part of the data requirements for good decision-making. This poses a tremendous challenge to leaders in development, politics, policymaking and management alike. Apart from the undertaking to build models of politics and development, there will be the need to secure the population's legitimacy for this trade-off, as they are critical in making political choices. Is there a great transformation in developmental economics ahead of us?

The First Wave of Reforms

In the last 25 years, some developing countries have been on the 'catch-up' trajectory in the development cycle. Many have persistently attained high growth rates over a period. The Growth Report[5] identifies 13 such economies with a sustained growth rate of seven per cent over a quarter century. Is there a formula? What is the underlying growth strategy? How is the framework built to sustain high growth rates over a long period? Clearly, domestic policies, important as they are, worked in an open integrated world economy.

Increasing global demand, together with abundant labour supply, enables 'catch-up' growth in the early stages of development. For small economies, this is a special challenge. High growth rates are possible through sustained transformation of the society and economy. These dynamics unleash a new energy of microeconomic undergrowth, sometimes referred to as 'creative destruction' – creating new frontiers while protecting the people adversely affected by this change.

In the preface, the *Report* states that growth is not an end in itself but it is a necessary, if not sufficient, condition for broader development. Could broader development take place without high growth rates? The *Report* is silent on this issue, while regarding inclusive development as a critical objective. This implies that the nature of development must focus on inequality and poverty. These challenges remain the key focal points of development, which can be pursued effectively by societies without high growth rates. This raises the question of what is the natural rate of growth of a specific economy. How could inclusive development take place in any growth scenario? After all, inclusive development may well have a higher priority in the social welfare of the population. If not, the democratic outcome may alter the social welfare function through the workings of the political process.

The *Report* calls for a long-term commitment by political leaders pursuing with patience, perseverance, and pragmatism. However, it is arguable whether the incentives facing political leaders support this required commitment. How can continuity in growth strategy be attained in a competitive political market where the very disruption of that continuity creates a new political opportunity? Why would the development agenda take precedence over the political agendas of political entities vying for political office?

Understanding the link between politics and development is crucial and is an important ingredient in constructing a rapid growth formula. A credible and strong political leadership must be able to emerge from the workings of the democratic system, which itself must have built-in incentive structures if this is to occur. Identifying deficits in the political economy is not enough. The democratic rules and behaviour by which leaders operate must be scrutinised to ensure that they allow for a development outcome.

A greater demand for good governance needs to be created. Unless this demand exists, there is less possibility for the emergence of a supply of good governance. Here, the interaction between policy, institutions and the market becomes a critical ingredient in the growth strategy, a lesson learned from the experiences of the reform process. The first wave of reform policies concentrated on issues of macroeconomic stability: putting the house in order. The main measures of macroeconomic stability were opening up the economy to become competitive, removal of persistent budget and non-budget deficits, control over liquidity and inflationary excesses, and altering the supply structure of private and public goods.

The Second Wave of Reforms

The second wave that 'institutions matter' came to the forefront as issues of effective regulatory systems. More market-based initiatives and new institutions to promote inclusive development became central to the new reform. The right governance now acquires a special meaning to influence market behaviour so that the public interest is paramount. Sustained high growth rates and inclusive development – like equality of opportunity, giving everyone a fair chance to enjoy the fruits of growth – are the anchors of the new legitimacy of right governance. Honest and transparent processes in both the public and private sectors add to that legitimacy.

Small states face a special challenge because of the high per capita cost of public services, limited scope for production diversification, and increasing risks to economic shocks. The *Growth Report's* analysis of small states is rather limited, even though these states comprise a significant portion of sovereign nations. Its prescription for small states is this: embrace the world economy, form regional clubs and outsource some government functions. In small states, short-term cyclical capital inflows cannot mitigate the risk factors of emerging fiscal deficits, loss in competitive advantage and secular decline in productivity.

In defining the current challenge of Caribbean small states, a recent report by the Foundation for Politics and Leadership stated:

> Caribbean societies are caught in a profound wave of change, as they respond to a different globalized order and to an emerging crisis within the borders of their own politics. The political and economic paradigms of yesterday have lost their legitimacy to promote workable solutions for a generation that is impatient and has high expectations. The realization of these expectations cuts across the social and generational space unleashing the inherent conflict with politics and creating new obstacles to advancing development.[6]

The new obstacles may also surface in the strategy for high growth if countries are unable to navigate through global challenges ahead. As the world faces up to the issues of global warming and climate change, efforts to satisfy the criteria of efficiency and fairness as a global solution have reached an impasse. The global search for solutions between growth, income equality and environment has also been stalled on critical financial issues. The changes in the global relative prices may affect a country's choice of sectors in its development strategy, and have a fiscal and balance of payments impact. Demographic changes and policy coordination in multilateral systems will add to the challenges of assessing global risks, uncertainties, and opportunities. In particular, changes in the world's currency reserve system may provide a new impetus for shifting power in the governance of the financial institutions to reduce the risks faced by developing countries and improve the efficiency of the global system. One imminent risk is the rise of protectionism in the face of the World Trade Organization's (WTO) commitment to a flexible multilateral trading system.

The *Report* identifies the 'adding-up' question: if many individual countries pursued export-led growth, would it work in the aggregate? The idea is dismissed as a fallacy of composition as there is little evidence in the pattern of trade that early entrants block late arrivals. Countries graduate to higher levels of labour intensity in their exports, thus keeping the door open at lower levels for new entrants. This may in fact be a fallacy as the very composition of trade may change to the demands of an information era, making it uncompetitive to tread the old path. In any event, high growth rates are sustainable by structural changes in the economy that is at the same time competitive. It is unlikely that old paths will remain competitive, an essential ingredient in a strategy of sustained growth.

True enough, there is no generic formula for countries to emulate as each country has specific characteristics and historical experiences that must be reflected in the growth strategy. Do the experiences of these countries help in the understanding of the general theory of development? Do we need to design a new vintage of embodied and disembodied growth models that will explain the present reality in development? These are questions open to scholars of model building in the economics of development. The 'success' stories of even China and India do not deny that development remains the central global problem of our times. It would be a mistake to call a victory too early, as the *Growth Report* is tempted to do.

Political Economy of Development
What can be learned?

The United Nations University World Institute for Development Economics Research (UNU-WIDER) conference on country role model carefully examined the issues of macroeconomic stability, reform of institutions, and the politics of development as the model countries look ahead at the economic and political challenges. There is a lot of normative analysis on this theme, and each group of countries exhibits special features that allow for some generalisation. A key focus is on the third wave of the reform process, the next step. Success stories of some economies are presented. This provides insights and may have shed some new light on the performance of different strategies for economic development. What emerged from the conference are propositions that may guide thinking to reflect on the current reality, hurdles, and pathways.

The Nordic experience suggests that the key to organising the economy is to organise the society for consensus, being adaptable to innovative change and strengthen good institutions to counter the adversities of the resource curse. With little political room, Finland was able to achieve a political compromise while preserving the democratic institutions and basic freedoms, and allowing for necessary capital accumulation, wage moderation and welfare reforms. In the non-Nordic developed economies of Europe, the focus was on changing the economic structure to sustain employment and reduce the demand for the welfare state. The key strengths lie in the competitiveness of the economy and the contestability in the political system. Switzerland devised the right political institutions, starting with the Swiss confederation in 1848 to the current 'direct democracy' model that paved the way for sustained economic growth of a consensus nature.[7]

Process and the microeconomic foundations of capabilities were paramount in the East Asian and Pacific economies. Economic development results from domestic capital accumulation and enhancing the capabilities of the population in this emerging part of the world economy. The Asian giants face the challenge of sustainable economic growth translating into economic development. These successes lay in dynamic learning and flexible institution building as components in a strategic approach to development. The ideas raised in the *Growth Report* are consistent with this approach, focusing on development as a process with strong microeconomic foundations embedded in the people themselves.

The transitional economies confused the critics in their ability to cope with the politics of changing the system, as they work the new institutions of a market economy. Here, shock therapy could not bring results, as the initial conditions did not prevail and private accumulation of wealth raised a new dichotomy between the roles of the state and the market. The key lesson for development is not to discard the existing strengths in the economy. Hungary offers an example of a neo-institutionalism/political economy approach to development where reform coalitions were built into a reform strategy shaping the reform waves.[8]

When the issue of development is applied to Sub-Saharan Africa, the main missing ingredient to success is getting the political economic model right. Here, the pendulum swings between taking control of the state and state failure. Augustin K. Fosu's article on the anti-growth syndrome traces the political and economic context of development in African countries since independence to the end of the last century.[9] It is an extraordinary account, succinctly showing the persistent conflict between the workings of political forces and institutions for economic growth.

The conservative policy framework gives way to more soft and hard state interventions, a phenomenon that appears to reflect in all the African case studies. This approach emphasises the challenges of macroeconomic management in a post-colonial Africa. Fosu argues that a common thread emerges where the institutional framework displayed an anti-growth bias retarding economic development. This experience gives rise to the importance of the institutional constraint in macroeconomic performance and the emergence of democracy and development models as a key learning requirement to understand change in Africa.

Latin American and Caribbean economies faced the development challenge of 'stability in fragility' as the reform process was fractured and incomplete. Here, more than anywhere else, the issue of theory vs. real change emerges, as good macroeconomic indicators do not necessarily imply a fall in inequality and poverty levels and improvements in other development indicators. The dichotomy between growth and development is stark as the entropy index (measure of diversification) suggests that the development cycle may recur. There is much uncertainty since development discontent may find expression in political populism.

The process of economic behaviour re-emerges in the discussion on ·Middle-East and North African economies. Development is seen as correcting mistakes on the roadmap to higher levels of development. These economies exhibit 'uniqueness' and their development hurdle is how to use the 'Dutch disease'[10] phenomenon to change direction and broaden the development process from fragility to sustainability. Stable leadership rooted in their history and culture currently provides the right politics for growth, if not development and democracy.

An overriding theme is the role of leadership and governance in economic development. Leadership and governance must be rooted in the right politics, reconciling economic outcomes with political democracy. A clear distinction between policies and institutions needs articulation, as policies do change when right institutions evolve. A key premise in formulating development strategy is to recognise the initial conditions and the successes of the past, as this becomes the departure point from the old paradigms.

There have been significant strides in the development performance over the last 50 years. Yet, the path ahead is still treacherous, given the uncertainties in the direction of global adjustment and global market failures, especially in the context of current financial crises and global recession. The misalignment of currencies and the upward inflationary pressures due partly to new aggregate demand is drawing the attention of world leaders. Rising food and fuel prices are a reflection of the stress in the fundamentals of the world economy.

The adjustment to this current global macro imbalance is unclear and poses new risks to developed and developing countries alike. It may lead to a shift in political power and a reaction as the political leadership in today's world is the new development challenge of tomorrow.

A New Approach to Politics and Development

The current phase of globalisation has deepened considerably. There are benefits of globalisation even for developing countries, as the Nobel laureate Joseph Stiglitz observes. 'Globalisation has reduced the sense of isolation of developing countries and…has given many people in the developing world access to knowledge well beyond the reach of even the wealthiest in any country a century ago.'[11]

Nevertheless, as Nancy Birdsall[12] points out, income inequality has risen in most regions over the last two decades, and consumption data from groups of developing countries reveal the striking inequality that exists between the richest and the poorest in populations across different regions. Globalisation is gathering momentum. However, the importance of the sovereign governments should not be overlooked as they still have the power to erect significant obstacles to globalisation, ranging from tariffs, to immigration restrictions, and military hostilities. The world is still made up of nation states and a global marketplace.

Louis Emmerij states that the fork before us is whether there is one theory (development) and one practice for the entire world, or whether there should be many theories in order to tailor-make development policies according to culture and habits of countries.[13] This opens up the question of the definition of development. It is here that Nobel laureate Amartya Sen's insights throw new light on the nature of development - development is about creating a set of capabilities and development is about 'freedom.'[14]

The scope is now widened, as Sen's interest shifts from the pure theory of social choice to a more practical approach that sees individual advantage not merely as opulence or utility, but primarily in terms of the lives people manage to live and the freedom they have to choose the kind of life they have reason to value. Sen's emphasis on freedom of choice naturally leads him to democracy as a preferred political system where a country does not have to be deemed fit for democracy; rather, it has to become fit through democracy. The pendulum has now moved to democracy and good governance as a critical requirement of development. However, there is still the search for a consensus on the precise indicators of democracy and good governance. What is clear is that the conduct of politics will influence considerably the measurement of these indicators.

In the search for these indicators on good governance, the notions of political tolerance and pluralism can differ remarkably, if government is viewed from a western liberal perspective or from the perspective of development outcomes. The World Bank with a Western liberal eye, measures the six components of good governance as voice and accountability; political stability and lack of violence; government effectiveness; regulatory burden; rule of law; and the control of corruption. These are important indicators, but miss issues like economic inequality, poverty, employment, technology, liberty and rights, capabilities and well-being.

In several developing countries, the institutional framework may not be mature. Yet the outcomes of governance may be high when measured by indices such as the human development and gross happiness. Therefore, a consensus on a set of good governance indicators must capture the dynamics of development that takes place in an ever-changing institutional framework.

The World Bank has measured a 'development dividend' of good governance. This dividend is a difficult proposition to isolate and to measure, but there is no doubt that good governance can deliver significant improvements to people, particularly if the demand for good governance could grow among the population in a steady manner. Here, the dynamics of the political culture becomes important, as good governance will thrive, if the demand for it increases. Often, this is a matter of political choice and the conduct of politics in any given situation. In spite of a growing proliferation of good governance initiatives, much work is needed on the issues of the nature, measurement, and supply of good governance.

An evolutionary view of the major waves of development is presented by Mika Mannermaa in her work for the Finnish Parliament.[15] Mannermaa states that the Agrarian era (ca. 6000 BC–1750 AD) attended to issues of community interest within the village context. The industrial era followed for the next 250 years driven by new means of production where models of representative democracy emerged as a governmental form. Today, the information era is upon us, creating an information society, yet to mature. It is characterised by innovations in communication technology. Networks, rapid changes and flexible thinking will now inform the political process, creating a democracy of 'minorities' that will undermine the 'majority' notion in representative democracy.

How will the conduct of politics be affected by this new wave of development? According to the Committee for the Future in the Finnish Parliament, the notion of 'instantism' (the expectation that things have to happen immediately) may see a shift towards electronic voting, and an increase in 'non-representative' civil society's influence in the political process. Consequently, the welfare function that reflects the developmental needs of the society may be at risk, adding new challenges to development and democracy.

In a path-breaking study two decades ago, Robert Scalapino identified the key link between politics and development in Asia at that time.[16] A large part of the 'success' of the Asian development in three decades can be attributed to the management of tensions and politics in these countries. To a western mind, the kind of political system may not fit the indicators of the democracy matrix, thus bringing into focus the link between political systems and economic development.

Yang Yao bases his explanation for China's record of economic growth on the notion of 'disinterested government'.[17] He defines a disinterested government as one that does not have differentiated interests among the segments of the society and is more likely to foster overall economic growth of the country instead of advancing the interest of certain segments that it represents or forms an alliance with.

This is because reform is seen as a historical evolution reaffirmed by the belief that the pursuit of egalitarian policies and an equal society is the trusted prerogative of the political elite that cannot be comprised by alliances with any segment of the society. Yao dismisses the 'one party system' as being anti-democratic, as there are democratic elements in China's political structure allowing for voice and accountability, and indeed other components of indicators of good governance.

Politics and economics have been central to the analysis of development and the western academic tradition has kept it so partly for pedagogical reasons. However, in the study of development, such a separation may conceal the dynamic inter connections between the economic and political factors. Could there be a synergy between economic and political logic in the study of development?

Waves in Economic Management: The Search for New Thinking

The inauguration of The Foundation for Politics and Leadership raises fresh hopes for a new direction for politics and leadership in the Caribbean. There is the beginning of an emerging consensus that was expressed by several commentators that the time has come again for a new point of departure in Caribbean development. David Jessop[118] calls for Caribbean think tanks, study groups and corporate retreats to look over the horizon and react to the new trends and developments that will shape the future.

There is no single or simple answer but there is an answer, and the search for real solutions must inform the creation of that future. The hopes are that the 'new direction' forum mentioned above would advance Caribbean thinking well beyond what was carefully documented in the 1990s West Indian Commission's report, *Time for Action* published in 1992. The report was a static expression of unfulfilled Caribbean dreams. What we need now is a roadmap for creating new energies in Caribbean development – a new departure point.

The Context of the Economic Debate

The history of political economy has always had departure points and shifts in the prevailing economic paradigm, putting the economy on a different path. One such departure point in the hemisphere and the Caribbean region was in the 1980s. In Trinidad and Tobago there was a shift from a commanding heights economy to a market-driven economic process. The economic strategy of the Washington Consensus was embraced and the answers to the following questions sought: What macroeconomic measures are required to stabilise the economy? How do we liberalise our markets to exploit opportunities abroad? Why do we need a better relationship between the private and public sectors?

The answers to these questions are the first generation reforms, a challenge of structural adjustment. The political process was emphasised culminating in a failed coup attempt in 1990 that threatened to derail the new direction. The first generation reforms were soon seen to be insufficient, giving scope to a second generation of reforms focusing on building institutions.

These institutional reforms required the change in the exchange rate regime, a new regulatory model in telecommunication and technology, meeting international banking standards, and creating new delivery systems for public goods like water, electricity, postal services, roads, bridges, education, and health.

Changing institutions became much more difficult than imagined as it also meant a change in the power structure controlling these institutions. Many talked about change, but few were really prepared to give up the power and the privileges that the change required for the common good.

Once again, the development results were disappointing and a populist discontent emerged as prices soared beyond the reach of large segments of the population, and poverty levels rose leading to violence and lawlessness. In the meantime, the integrity of the political process was questioned as bribery and corruption drew the national attention. This is the context of the development path in Trinidad and Tobago since the turning point of the 1980s when the country embraced a reform agenda, similar to that taking place in the wider Caribbean and Latin American region.

The Expression of the Crisis

Protest politics emerged in the first decade of the 21st century leading to the election of 'leftist' governments in Bolivia, Brazil and Venezuela. In the Caribbean, 'change' governments came into office in Barbados, Jamaica, St Lucia, Belize and recently Grenada. Globally, there was a fervent passion for political change as expressed in Australia, Kenya, Zimbabwe, and France and the United States. These political changes were taking place in the midst of an evolving global and national crisis.

In the April 2008 issue of The *Economist*, the cover page headline read 'Fixing Finance…and the risks of getting it wrong'. The 'home rage' in America's mortgage market raised issues of confidence and faith in open financial markets. First, there was disbelief and denial, then fear, and then came anger because three decades of public policy was dominated by the power of the markets. Finance stumbled with sub-prime lending, the credit crunch, and weak business and consumer confidence; laying the conditions for the onset of a recession in the United States. Other countries like Canada, Mexico, the United Kingdom, and Japan were at risk of contagion effects.

Action was taken to neutralise market fears by bringing real interest rates to near zero. The US dollar weakened in response to stabilising a rising trade deficit. In the economy, between 2002 and 2007, the energy sector's contribution to GDP rose from 26.2 per cent to 43 per cent, the total revenue from 29.9 per cent to 56.0 per cent, and exports from 73.3 per cent to 89.4 per cent. In Trinidad and Tobago, this increased the exposure to adverse financial shocks and emphasised the 'natural resource curse' and vulnerability of this energy-based economy.

Particularly worrisome was the growth of the non-energy deficit or the level of net domestic fiscal injection from 7.6 per cent in 2003 to 15.4 per cent of GDP in 2007, which increased further in 2008. This was a key source of domestic inflationary pressures. These statistics confirmed that the US economy was facing structural imbalances that reflected a sustained inflation surge and the creeping up of fiscal pressures that would soon create a chronic deficit in public finance.

Confidence and Risks in the Global Economy

Underlying this development was the huge risk of the global economic imbalances – few rich countries were receiving large current account deficits. The United States deficit was about three and a half times larger than the deficits of all other countries of the Organisation for Economic Co-operation and Development (OECD) combined. It is estimated that the average growth rate of energy during the next years will be about 5.5 per cent, and given the supply constraints, this will lead to dramatic price escalation. Global growth will be negatively affected. There will, however, be more resilience in the major markets of the developing world.

Historically, resource rich countries fall into a downward spiral and once the cycle has begun it is hard to stop. Economist Joseph Stiglitz, in *Making Globalization Work*[19] argues: 'the political dynamics of resource-rich countries often lead to high levels of inequality; in both developed and less developed countries, those controlling the natural resource wealth use that wealth to maintain their economic and political power – which includes appropriating for themselves a large fraction of the country's resource endowment'.

Can you imagine Trinidad and Tobago without an energy sector? We are sitting on the cliff of a crisis economy in a global economy that is on the verge of major macroeconomic adjustment. A key element of this adjustment will come in reforming the global reserve system and in the expected global crisis in food and water.

The global reserve system is at the heart of the weakness on the global financial system. In the dollar denominated reserve system, the reserves are tantamount to borrowings of the US. The return on these lending is much less than it would have been if it were invested in other commercial projects. Stiglitz estimated[20] that the cost of holding reserves is in excess of US$300 billion per year. That represents four times the level of foreign assistance from the whole world.

The key risk issues ahead are a global recession, adjustment in macroeconomic imbalances, global reserve reform and the erosion of competitiveness. These risk factors pose challenges to the resilience of Caribbean economies, already vulnerable to external shocks. On the local radar screen, new expressions of internal balance will surface because of the coming trends in economic behaviour.

The twin deficits in the fiscal and current account may once more recur as a key policy concern. The reasons why this may now emerge as a risk are the emergence of a growing non energy fiscal deficit, notwithstanding the persistence of buoyant revenues, the continuous fall in competitive advantage on an economy-wide basis, and a secular decline in productivity in the Caribbean economy over the last 25 years.

These risk factors may be mitigated in the short-term by energy financial inflows. However, recent developments in the behaviour of energy companies operating in Trinidad and Tobago by cutting expenditure and seeking more tax breaks, would suggest an end of sustained growth in this sector. This is further reinforced by the revelations of the limitation on gas supplies in the wells and the high depletion rates in the industry.

Crossroads and Changing Directions

The economy is now at another crossroad in choosing an economic path for the future. We now stand at yet another point of departure. The gains made during the first and second generations may have reached the end. The Caribbean Community (CARICOM) has long since reached its limits. In spite of the recent breakdown of the Doha Development

Rounds of trade negotiations, the Caribbean countries remain defensive in their trade negotiations. In short, the economic space in which the region operates is perhaps receding. 'New thinking' in the political economy is now a necessity.

What are the new pillars for building another generation of economic leadership? In the immediate future, preparing for the adverse risks ahead is the key challenge. There are positive risks that we must address upfront. How do we go about that task?

Energy flows converted into public investment is limited in its returns. This is so because such public investment, rather than generating income and output in the national economy, makes more demands on further recurrent expenditure. Infrastructure development for building productive capacity in a competitive economy is the direction in which we should be heading.

This calls for a radical altering of development strategy to deal with structural inflation; that spells serious economic instability. Such instability may lead to social pressures that cannot be contained by the political process. Economic leadership must shift from targeting a dateline for development, to managing risks on a current basis – risks associated with the falling dollar. And the expected fortunes of the energy sector must be carefully simulated in a model with foresight.

In this forecast the following risks must be factored: the exchange rate and interest rate volatility; shortages and price rises in an overheated economy; the fall in the real value of the local currency; and the change in food and fuel prices on relative prices in the world.

New directions in building institutional capacity for delivering public goods must be on top of the economic leadership agenda. The old institutions may have lost their relevance, calling now for new models for cooperation among private, public, and civil society. The role of the state must respond to the delivery and equity issues confronting the society. The bureaucracy and the judiciary are essential activities that must be included in the matrix of governance fundamentals.

New directions are required in the models of political leadership. Kelvin Dalrymple,[21] former Chief Research Economist of the Caribbean Development Bank (CDB) in discussing the role of leadership in economic development, characterised the models of Caribbean leadership as personality, autocratic, dynastic, crisis, and situational. The political structures that support these styles of leadership must be assessed in the context of development and right politics. The economy is riding on a cliff, with the expectation that the bubble will grow in response to global rise in prices and non-performing energy output in the local economy. The fall is inevitable. At that time, the stabilization fund (still under-funded) may have to be accessed and the national debt increased. Where do we go from here?

Choices for the future

The *Foundation for Politics and Leadership* provides a forum to critically define the issues and construct solutions. To do so, the following questions provide a framework for an action agenda:

- How do small nations sustain development in a constantly changing global information and competitive market environment?

- What is the relationship between a state-centred economy, use of state funds, natural resources, and sustainable development?

- What is the relationship between the state and the development of a market economy and healthy private sector? How can the new network power – social networks and connectivity – be used as a catalyst for creating new leadership in development?

We have arrived at another point of departure. First, it was a programme for adjustment, then the creation of institutions. Now, the challenge is of constructing the structure for a knowledge-based economy and introducing a risk management approach to economic leadership.

The time has come to introduce a paradigm shift in the economic leadership. Trinidad and Tobago is a classic resource-based economy. In such economies, development is elusive as economic linkages are missing and growth is limited by the cycles in world prices. The imperative is now to search for new choices for the future. Resource- and investment-driven industrialisation strategies cannot deliver sustained development.

Today, knowledge is a major driving force in development, fuelled by changes in the globalised economy in the new information era. The building of a knowledge economy has become possible due to the creation of knowledge through research and advances in technology, investments in education and a new openness to innovation. At the heart of this is the search for competitiveness and sustainable development. Investment in knowledge infrastructure, including human capital, offers a new wave in economic restructuring with higher value-added products with closer customer linkages. Finland was able to transform from a natural resource-based economy into a knowledge-based economy in a short period, recently ranking first in the World Economic Forum's competitive index.

Structural transformation to a knowledge driven economy may better prepare us for a secure future. Small economies can build a competitive edge by focusing on infrastructure that enhances productivity; incentives that facilitate technological leapfrogging; and investments that quickly penetrate the global market. Once these goals are set, a programme to direct private and public national expenditure towards these choices must be implemented. This will demand a deep understanding of the political economy of change including the challenges of building capacity in the education, information, telecommunication, and innovative sectors.

A risk management approach to macroeconomic management should be adopted. The basic elements of the first and second generation reforms must be kept, but a third point of departure is now mandatory. The world economy is not standing still and global markets are more integrated. This raises adverse risks and positive opportunities in economic management. Visioning and consensus-making mechanisms must be seen as a continuous process in framing strategies and executing plans.

The first question is whether small states will be able to survive. Limited by geographical space and capacity, it seems to be an impossible target, especially in a world based on reciprocity and competitiveness. Lino Briguglio[22] makes a strong argument that small states have been surprisingly resilient as they respond to their vulnerability to external shocks, their inherent narrow range of exports, and structural openness. This resilience, Briguglio claims, is based on policy interventions in four principal areas, viz., macroeconomic stability, microeconomic efficiency, good governance, and social development.

This provides a framework upon which a risk management matrix could be designed for decision-making in the present. The question for small states now is whether resilience is the necessary condition for sustainability?

A Political Economy Perspective of Small State Development

The political economy perspective sets the backdrop for the future agenda discussed in this book. The new feature to this perspective is a regional approach to small state economic resilience. Small European states share the common characteristic of having achieved a high degree of economic and political success. In addition, like all other small states, they have to continuously adapt to the changing world economy. How have they succeeded in their development? In *Small States in World Markets*, Peter Katzenstein[23] provides an analysis of the industrial adjustment strategy of small European states of Sweden, Norway, Denmark, Netherlands, Belgium, Austria, and Switzerland.

Katzenstein describes how these states have coped with changes in the international economy. The social agenda asks to build social cohesion and to promote basic needs and capabilities; it asks for the delivery of basic social services to consider regional social impact, and to establish the Caribbean Court of Justice (CCJ). The political agenda wants the reform of systems and governmental institutions, electoral reforms, a demand for greater accountability, and the effectiveness of public policy.

The CARICOM Single Market and Economy (CSME) agenda requires the inclusion of the development dimension in Economic Partnership Agreements (EPAs), the set up of regional institutions for good governance, and the formulation of a management approach. The private sector agenda should include private sector leadership and involvement, encourage investments and entrepreneurship, provide incentives for Small and Medium Enterprises (SME) development, and institute governance of private sector and microfinance. The scholarship agenda is about linking political and economic logic, about more process analysis, about directions for capacity building and good governance. It deals with charting demands for good governance and generating new ideas to cope with global changes.

Due to their small size, these European states are dependent on the international markets. They have pursued a policy of adjustment with economic change through a variety of economic and social policies that prevent the costs of change causing political crises. They have cultivated a strategy that responds to, and reinforces, domestic goals that mitigate the political impact of economic changes. The leadership in these states has maintained the legitimacy of the political arrangements through good governance policies.

As Katzenstein notes, the yardstick for measuring their success is the extent to which social coalitions, political institutions, and public policies facilitate shifts in factors of production that increase the economic efficiency with due regard to the requirements of political legitimacy. This form of social partnership covers all areas of economic and social policy that is able to diffuse conflicts and accommodate the different interests of the stakeholders. This model of 'democratic corporatism' (or social partnership) demonstrates a culture of compromise reflected through their political arrangements, reinforcing the shared interpretations of the collective good.

The social partnership provides these European states with the space to respond to changes in the international economy. In their effort to cope with constant change, they pursue a combined strategy of liberalisation, domestic compensation (or distribution) and flexible industrial adjustments. Hence, their strategy is flexible, reactive, incremental, and constantly improvising to cope with change. Their policies are aimed at identifying and anticipating changes in the international economy and helping the social partners (private sector, trade unions and government) to adjust to the changes without causing political instability. In another comparative historical study of development of European states, Dieter Senghaas[24] tries to uncover the development paths the countries have followed, and why some parts of Europe developed while others did not. This Eurocentric analysis draws lessons from varied recent history of European development. His discussion focuses on Friedrich List's theory of how 'delayed development' is possible in a world economy characterised by growing development differentials. Senghaas examines the relationship between various types of development paths: 'associative' (export-led), 'dissociative' (opening up of domestic potential) and 'auto centric' development or 'peripheralization'.

Among the smaller states of Europe, Belgium, Austria and Hungary pursued a dissociative strategy. Switzerland and the Netherlands adopted an associative development path. A third set of small states – Denmark, Sweden, Norway and Finland – have pursued an associative-dissociative development history. These states illustrate how a redistribution process preceded industrial growth in successful delayed development. This 'distribution before growth path' in Europe contradicts conventional development theory that puts growth first and redistribution later.

Briguglio in *Small States and the Pillars of Economic Resilience*[25] defines the economic resilience of small states as the ability to generate and manage a relatively high GDP per capita when compared with other developing countries. This ability, given the small states' vulnerability, is associated with policy-induced measures to adjust to external shocks. These policy measures, called pillars of resilience, are macroeconomic stability, microeconomic market efficiency, good governance, and social development. Deficiencies in any one of them is likely to compromise a country's ability to withstand exogenous shocks.

The macroeconomic aspects of resilience building are stability, stewardship, and competitiveness. The regulatory framework needs to promote competitiveness, stability, and predictability. Since small states have limited scope in setting discretionary fiscal and monetary policies, they would need to concentrate on factor and market flexibility. The policies to promote microeconomic efficiency have to focus on market efficiency and right resource allocation. There is a greater role for the private sector in developing small state resilience. Creating a favourable environment for the growth of a healthy private sector and entrepreneurship is crucial. Policies have to promote competition in domestic, regional and global markets.

In a chapter of *Small States*, Claudius Preville[26] has noted that development has a wider connotation than economic resilience. He associates resilience building with social and environmental concerns that cannot be considered in isolation from the economic realities. Furthermore, social cohesion negatively affects small states experiencing political and/or ethnic conflicts. Policies need to take into account the wide divergences in income among the different groups.

A social policy that promotes social cohesion enhances the chances of economic success. In another study, Sudha Venu Menon[27] shows how the multicultural small state of Singapore is a classic example of good leadership and public management in realising the country's development goals. Governance and leadership are put forward as central forces in fostering economic growth in that country.

The Agenda for the Future

Leadership and governance have been important to the development of appropriate institutional frameworks for sustained dynamic development and constant innovation to adapt to changing external realities. The social partnership policies of certain small states have provided the basis for economic resilience. From Briguglio et al. we can infer that in the area of good governance, small states need measures that are more specific to their respective contexts. The important elements of governance are openness, transparency, government accountability, administrative efficiency, respect for human rights and the rule of law.

Venu Menon's report also notes the importance of leadership and governance in the development of small states. A recent newspaper column states that history provides us with a plethora of evidence pointing to a country's development owing to the leadership, irrespective of whether is it in the history of Western advanced countries or the post Second World War emergence of nations.[28] Leadership is vital in meeting the goals of development. So is good governance.

The last report on the Wilton Park Conference observes that the era of preference is now effectively over and globalisation poses the major challenge to the Caribbean region.[29] The region must therefore develop strategies and policies to enhance resilience. The report raises the following urgent needs of the region: to develop of modern skills like information technology, to enhance entrepreneurship skills and education, to promote small and medium enterprises, to address food and energy security, and to make the region more attractive to investors. The report notes that the promotion of good governance is an important issue. The region has also seen recent changes of governments with a new generation of leaders and the expectation of fresh thinking. What should be the fresh thinking for leadership and development of small states?

The New Political Economy Agenda

Merilee Grindle[30] makes a pertinent point that the reform of the state in the Caribbean and elsewhere demonstrates the importance of ideas in the politics of promoting reform of the state, something that Owen Arthur and Vaughan Lewis also reiterate. In the first chapter of the book the authors make an important point that a fresh thinking of leadership and governance in the development of small states must not only be sensitive and responsive to vital national and regional interests, but also take cognisance of shifts in a changing world order.

The key factors in the new political economy of development are leadership and good governance. Political leadership today must face up to the new notions of formal and functional sovereignty and the exercise of pooled sovereignty in relations between nation-states. Development involves some of the hardest choices between the development path and distribution of public resources. In the current context, governance is about the way in which trade-offs are made between keeping pace with global developments and being sensitive to local and regional aspirations. Global economic trends are bound to impact on domestic and regional politics. The future problems will be in the area of human security that will need to be addressed by a combination of innovative domestic policies and international cooperation via various dialogues and formal institutional agreements.

The task of leadership is to find a synergy between economics and politics in the development of small states. Managing natural resources in a sustainable manner is another major agenda for small states. The economic growth prospects of small island states will depend on management to mitigate the future impacts of climate change.

The Social Agenda

Good governance or quality governance relates to the quality of leadership that can forge 'social cohesion' in a plural society. The future agenda of leadership would have to promote the basic capabilities that cannot be left solely to market forces. Social objectives can contribute to economic growth and human capital. This implies improving government resources and the capacity to implement social policies and deliver basic services. This calls for a fresh look at appropriate governance structures and delivery mechanisms.

The choices about future governance and development should involve a 'regional social compact'. It is necessary to demonstrate renewed commitment to building a regional institution that will foster economic growth and development, namely, the CCJ. This institution will ensure the legal commitment and obligation to implement decisions taken at the regional level after substantial consultation and negotiation among relevant parties. The future of the Caribbean will be brighter once we find the confidence to make something as vital as a regional court function as intended, rather than remain in its present uncertain state.

The Political Agenda

Many small states are today facing the challenge of political reform of the system and institutions of government. During the past 50 years since the Caribbean states attained independence, the Westminster system of governance has been subject to intense scrutiny and the call for fundamental political reform has emerged. This is currently a serious issue in popular, political and academic circles. Of significance is the issue of electoral reform and how governments are elected, which has become a key issue in sustaining democracy in these small states.

At the beginning of the 21st century, the intersection between politics and technology is now part of the new political scenario in connecting minds and shaping political behaviour. Electronic voting is already being promoted as a viable system in this global community. So too are changes in the new media that will enhance the information flow in the quest for good enough governance. Electoral reform is a major requirement for small states attempting to bring people closer to government and so strengthen the pillars of democracy.

The process of constitution making has come to the fore as nation states strive to alter their worn out constitutions, embrace new approaches to stop the abuse of power, demand greater accountability of the executive power and enhance the effectiveness of public policy implementation. In addition, plural societies face special challenges in reforming constitutional structures that promote social cohesiveness, national character, and justice.

The Caribbean Single Market Economy Agenda

There is the 'unfinished business' of matching the institutional arrangements of CARICOM to the political strategising and implementing the single market economy and its external negotiating requirements. The task ahead is to relate and support the CSME through a process of political legitimating decisions made in these respects, an essential task for the political leadership. Furthermore, the international economic environment will have an impact on this process through the EPA, for example.

Against the backdrop of the CSME, individual state governance as well as regional governance need to be addressed. Given the deepening of interdependence, the regional institutional capacity for good governance and management has to be improved. In this context, chapters five and six in this book alert us to the leadership's failure to include the development dimension in making trade-offs with a flawed CARIFORUM–EPA process.

This trade-off works against regional integration and development goals. The fresh thinking should be in terms of consolidating regional governance. While it is important for the region to reorder its relations with the rest of the world, leadership and governance will have to place the development goals of the region as the guiding principle of the relationship. A new CSME cannot be achieved and made to work relying on the existing regional organs such as the Council for Finance and Planning (COFAP) and the Council for Trade and Economic Development (COTED). Establishing a regional development fund would go a long way fostering new institutional capacity.

The Private Sector Agenda

A Caribbean Business Council should be created since a new CSME will also be driven to a large extent by the private sector. This Council will facilitate greater private sector leadership and involvement in all aspects of the creation and management of the CSME. Given the need to expand the private sector and to create jobs in small states, the new agenda is to provide incentives to encourage investment and entrepreneurship. New and innovative approaches are needed to ensure that there is a continuous process of building local capacity in the region.

In an environment of limited alternative employment opportunities, self-employment and SMEs will continue to grow in the region and improve in competitiveness. Addressing their credit needs is crucial to fostering their development and promoting entrepreneurship. Microfinance is one way of achieving this goal. Microfinance is important for small Caribbean states when considering the contribution of SMEs to GDP, employment, access to credit, and the social benefit it brings.

The current regulatory environment in the region does not favour the microfinance sector, as there is no policy or regulatory framework specifically addressing the unique and specific needs of the microfinance. The CSME will also impact the small and medium enterprise sector and the microfinance industry. The small and medium enterprise and microfinance sectors will become central to the region's future development policy.

Governments and financial institutions at the national and regional levels have to take a fresh regional look at the financial regulation to put microfinance and small and medium enterprise policies within the Caribbean region's development goals. The way forward is to create an enabling policy environment to support an integrated approach to small and medium enterprises. This implies improving the institutional governance for the private sector and microfinance.

The Scholarship Agenda

Global trends are constantly changing. In order to be resilient, small states will need to keep pace by generating new ideas to cope with the changes. This calls for a regional scholarship agenda that raises the following fundamental issues for the future of leadership and development of small states: How do we reconcile economic/development outcomes with political democracy; What are the new challenges to development and what should be the appropriate responses?

As guidelines for the scholarship agenda, the following propositions are presented:

1. the need to get a frame of analysis that links the political and economic logic;

2. global forces are disrupting and this requires a shift from pure policy analysis to process analysis;

3. the search for a new great transformation in economics as Polayni[31] did, requires a proper understanding of the working of the democratic political process; and

4. creating the right political capacity (structure, institutions, and incentives) is an essential task for furthering the goals of good governance. Unless there is a demand for good governance, there will be less chances of having a supply of good governance.

Notes

1. Adapted from Winston Dookeran & Akhil Malaki, *Leadership and Governance in Small States, Getting Development Right* VDM Verlag Dr Muller, 2008. Introduction; Chapter 3 - Politics & Development: A strategic conversation on the missing politics in development; Chapter 11 - Waves in Economic Management: The Search for New Thinking; Chapter 13 - Epilogue: A Political Economy Perspective of Small State Development.
2. Ricardo Hausmann (July 2010), based on a workshop facilitated by the Finance Minister at the Ministry of Finance of Trinidad and Tobago, *Modified Suggestions and Concepts* of Dr Ricardo Hausmann based on Complex Dynamic System Behaviour.
3. See speech by Winston Dookeran on July 28, 2010 'Risks and Challenges, The Economy' at the American Chambers of Commerce of Trinidad and Tobago (Brochure: *Moving from Promises to Performance, The Underpinnings of the 2011 Budget,* Minister of Finance, September 30, 2010) for practical application of Getting Development Right.
4. Nancy Birdsall, *The World is Not Flat: Inequality and Injustice in our Local Economy*, UNU-WIDER Annual Lecture 9, Marina Congress Centre, Helsinki, October 26, 2005. She argues that global markets alone will not increase wealth and welfare in the global economy, and there is the need to address the fragile global polity. Available online: http://www.wider.unu.edu/publications/annual-lectures/en_GB/anual-lectures/
5. Commission on Growth and Development (2008). *The Growth Report: Strategies for Sustained Growth and Inclusive Development.* http://www.growthcommission.org.
6. The Foundation for Politics and Leadership, a think and action initiative, was launched in Port of Spain, Trinidad on June 4, 2008. Homepage: http//www.fplcaribbean.com
7. Beatrice Weder and Rolf Weder, 'Switzerland's rise to a wealthy Nation: Competition and Contestability as key Factors'. Paper presented to UNU-WIDER Conference on Country Role Models, Marina Congress Centre, Helsinki, June 13–14, 2008. See (www.wider.unu.edu/research/projects-by-theme/development-and-finance/en_GB/country
    They had this to say:
    > the Swiss political system with its direct democratic elements and the implemented principle of subsidiarity created political contestability that maintained government efficiency and led to political stability throughout history.

8. Lázló Csaba, 'Country Study Hungary'. Paper presented to the UNU-WIDER Conference on Country Role Models, Marina Congress Centre, Helsinki, June 13–14, 2008.

9. Augustin K. Fosu, 'Anti-Growth Syndromes in Africa: A Synthesis of the Case Studies'. In Ndulu, B et al., *The Political Economy of Economic Growth in Africa 1960-2000*. (Cambridge: Cambridge University Press, 2008) 137–72.

10. Dutch disease is a concept that purportedly explains the apparent relationship between the increase in exploitation of natural resources and a decline in the manufacturing sector.

11. See, IMF Staff, *'Globalization: A brief Overview'*, with a reference to Joseph Stiglitz's *Globalization and its Discontents*, (New York, 2003), 4. Available online: http://www.imf.org/exteranal/np/exr/ib/2008

12. Birdsall, *The World is Not Flat.*

13. Louis Emmerij, *'Turning Points in Development Thinking and Practice'*. In George Mavrotas and Anthony Shorrocks, eds. *Advancing Development: Core Themes in Global Economics, Studies in Development Economics and Policy*. (Hampshire: Palgrave Macmillan) 2007.

14. Amaryta Sen, *Development as Freedom* (Oxford: Oxford University Press, 1999). See also, Wyne E. Nafziger, 'From Seers to Sen: The Meaning of Economic Development' in Mavrotos & Shorrocks, eds *Advancing Development.*

15. Mika Mannermaa, *Democracy in the Turmoil of the Future*. A publication of the Committee of the Future, Parliament of Finland, 2007.

16. Robert A. Scalapino, *Politics of Development: Perspectives of 20th Century Asia*. (Harvard University Press, 1989).

17. Yang Yao, 'The Disinterested Government: An Interpretation of China's Economic Success in the Reform Era'. Paper presented to the UNU-WIDER Conference on Country Role Models, Marina Congress Centre, Helsinki, June 13–14, 2008.

18. David Jessop is the Director of the Caribbean Council of Europe and a regular commentator of Caribbean issues in several forums.

19. Joseph E. Stiglitz, *Making Globalization Work*.(New York: W.W. Norton & Company), 2007.

20. Ibid.

21. Kelvin Dalrymple, former Chief Research Economist, Caribbean Devlopment Bank, Barbados: 'A catalyst for development resources in the Caribbean', High-Level Roundtable on International Cooperation for Sustainable Development in Caribbean Small Island Developing

States, Bridgetown, Barbados March 25–27, 2008. See http://www.un.org/esa/sustdev/sids/2008_roundtable/presentations.htm

22. Lino Briguglio, Gordon Cordina, Nadia Farrugia and Constance Vigilance, eds, *Small States and the Pillars of Economic Resilience.* (Islands and Small States of the University of Malta and the Commonwealth Secretariat, London, 2008) 11–34.

23. Peter J. Katzenstein, *Small States in World Markets.* (Ithaca: Cornell University Press, 1985).

24. Dieter Senghaas, *The European Experience: A Historical Critique of Development Theory.* (New Hampshire: Berg Publishers, 1985).

25. See note 22.

26. Claudius Preville, 'CARICOM's Orientation in External Trade Negotiations and Resilience Building' in Lino Briguglio et al., eds, *Small States and the Pillars of Economic Resilience.*

27. Sudha Venu Menon, *Governance, Leadership and Economic Growth in Singapore.* Munich Personal RePEc Archive (MPRA), Paper #4741. http://mpra.ub.uni-muenchen.de/4741 (August 2007).

28. The *Sunday Times 'Leadership for Economic Growth.'* Available online: http://sundaytimes.lk/080817/Columns/eco.html (August 17, 2008).

29. Report on Wilton Park Conference 900 (March 2008*), Caribbean States in 2020: Sinking, Surviving or Prospering?* http://www.acp-eu-trade.org/library/files/Wilton-Park_EN_030708_Wilton-Park_Caribbean-States-in-2020.pdf.

30. Merilee S. Grindle, *Going Local: Decentralization, Democratization, and the Promise of Good Governance.* (New Jersey: Princeton University Press, 2009).

31. Karl Polanyi, *The Great Transformation: The Political and Economic Origins of Our time*, 2nd edition (Boston, MA: Beacon Press) 2001.

CHAPTER 3
POLITICS, DEVELOPMENT AND SOVEREIGNTY

Crosscurrents in Caribbean Policy Analysis[1]

The Challenge for the Caribbean Political Economies

Imperatives for the region are clear and arguments for integration and regionalism are strong. This calls for building institutional and private sector linkages. This chapter presents the Caribbean context and history in light of the liberalisation of the world economy.

The problem of integration without convergence must however be addressed. Sovereignty and regionalism are not mutually exclusive. Nations do not lose from relinquishing some sovereign power in regional integration, as fellow regional states must also do. The resulting economic benefits will actually strengthen governments' ability to act at home. This must translate into a culture and psychology of openness, with regional structures seen as joint problem solving processes – a partnership.

It is operational sovereignty that must be given up in exchange for greater legitimacy and international viability, actually strengthening the state's reach. There must therefore concurrently be an acknowledgement of the state role in building institutions in the move toward generally beneficial market oriented policies.

The Caribbean is a complex, enigmatic region, characterised by great disparities in size, population, geography, history, language, religion, race, and politics. Notwithstanding these important differences, the economic parameters of the countries in the region are largely similar. They are primarily small economies with narrow resource bases and high trade-to-output ratios, whose GDP is largely related to the export of primary resources and agricultural commodities.

Despite persistent efforts, most Caribbean nations still depend on preferential export markets. Compared with other developing countries, living standards are relatively high, though this is due more to periodic windfalls and protected markets than to the region's productivity or international competitiveness.

The defining frameworks of Caribbean political economy over the last 40 years have been the triangular trade of the pre-independence period, the era of multinational corporations and American hegemony, and more recently International Monetary Fund-World Bank (IMF-WB) structural adjustment programmes. Out of these frameworks came theories of exploitation, neo-colonialism and marginalisation respectively, and the export of protest diplomacy.

Then followed heavy political and moral overtures for protection, special considerations, aid, trade, and investment support from the developed world. Reacting to their history of colonialism, the mandates of nation building, and conditions at the times of their independence, Caribbean nations pursued inward development paths for increasingly state dominated economies.

This approach may have been feasible in the 1960s and 1970s, given prevalent developmental thought and the geopolitical structure of the world economy of the time, but it is no longer sustainable. For decades, the plantation economy has only adjusted around a persistent low-level equilibrium, resulting in lower incomes. Although the region's resource-based industries were integrated into the global economy, they formed economic enclaves within their domestic economies, which transferred little development benefits. Caribbean countries remain highly sensitive to exogenous forces, such as exchange-rate manipulation, economic crises and foreign price shocks, all of which can, and do, adversely affect their critical foreign exchange, largely export-derived public revenues, and competitiveness.

The liberalisation of the global economy is now eroding the preferential terms of trade on which Caribbean living standards are built. Faced with negative terms of trade, the need for technological advancement, stresses in its political systems, and changing political and economic ties with the rest of the world, the Caribbean is confronting its most severe challenges since many of its nations became independent a generation ago.[2]

Political and Economic Imperatives

Any future Caribbean economic strategy must be premised on the creation of a dynamic, sustainable export centre that is not reliant on trade preferences. Whilst negotiated treaties push for action, sustainability must be founded on market forces. Yet, no meaningful steps have been taken to address this crisis and to create a new generation of exports.

How will these new exports relate to the region's domestic capacity, to the unit cost of production and to technology requirements, and how will this transformation be financed? How will the region respond to the worldwide liberalisation of financial markets to safeguard its foreign exchange reserves? What new policy framework will meet the looming crisis faced by the region's smaller islands, many of which are almost entirely dependent on the exchange they receive from sugar, bananas, citrus, cocoa and coffee? Furthermore, are the steps now being taken sufficient to push-start the economy into an integrated world economy, so that it can gain a more equitable share of world commerce?

These questions have not been completely answered. Despite a great deal of rhetoric and debate, the region is yet to find ways to change its industrial structure, so that transnational Caribbean enterprises can perform on a more competitive basis in the world economy. The growing gap in the Caribbean between expectations and performance, and the rising tension between intention and reality, has widened the space between the art of politics and the discharge of governance. Political rhetoric tends to base new promises on old premises. In this politics of illusion, past hopes remain unfulfilled, and tentative new hopes have little expectation of action.

In the face of seriously deteriorating conditions and the abandonment of many social goals, the sense that the Caribbean is unprepared for the future is a deep source of anguish for its people. Not only has this resulted in disillusionment with institutions and politicians, but the very role of the state and its ability to govern have come into question.

The Caribbean must build its income-generating capacities and reposition itself in world markets by expanding the range of its economy. Accomplishing this task requires new theoretical models to address practical policy issues, implementation, and international relations; outward and forward looking strategies; new approaches to the region's persistent problems; and a plan for integration, based on contemporary realities, that will increase the region's political clout.

To be effective, any Caribbean integration must move beyond a sole focus on trade and once again consider stronger political connections. This new paradigm should link productive structures, promote interaction between different countries' private sectors, and technological and process innovation to reduce businesses' costs, increase institutional flexibility, and promote the region's social capital. The alternative is further economic and political marginalisation. But specific targets and methods, and means of securing new integration paradigms, remain uncertain.

Sovereignty and Regionalism

The forces transforming the global environment are pulling the international system in two seemingly contradictory directions.[3] On the one hand, the world is moving towards multilateralism and integration, with a strong commitment to open markets and international institutions. On the other, it is entering a new era of regionalism, as nations seek to guarantee their markets. Strategies, policies, and institutions that are not in harmony with international regimes and regional common interests are dangerously short-sighted and are becoming untenable.

National interests have not merged with the realities of international relations. Rather, the limits of the nation-state and sovereignty, of internal and external, domestic and international parameters, must now be understood in terms of a complicated two level framework. These developments raise fundamental questions of economic and political philosophy.

Governments in both the developing and developed world are facing the increasingly difficult task of managing their national economies in order to improve macroeconomic performance, increase public investments in job creation, education, and health care, and develop policies and institutions that will address the issues of poverty and inequity, in an increasingly laissez-faire environment. Political systems are undergoing stress, as the economic forces for integration outstrip their capacity to make the requisite political adjustments.

They are likely to endure only insofar as they are able to adapt. In the Caribbean and other developing regions, this scenario is further complicated by structural adjustment policies, which many argue are undermining the conditions for development.

Others fear that building the requisite regional institutions for addressing these problems will result in a loss of national identity and sovereignty. Further, as regionalism is by definition discriminatory, economists and decision-makers are concerned about the possible trade-diverting effects of the future regional landscape.[4] In this, two points should be considered. First, as Bhagwati[5] indicates, we are now seeing a resurgence in regionalism. The first round essentially collapsed in the 1960s, primarily because the United States was still intent upon following a multilateral course.[6] The lowering of trade barriers worldwide however, has extended the 'new integrationist' agenda far beyond matters of security, trade and markets, towards convergence on such matters as common regulatory systems, environmental and labour standards, and institution-building.

This is leading towards a type of interdependency that can be seen in the new financial geography, where cross-border trading and capital flows make it increasingly difficult to distinguish international banks from domestic ones. Furthermore, the removal of strict capital controls in many countries has placed emphasis on further integration, with the establishment of global safety nets for international trading, external policy coordination, and common fiscal and monetary policies.

The second point to consider is that regionalism need not necessarily be a stumbling block towards a multilateral trading system. The European Community, for instance, furthered the General Agreements on Tariffs and Trade (GATT) negotiations, and it may very well be that the Western Hemisphere, European, and Asian trading blocs will be better able to carry out the negotiations leading to global free trade than the 120-odd nations that are signatories under the General Agreement.[7]

The danger, of course is that this will not happen and that by turning inward, they will fracture the global system. Regardless of the outcome, governments and other actors can no longer define their interests primarily in terms of their geopolitical boundaries, but must increasingly do so in regional and even global terms.

Regional integration is a necessary step for solving the Caribbean's problems, but its countries resist taking the next step. The goal has been to reduce tariffs and to maximise internal trade, but without establishing external linkages that would increase the Caribbean's international and regional trade.

The result has been integration without convergence. Institutions may be efficient, but in terms of achieving the real goals of integration, are certainly ineffective as they are based on outdated premises.

This is due, at least in part, to the region's insularity: divisiveness remains a prominent, even institutionalised feature of the domestic political scene. The cultural basis for a new integration process must address matters of Caribbean identity and social capital, so that it will be more durable, and premised on the integration of peoples, not just policies. In this, integration should also be less anxious about trade, investment, and the creation of human and physical capital, and place a greater emphasis on what Robert Putman terms 'social capital,' a vital ingredient in the mix for economic development.[8]

This psychology also extends to the construct of sovereignty in the context of the region's nations that are still engaged in the task of nation-building. But difficult and painful as integration might be, collaboration and agreed-upon agendas, and shared responsibility for the promotion of common interests do not mean that the nation-state will disappear, or that national sovereignty will be lessened; in fact, the outcome may well be the reverse.

Sovereignty is often confused with notions of size and unilateralism, but its essence – the capacity to make effective, intelligent, and timely decisions that promote a nation's welfare and autonomy – is altogether different. In Robert Keohane's analysis,[9] sovereignty is twofold: formal and operational. In terms of formal sovereignty, 'a state has a legal supremacy over all other authorities within a given territory, and is legally independent, except where it has accepted obligations under international law.' Nations sacrifice some operational sovereignty or 'legal freedom of action' when they enter into international agreements, but they do so in return for reciprocal limits on other states.

If entered into wisely, such agreements will increase economic well-being at home and enhance government's options and its ability to govern. Far from limiting the state's power, therefore, the establishment of regional common interests and joint problem-solving processes where the grounds for interdependence exist may heighten national autonomy, particularly when these agreements are entered into with a view as to how benefit can be gained from a greater integration within the external world, while at the same time supporting the multilateral process.

Building Negotiating Space

In the Caribbean we have rationalised that our small size constrains development, but in fact, size is not in itself an issue. Hong Kong and

Singapore have achieved high levels of prosperity and growth without significant natural resources, preferential trade accords, or proximity to the United States and European markets.

They did so by linking their economies with the world economy and achieving external economies of scale, rather than relying on internal forces. They determined their cultural strengths and built on them, developing policies and strategies that unleashed the microeconomic forces for growth, and complementing these with the macroeconomic framework.

This was a matter of clear goals, skilful strategies, and sound policymaking, not market size. China, on the other hand, with its authoritarian government, large internal market and substantial resources, was unable to modernise its economy outside the global framework. Other large nations, including India, Indonesia, Brazil, Russia, Pakistan, Bangladesh, Nigeria, and Mexico, have also not been able to do so, though they have excellent resource bases.

The point, then, is that the political and sociological legitimacy of the nation-state are not threatened by changes in operational sovereignty per se. Rather, today's world requires that the nation-state cede more of its operational sovereignty, in order to uphold its legitimacy and viability. Historically, the American attitude towards the Caribbean has been conditioned by the geopolitical significance of the region's proximity, and this is still true, despite the end of the cold war. The regional agenda has decisively widened, however, and there is now a convergence of interests on such issues as drug trafficking, money laundering, immigration, the management of common resources, environmental degradation, and the strengthening of democracy.

The Caribbean must establish a new relationship with Washington in the light of these circumstances, and since resources and attention have shifted from the region, it will be taken seriously only if it negotiates as a unified entity. Furthermore, if the Caribbean is to strengthen its negotiating position at a time when both the United States and the European Union are preoccupied with matters unrelated to Caribbean development, it must speak with a greater voice. The Caribbean and its neighbours in South and Central America need to work together in greater harmony, if not always in total agreement. Regionalism is an inescapable feature of the landscape, and the asymmetrical integration of the Caribbean nations with its larger neighbours does not, as many fear, present a bona fide threat to Caribbean identity.

On the contrary, it will enable the Caribbean to distinguish what is uniquely its own, while at the same time facilitating the emergence of a trans-Caribbean identity that encompasses the Caribbean littoral. The Association of Caribbean States (ACS), created soon after the West Indian Commission report had recommended that CARICOM achieve greater cooperation and economic integration within the Caribbean Basin, was an effort to respond to global conditions.[10]

But without an explicit agenda or clearly identified targets, the precise function of the ACS is unclear, and it is in danger of becoming an expansion of outdated and ineffective structures that cannot deal with present crisis.

Open Regionalism and the Regional State

The best model that the Caribbean can consider at this juncture is a form of open regionalism, which encompasses a number of the above issues and trends.[11] In a time of great uncertainty regarding the eventual outcome of the multilateral and mini-lateral trading systems, open regionalism encourages nations to form sub-regional trading blocs in ways that facilitate the linkages with others, thus synthesising the globalisation trends.

While an open regionalism includes some preferential elements, import barriers are low, and it allows for the open-ended participation of its members in other trade agreements and regional schemes, so that these various groupings will function as building blocks towards global accords and an open and more transparent international economy.

The first round of regionalism led to a form of integration that widened the production base, erected trade fortresses, and began to build on policy convergences. This cycle is now over, and the integration process being pursued by CARICOM, has reached its limits. The current round of regionalism, however, which combines the integration of production with open markets, is representative of an intermediate position in a global move towards a more open multilateral trading system.

The Caribbean must accept the realities of the new global economy, and a policy environment must emerge to provide a development buffer zone, as we strive to emerge on a higher international platform. In this context, the establishment of the ACS can be seen, not as an integration process per se, but as an attempt to strengthen the region's negotiating position in international diplomacy.

This poses an opportunity for the Caribbean to move away from its traditional posture of protest diplomacy towards a more affirmative stance, in which its vital interests are identified and promoted in anticipation of changing balances in world politics. A non-sovereign, 'regional state', could exhibit the same sort of cooperation in world affairs that the Scandinavian countries often demonstrate; and perhaps move towards regional cooperation on economic policy matters. The funding policies of the international financial organisations may well be more appropriate to this regional state.

Post-Structural Adjustments

Since the oil crisis in the 1970s, the path towards development in many of the world's poorer countries has been hindered by deteriorating terms of trade for export commodities and inappropriate development policies. These difficulties culminated in the debt crisis of the 1980s, and many developing countries had to restructure their economies along the lines of structural adjustment policies. These programmes consist of both short-and medium-term measures for improving the overall economic situation by such means as cuts in public spending, contraction of the money supply, changes in import restriction, devaluation of the currency, and the privatisation of state enterprises. In general, this new orthodoxy views the market as the major instrument of reform, while the state is seen as the key obstacle to development.[12]

The structural adjustment policy debate in the Caribbean has centred around the sequencing of measures and a time period for these policies to work, when it should have focused on substance. After a decade of adjustment, development still remains an elusive goal. This is largely a static model, based on two-dimensional premises that cannot be supported. The neoclassical policy prescriptions for getting the right prices, such as reducing costs, getting the right technology, flexible exchange rates, and removing price controls and subsidies, are all well and good in themselves, but competition is a complex, dynamic phenomenon in which price is only a single element.

Moreover, whilst strict fiscal and monetarist measures may promote stabilisation, they will not unleash the internal forces for change that will result in growth; and while the divestiture of state enterprises, for instance, may be necessary to balance the books, unless privatisation takes place within a post-structural adjustment framework for development, it will not result in a new platform from which output, income, and well-being can be increased.

Furthermore, such a framework must engender the dynamics for endogenous growth, so that the industrial structure of production will yield a high-level equilibrium and momentum for sustainable development. Similarly, the measures for 'getting the state out of the way' ignore the need for enhanced state role in building meaningful regional institutions that will create and promote an environment of growth. The state is needed to enforce regulations, formulate and implement policy, build international linkages, forge collective public and private sector initiatives, and promote human resource development that will bring the disadvantaged into the development process.

The world that we now inhabit will likely call for constant economic adjustment; but if the foundation of social life is not to be further eroded, this process must be countered with a 'high-energy politics...capable of... repeated basic reform,' involving intensified public participation and democracy.[13] Correcting economic accounts regardless of social costs can only destroy the basis for future growth. The state must be redesigned, but not eliminated. In the Third World, the state has always played a central role in economic development and economic adjustment. What is now required is a balance between the free market forces and the state. The international financial institutions have come around to this view. Interventionist strategies, such as incentives and subsidies, have become the core of East Asian development and propelled growth. These movements are cyclical, as W. Arthur Lewis pointed out, and there is nothing inevitable about the process.

Caribbean Political Economy

Development in the Caribbean entails a comprehensive political economy of change, including the development of endogenous growth capacity to drive the economy. Only then can the region benefit from the new and flexible world economy, in which ends and means are readily adjusted to changing opportunities in different countries. This will require an integration model that transcends trade and converges at the institutional level, and facilitates backward and forward, macro- and microeconomic linkages. Eventually a virtuous circle should be created, in which the region can expand its political space and gain greater negotiating strength in the international arena. Merging into a greater political-economic entity should help to free individual states from rent-seeking power bases, bring about greater economic efficiencies, and allow governments to concentrate on governance.

Sustainable development is an affirmative political-economic process, linking economic logic - the measures needed to pursue economic efficiency in both international and domestic spheres - with political logic, in a synergism that allows them to reinforce one another. Merely opening the economy to the outside will not induce sustainable growth. On the contrary, it will result in further social and economic destabilisation.

As integration progresses and the state reduces its direct role in the economy, public policy will have an even greater impact on society. There will be winners and losers. To address this situation, government must be strong enough to manage the transition and alter the opportunity structure, so that lower and middle income groups will not bear disproportionate burdens. The government must also ensure that poverty issues are systematically addressed with visible effect.

A society is largely defined by citizens who possess a common identity and a common loyalty to shared ideals. Caribbean society must create a new sense of civic identity in which people feel free to express themselves, speak their own languages, practice their cultural traditions and transmit these to their children, as they embrace common goals with the larger society.

The agenda before us is enormous, but we can neither succumb to the forces of history, nor surrender to the new vulnerabilities that will surface in the path ahead. Our resilience must be founded in our sense of Caribbean identity, with an enduring commitment to confidence in our future.

Notes

1. Adapted from Winston Dookeran and Akhil Malaki, *Leadership and Governance in Small States, Getting Development Right* VDM Verlag Dr. Muller, 2008. Introduction.

2. Winston Dookeran and Ramesh Ramsaran, 'The Caribbean Quest: Directions for Structural Reforms in a Global Economy', *Nordic Journal of Latin American and Caribbean Studies*, Institute of Latin American Studies, Stockholm University, 1998.

3. These include the end of the Cold War; the worldwide dismantling of trade barriers and the integration of markets; the globalisation of capital, production, distribution and exchange; technological advances; and the convergence of common interests and concerns

4. Examples of the confusion surrounding these issues are readily apparent. The MERCOSUR trade bloc (Argentina, Brazil, Uruguay and Paraguay), for instance, which formed the world's second largest customs union in January 1995, will not establish a supranational court to settle trade disputes, as some members felt that it would reduce their sovereignty (see Angus Foster, 'Difficult Choices Ahead for Mercosur'. *Financial Times*, December 19, 1994.). They feared that the World Trade Organization (WTO), by eliminating the one-country veto and establishing tribunals to rule on trade disputes, would dilute US Sovereignty and force changes in a wide range of US Environmental and labour laws (see Mitchell Zuchoff, 'At GATT's Core: A Debate about Money, Sovereignty'. The *Boston Globe*, November 27, 1994). In a recent nationwide referendum, Norway voted not to join the EU, feeling, at least in part, that its resource base was strong enough to keep foreign bureaucrats from interfering in its 'internal affairs.' CARICOM Heads of Government were determined to keep the community's expansion under the ambit of elected governments, in part because they feared a devolvement of their sovereignty. In each case there were serious debates as to what constituted the national interests and how integration would affect national sovereignty.

5. Jagdish Bhagwati. 'Regionalism and Multilateralism: An Overview'. Discussion Paper Series No. 603. Washington, DC: World Bank, April 1992.

6. The most notable exception to this, of course, was the European Common Market, now the European Union (EU), which the United States supported primarily out of regional security concerns. The same can also be said of the former Union of Soviet Socialist Republics (USSR) and the Council for Mutual Economic Assistance (COMECON).

7. The Free Trade Area of the Americas (FTAA), formed in December 1994, sought hemisphere-wide free trade by 2005 but did not succeed. The EU has expanded its borders into Eastern Europe and the southern Mediterranean; and eighteen members of the Asia Pacific Economic Cooperation (APEC) forum have signed an agreement to establish a future free trade zone among developed nations.

8. Distinct from human capital and social expenditures, social capital, as defined by Robert Putnam, '...refers to features of social organization, such as networks, norms and trust that facilitate coordination and cooperation for mutual benefit. Social capital enhances the benefits of investment in physical and human capital...and seems to be a precondition for economic development, as well as for effective government. *Development economists take note: Civics matters.*' (Taken from Robert D. Putnam 'The Prosperous Community, Social Capital and Public Life' in The *American Prospect* No. 13 (Spring, 1993, 35–37). While social capital is specifically concerned with the grounds for public policy and institution building, on another level it is reflected internationally in the emerging norms for cooperation, multilateralism, and shared concerns and responsibilities, as opposed to traditional opportunistic, unilateral models of international relations.

9. See Robert O. Keohane, 'The Study of International Relations', *Political Science and Politics*, September 1, 1999.

10. Prime Minister A.N.R. Robinson of Trinidad and Tobago took the initiative in establishing the West Indian Commission in the late 1980s in order to examine the issues facing the future of the Caribbean. Its 600 page report, *Time for Action* contained more than 200 specific recommendations (West Indian Commission, 1992).

11. For a discussion on how Caribbean open regionalism might be built, see Dookeran: 'Caribbean Integration: An Agenda for Open Regionalism' *The Round Table: The Commonwealth Journal of International Affairs,* University of London, July 1994.

12. The five basic strategies of structural adjustment programmes include the reduction of domestic demand, resource allocation, the increase of foreign savings, the increase in domestic savings, and increased economic efficiency in the use of resources. (See Roger D. Norton, 'Agricultural Issues in Structural Adjustment Programs. FAO Economic and Social Development Paper No. 66, Rome, Italy, 1987.

13. See Roberto Mangabeira Unger and Zhiyuan Cui,'China in the Russian Mirror' in *New Left*, Volume a, Review I/208, November-December 1994, 78–87.

CHAPTER 4
FOUNDATION FOR POLITICS & LEADERSHIP

Educating the Citizen, Innovative Governance, Developing Leadership

Economic growth is the engine of development, but development is about people, about enlarging their possibilities, improving their quality of life, and enhancing their capabilities. The Foundation for Politics and Leadership[1] has emerged as a solution and action oriented vehicle focusing on educating the citizen, innovative governance,[2] and developing leadership.[3]

Foundation for Politics and Leadership

The Foundation seeks a new direction. It works for the right political system for development, promoting the harnessing of the energies of diversity, encouraging competitive leadership and advising on a 'make-it-happen approach' to change and success through three major initiatives: The School for Politics, The Centre for Creative Leadership, and The Intelligence Network.

The Foundation is the first policy centre and facilitator of collaboration in the Caribbean, dealing with politics and leadership. It is a vehicle bringing together leading minds – academic and practical, international and regional – on politics and leadership in the Caribbean to shape useful and practical policy initiatives and facilitate political consensus.

The Foundation unites the wisdom and experience of earlier thinkers and development practitioners with the imaginative energy and social commitment of a new generation. All sectors of Caribbean society can make valuable contributions and are invited to participate. The only criteria are a belief that the Caribbean can be better served by its leaders and an understanding that people are both the contributors and beneficiaries in the development process.

A New Direction
In the Caribbean, a sustainable culture supporting integrity, equity

and political rights in the working of the electoral and political order is undermined by an oligarchy of corruption in establishment politics that continues to dominate the present power structure. There is no silver bullet intervention that will easily confront the real challenge of failed leadership and collapsing institutions now typical in the governing process in most of the region's systems of democracy. Societies rooted in pluralistic divisions retreat rather than advance when faced with the challenge of embracing a new political and social belief system. The forces against change unleash their power that makes the winners impotent in the political battlefield.

Getting the right political system, transcending divisions, restoring the integrity of institutions, directing social justice, and achieving sustainable economic growth must become a new uniting mandate in addressing the complexities of societal change and building confidence in the future. Re-orienting the thinking of decision-makers to challenge old, narrow agendas and priorities can be accomplished effectively through the action of civil society organisations.

Political systems, regardless of their constitutional structures, can be, and are, easily twisted and manipulated by leaders. The analysis of right politics must distinguish between political culture, political systems and the gap between political logic and economic logic. The Foundation for Politics and Leadership focuses on exploring the relationships between the right politics, good governance, sustainable economic growth and creative leadership for small nation states and their public and private institutions.

The Foundation is guided by a set of shared values to foster a political culture based on respect for the people; to commit to individual rights, transparency, accountability, integrity and decency; fiscal discipline and balanced development; and to ensure fairness and equality. The Foundation's core value is that the government must be the servant of the people. The economic benefits of development should be equitably shared by all and every citizen must be assured of equal justice. The Foundation encourages leaders to be learners and to place their country above their self-interest by serving those they lead.

The Foundation serves as guide and directly assists the activities and search for a new future by identifying critical issues, providing actionable solutions and developing creative leadership for execution at the national and community governments, public and private enterprise levels. There are critical political, economic, citizenship, and global challenges that demand a thoughtful action agenda for the Foundation in finding a new direction for the development of society.

Politics

The primary focus of the Foundation is to examine the exercise of political authority and its impact on development in the Caribbean. The Foundation informs stakeholders about the ways in which political authority is exercised and puts forward alternatives that will accelerate the development process.

The following questions provide a framework for an action agenda:

- how does politics drive development, or more precisely, how does the right political system drive sustainable development?

- how do we define good governance?

- how does the leadership make a difference in achieving good governance and sustainable development, in both public and private enterprise?

- what are the linkages between politics and sustainable economic growth?

Economics

The Foundation defines the critical economic issues and search for actionable solutions. The following questions provide a framework for an action agenda:

- how do small nations sustain development in a constantly changing global information and competitive market environment?

- what is the relationship between a state-centred economy, use of state funds and natural resource and sustainable development?

- what is the relationship between the state and the development of a market economy and healthy private sector?

Citizenship

The Foundation defines the critical citizenship issues and encourages participatory governance. The following questions provide a framework for an action agenda. How do small nations develop and secure the supply for an increasing demand by citizens for good governance? What is the relationship between the political system and participatory citizenship in small nation states? How can the citizen be democratically empowered to participate in all levels of government?

Global Environment

The foundation will seek to define the critical global environment and International Relations issues and point towards new directions. The following questions provide a framework for an action agenda:

- how can small states contribute to solving global issues?

- what is the relationship between local and global environment issues and approach in dealing with global humanity challenges including fighting poverty, education, diseases and other global issues?

- what is the relationship between local and global common issues and approaches in dealing with global warming, fisheries depletion, deforestation, water deficit and others?

- how small states could cooperate and coordinate their efforts in regional and global alignments to protect their vital security, sovereignty and economic interest?

- what is the relationship between local and global regulatory issues and approach in dealing with illegal drugs, intellectual property, international labour and migration rules, and trade, investment and competition rules amongst others?

The Initiatives.

The Foundation seeks to create the right political system for development, promote diversity, encourage competitive leadership and advise on a dynamic and decisive approach to change and success. To achieve these goals the Foundation will work through two major initiatives, The School for Politics and The Centre for Creative Leadership, in addition to the Foundation's Network Activities.

The School of Politics will develop civil leadership, foster democracy, improve governance and strategise for sustainable growth all in the context of political systems. The school will use customised short courses, seminars, public forums and programmes, and use strategic alliances with established institutions as part of the delivery system. The school will focus on educational programmes on the workings of the governance systems, responsibilities and rights of political leadership and constitutional structures and political culture in society.

The Centre for Creative Leadership supports and helps to develop solution leaders in government, public and private enterprises. This will be achieved through strategic advising services and a customised leadership development programme supporting decision-making and solution execution by leaders/executives by focusing on leadership competencies and their impact on organisational performance. The leadership development programme is a senior executive-led strategic and intervention to build a high performance and globally competitive public or private enterprise, customised and solution focused to fit the client's needs. Participants learn by doing individual and team real life projects.

The Foundation's Network activities will develop and maintain a network for intelligence and services through sourcing, co-ordinating, researching information and networking with 'caring' people and communities of practices locally, regionally and globally. The Network will focus on timely and customised intelligence to selected stakeholders through networking, educational programmes and public events. Public seminars, open forums and conferences, will bring together innovators, creators and activists and presents the Foundation's information in an easy-to-explore form, and featuring all the information, understandings, practices and resources used and produced; and the ideas and innovations from every conversation and every interaction, which could enhance good governance. Publications, including magazine articles, books, reports, brochures, newsletters, videos, and films will also be introduced.

Innovative Governance:
Breaking Global Deadlock for Small States - A Proposal[4]

The Role of Leadership

A major goal for the Foundation is to promote good governance adapting to today's challenging global information driven environment. This section presents a proposal on innovative governance and asks development questions facing small states in light of the relationships between global and local issues and responses to challenges. It presents a new framework for political economy in small states, considering regional issues, leadership and developmental imbalances where there are needs for growth and inclusiveness.

Politics is about the distribution of power in a society and political economy is about investigating the resulting compensation to 'winners' and 'losers' in the distribution of power. In light of globalisation's inequalities, a new social contract must be formulated along with an action plan to investigate problems and ensure solutions for small states in the Caribbean. A special emphasis should be placed on regional integration and partnership for small island state solutions, involving organisations such as the Foundation's Centre for International Governance Innovation.

The current global financial crisis is the result of serious shortcomings in domestic financial governance that have also highlighted gaps in the global governance of international finance and capital. The world is interdependent in areas as diverse as financial markets, trade, infectious diseases, climate change, terrorism, product safety, food supply and water tables. Our collective capacity to manage this interdependence through pooled or coordinated policy responses has fallen behind the rise in the numbers and intensity of the interventions among these interdependent sectors.

Existing institutions and arrangements can no longer cope with the growing number, range and gravity of the major global problems. What is required is bold leadership by heads of government with a vision for the community as a whole and then inspiring individuals and groups to transcend their immediate self-interest in identifying both intellectually and emotionally with the shared vision. This new leadership must set standards of conduct and benchmarks of progress, explain why these matter, and encourage everyone to strive for and achieve these standards and goals.

Leaders are needed to rise to the challenges of the 21st century. An urgent first step is to redesign the architecture of global governance, from peace and security, to development and finance, environmental protection and resource conservation, and human rights and humanitarian protection.[5]

The Key Questions[6]
- how can small states contribute to solving global issues?

- what is the relationship between local and global issues and approaches in dealing with global challenges including the fight against poverty, education, diseases and others?

- what is the relationship between local and global common issues and approaches in dealing with global warming, fisheries depletion, deforestation, water deficits and other problems?

- how could small states cooperate and coordinate regional and global alignments to protect their vital security, sovereignty, and economic interests?

- what is the relationship between local and global regulatory issues and approaches in dealing with illegal drugs, intellectual property, international labour and migration rules, trade, investment, and competition rules among others? How do small states sustain development in a constantly changing global information society and a competitive market environment?

The Framework[7]

The work of political institutions, the political economy approach, and the politics of the future are difficult subjects to integrate into a development agenda.[8] A new framework is needed to take on many aspects and challenges. Regional issues must be considered and this framework must be responsive and adaptable to new challenges in leadership, politics and regional governance. The imbalances between 'winners' and 'losers' in the developmental process must be considered and the means to entrench sustained growth and inclusiveness be investigated and implemented. Any new framework must be sensitive and responsive to national and regional interests and be cognisant of shifts in the world order.

The polity of a society strives for the 'best balance' between political and economic goals (reconciling the political and economic logic), whilst reflecting the values of that society. Often, this equilibrium is unstable and constrained by the powers of the institutions in the society and the state. The application of the calculus of political economy allows the society to find the right balance that will promote sustained growth and development. Development is about closing the gaps in social equity and increasing the growth potential of the society whilst compensating the losers in the process of reshaping the society's social welfare.

The politics of development is often viewed in narrow terms of the distribution of income and opportunities. Looking at inequality and injustice in our global economy, higher weights should be assigned to these goals in the policy paradigm of development. Globalisation is a disequalising force. The market works by rewarding countries and individuals with the most productive assets; it fails by negative externalities for the vulnerable and increasing the risks faced by the weak. The market, through rules and regimes, systemically favours the rich.

To address these inequities a global social contract is needed to deal with unequal endowments and to build sound institutions that will supply global public goods; construct global regulations to address market failures and better represent developing countries in international organisations. These elements in the global social contract raise critical political issues.

Politics in development is likely to get deeper, as each political choice will have different development outcomes. As such, analysis of the political choices becomes an essential part of the data requirements for good decision-making. This poses a tremendous challenge to leaders in development, politics, policymaking and management alike. Apart from the building models of politics and development, there will be the need to secure the population's legitimacy for this trade-off, as they are critical in making political choices.

A strategic action agenda identifying specific work programmes for innovative governance must be designed.[9] Following is a brief outline of the objectives, approach and key activities. The organised entity would co-ordinate new and ongoing work on the Diaspora issue, involving coordinating work with partners. Those involved would act as project ambassadors. This would be part of a programme encouraging multinational and multilingual dialogue amongst the English-speaking and non-English-speaking Caribbean.

Apart from these objectives, the approach would be to stimulate discussion on the Caribbean within the context of Caribbean research papers with a focus on understanding policy recommendations, and impediments to implementation. The aim is to lead a discussion on Caribbean economic co-operation and develop a position statement and framework to guide the strategic action agenda.

Specific activities would then involve disseminating the Centre for International Governance Innovation (CIGI) papers and other

Caribbean research papers and getting feedback, engage non-English speaking Caribbean, and benchmarking Caribbean experience and research using successful Diaspora experience. This would all be part of preparation for a workshop on leadership and strategic thinking for small states, including the Caribbean.

Developing Solution Leadership:
A Programmatic Strategic Intervention

Leadership Development Programme

The Foundation aims to develop public and private enterprise leaders, including political leaders who are successful in a turbulent global and local information environment.

All leaders must develop, both in business and in politics, harnessing and building systems to create, filter and act on knowledge. New competencies are required. The political leaders need incentives which already drive business leaders' performance. In order to build prosperity in small states, consensus based leadership must be at the forefront of development and competitiveness.

Solution leaders have a global mindset and are open to the challenges of the new frontier of the one-world information environment. They are anxious to gain and practice competencies to solve global and diverse local problems. They are learners, continuously training, developing and educating themselves as well as others.

In the Foundation's leadership programme, leadership behaviour, mindsets and competencies in the context of local cultures; including leadership types, programmed and unconscious management and business behaviour are explored. The challenge of knowledge transfer in the context of competency driven leadership is treated as a strategic change intervention involving all key executives of an organisation. The objective is to develop leaders to build and maintain a high performing, globally competitive enterprise.

Solution Leadership can be taught and learned. Complex thinking can be learned and must be the driving force behind the development of solution leaders. Solution leaders think and learn, lead and manage in both global and local space and in the context of local societies in which culture matters.

This Leadership Development Programme is managed as a strategic

s competency driven modular programme focuses on
ion leadership competencies:

ing – Intelligence Scanning;

ring – Fostering Personal Growth;

- *Coaching* – Developing Professionals;

- *Leading* – Creating the Future (Direction);

- *Competing* – Developing Industry Expertise;

- *Managing* – Executing Organisational Solutions; and

- *Teaming* – Managing Team Projects.[10]

This leadership model rests on four dimensions of leadership: circumstance (the environment), culture (the society), competency (knowledge) and character (values). Each of these dimensions has its own dynamics and tends to dominate a leadership type but in reality these leadership types are mixed.

Developing solution leaders requires a formal customised solution leadership programme. Such a programme becomes a strategic intervention at the highest levels of the enterprise. This intervention should focus on managing knowledge transfer from both 'outside' and 'inside' the organisation. The Solution Leadership Development Programme (SLDP) is designed to provide an integrated approach to leadership development. The model reflects seven essential leadership competencies required to navigate the landscape of the complex and unpredictable 21st century global realities.

Whereas education/training only develops knowledge (individually and without transfer), the competency-based approach demands not only development of critical competencies themselves but also changes in behaviour in terms of attitudes, values, skills, belief-systems, assumptions, principles, and experience. This is accomplished, not by passive teaching but by active learning: learning by doing. This programme is a strategic intervention. It is designed to develop a pool of leaders and is aimed at dramatically improving the organisation's work culture and systems via senior management participation and ownership. Participants learn through action. Participants individually and in teams should produce real life projects approved by senior executives.

Programme Challenges[11]
Assumptions and Design

The SLDP is a unique programme based on deep principles of Complexity Science applied to an organisational environment, and the avoidance of the pitfalls of traditional approaches to transformation. Training, by itself, cannot produce organisational change, it must be part of a wider integrated structure specifically designed to support knowledge transfer and organisation change.

Unlike traditional training and development programmes, senior management is involved in all aspects of the SLDP from design to stakeholder selection, participation, and evaluation. This provides the critical link necessary for transfer of knowledge into the organisation (not just individuals). Building organisational capital requires meeting global standards and simultaneously creating a Professional Business Culture.

The following are some key considerations that influenced the design of the programme:

- being customised to the environment, goals and values of the organisation;

- providing content that is relevant for developing nations and their private and public sectors;

- being conceptually integrated;

- producing leaders that can compete in their industries with any other leaders from developing nations, and at times, be on par with leaders from developed nations;

- producing professional managers who are confident, influential, critical thinkers, that can model the behaviours they expect their subordinates to adopt;

- producing managers that will immediately translate their learning into improved performance in their current posts in both operational and project-based activities; and

- having an application component where participants practice their new skills in a real business environment.

The Programme provides balance in immediate vs. long-term performance improvement; leadership vs. managerial skills; intellectual vs. emotional development; and individual vs. team development. The Programme should be delivered in such a way as to:

- provide little distraction from the participant's substantive duties;

- confirm that learning has taken place in the classroom via an assessment (online tests when possible);

- provide many channels of feedback and methods of assessment;

- provide a 'certificate of achievement' from a major tertiary educational institution upon successful completion of the programme; and

- take nine to twelve months and at the lowest cost possible.

The SLDP model makes several assumptions. It is for the developing nation; based on producing leadership to face challenges of the 21st century global economy. It is targeted at highly capable managers who are likely to be promoted to executive positions in the space of a few years.

Finally, it can work in any sector (private, public, NGO), with the necessary adjustments. The organisation's human resource leadership plays a critical role in the implementation, administration, and eventual assessment of this programme.

Leadership

When assessing leadership behaviour and its influence of organisational systems we should consider it in the context of the dimensions of leadership – circumstance, culture, competencies and character – should always be considered in the assessment of leadership behaviour and its influence of organisational systems. What is their influence on the behaviour of the leader and organisation's? What are the circumstances that influence the leader and the organisation's behaviour and performance? What is the influence of the leader's and the organisation's culture on performance? What influence does the leader's competency have on the organisation's performance? What influence does the leader's character have on the organisation's performance? These are the questions to be taken into account.

Change and development require the interaction and expression of power as politics. The concept and imperatives of sovereignty and regionalism – vital for small, recently independent states – must be able to compete. Yet political power is quickly distorted and maligned. To combat this the Foundation offers principled politics built into the system at ground level by flexible and action oriented leadership.

Solution Leader Competencies

A Portfolio of Expertise

In this information driven, interconnected global economy, individuals and professionals must match the rate of change with the rate of learning, by learning new competencies. A major paradigm shift in the new economy is turning employees into students and every such employee/student is a learning centre.

The employee is in charge of his/her continuous education and upgrading of competencies. The high performance, globally competitive organisation invests in intellectual capital by providing access to continuous on the-job-learning and by creating corporate universities or learning centres. These corporate learning centres act as the connective tissue of the organisation. They link employee learning to overall organisational strategy and are beginning to drive business. Competency development takes on strategic priority. Competencies are embedded in an organisation's cultures. In a sense, an organisation is as good at what its culture allows its employees to learn.

Competency component terms vary widely in definition. The SLDP model is based on four organic components or ingredients: Skills, Knowledge, Experience and Beliefs.

- skill is the ability, expertise and capacity to perform a specific, routine task. The capacity to perform a series of complex or higher order tasks or solve a complex, previously encountered problem drawing upon all components of a competency.

- knowledge is the learned information (facts, concepts, principles, or procedures) needed to execute a skill or solve a problem. Aptitude is an individual's ability to learn or to develop proficiency in an area if provided with appropriate education or training.

- experience includes knowledge, skills, or mindset (values, beliefs, attitudes) picked up or refined by direct participation in activities or events. Emotional intelligence involves emotional reactions or interpretations of facts, situations, or people. Attitude is a person's disposition or preference to think, feel, or act in a certain way toward an idea, person, behaviour, or event based on their internal beliefs, values, or feelings.

- beliefs are a set of subjective or unproven assertions or conceptualisation usually based on one or more fundamental assumptions that may drive actions. Values guide our actions and may be conscious or unconscious, formal or informal.

High performance organisations must adapt rapidly to the changing environment to stay healthy and competitive. They must be flexible in their structures, relationships, processes and management competencies. The leader-manager must be a multi-skilled and competent professional – a genuine generalist capable of learning. Such a generalist must possess a portfolio of expertise that is continuously changing. As one skill set becomes obsolete another replaces it.

Complex Thinking – *Understanding the New Frontier*

Solution Leaders create the future by giving directional guidance to the organisation. In doing so they must have a global perspective and act as if all change is part of an interdependent one-world information environment. They seek solutions in the context of global change, accepting that global and local change is interwoven, and they require a deep understanding of the web of life on this planet. According to the Heisenberg Principle,[12] a principle from quantum physics, the observer changes the observation and the active involvement when observing a problem not only changes the problem but also to a large degree determines the solution. Consequently, leadership by altering perception not only shapes reality but also transforms perception into reality.

A major science driven paradigm shift has occurred, whose powerful nature is best understood on a global scale with anticipation of local changes. Any paradigm shift can cause violent disruption in local human communities and in order to deal with the emerging issues, solution leaders need to be capable of adaptive complex thinking.

For the purpose of the SLDP model, mental activities can be divided into four categories of thinking and learning: creative, critical, strategic, and adaptive complex. Creative thinking embraces out of the box ideas. The organisational challenge for creative thinking is to transform individual creativity into organisational productivity. Critical thinking is rational and systemic problem identification and solution and it is at the core of traditional learning. Strategic thinking requires directional and goal oriented change driven mental activities and it is a key element in a 'Solution Execution Approach'. Complex thinking is grounded in the dynamics of complex adaptive systems and adaptive complex enterprise behaviour but also emerges out of the interaction of the other three types of thinking.[13] Adaptive complex thinking is vital to the system's learning processes and it is essential to adaptation.

Adaptive complex thinking requires re-training and re-education and a new learning perspective. One key component rests on intuition and the challenge is to make intuitive interpretation part of a formal approach in understanding a dynamic information rich world.[14] For most individuals, practising complex thinking will require a paradigm shifting mental exercise, a different view of the dynamics of the real world. The real benefit of adaptive thinking is understanding and identifying problems, and then making appropriate and timely decisions and executing the solutions in the context of the global information driven market.

Complex thinking include non-linear thinking, action learning, open-ended communication, and form-breaking creativity. A different mindset is required – a global mindset free to explore the human potential, and limited only by imagination in the new age of information and knowledge.

Always contextual, complex thinking accommodates the ability to shift attention back and forth between system levels as well as between systems. Complex thinking demands a holistic and integrated approach and it is closely associated with creative thinking. It accepts emergent properties within the same system and between systems. A dialogue or discussion between two or more people (systems) can develop brand-new insights and ideas will emerge in a way an individual alone would have not been capable of developing.

Complex thinking is network thinking as a human system is a network of relationships; it is a shift from objects to relationships. In the systems view we realise that the objects themselves are networks of relationships, embedded in larger networks.[15] Complex thinking is always process thinking, it requires an understanding of the nature of self-organisation – pattern of ordered relationships. Self-organising systems deal with novelty, open systems far from equilibrium, and non-linear interconnectedness of system components. It deals with feedback loops that simultaneously maintain and grow the system.

Complex thinking also intervenes in reality. The scientific paradigm of scientific objectivity shifts to include the process of knowing. Unlike the assumption of the traditional scientific method, the human observer becomes a critical and an integral part of scientific theory. It shifts from 'scientific certainty' to theories that are limited and approximate. Adaptive complex thinking operates in the realm of probability.[16]

Tipping Point Decision[17]

Adaptive complex thinking allows the future to emerge, and for human systems to learn their way to the future. Solution leaders must engage in action thinking to solve problems and create the future. The most critical aspect of leadership in today's one-world, speed driven information environment is a leader's decision-making capability. Through decision-making, which is the most information intensive process, a leader creates and maintains 'power' to influence actions. The most critical decision is a tipping point decision.

In complexity science, a tipping point decision is where an existing system bifurcates, separating the old path and space from the new emerging path and space. Tipping point decisions create a new space and can only be made by a leader sensitive to the underlying energy released from tension between the emerging new system and the existing old system. Tipping point decisions are not only information intensive but are extremely time sensitive – they must be made in the now space.

In today's world, a leader will be judged by the capability to make such tipping point decisions. A leader's first reaction to a tipping point bubbling-energy space is to fall back on survival traits. These typically take the form of delaying the decision in the hope that clarity will emerge with more information; deferring to others as a participatory team exercise and seeking advice; pretending there is no emergency or crisis and letting others or events make the decision; and rationalising the situation.

A tipping point decision is frequently hidden in the chaotic and operational details overwhelming a leader's concentration on a crisis-threatening event. Tipping points are real events that can and must be influenced by a leader's judgement. No one else can do it, because the real power of a genuine leader is the capability to create the environment for the necessity of tipping point decisions to emerge in the first place. The very existence and actions of a strong leader is the creation of an information rich space, a new space where opportunity and risk demand tipping point decisions.

Learning – *Adapting to the Environment*

Learning is not merely an intellectual exercise but is a critical production centred process in the context of information driven global market. Survival, growth and sustainable performance depend on individuals', organisations' and societies' willingness and capacity to learn. Learning is a transformational process whereby each system transforms information and data into value. From this perspective, learning is an information process within the system that creates value.

In this context, an individual's learning is viewed as a production process where the production takes place in the mind. Through the learning process, the individual takes information (data) and under the right conditions transforms it into value, value for self and for others.

From a personal point of view, the value created by me for myself is my knowledge, and value created for others is service value. The latter value I share with others, it is the value I help create in the 'minds of others' through my knowledge in the form of information. My knowledge is the input, the information that others can use and in turn create value. Finally, value is perceived and created in the minds of the active participants. In this sense, value and specifically service value, only exist in relationships, only quality relations can sustain quality value, through a continuously flow of quality information.

The Seven Critical Leadership Competencies

Profiling – *Intelligence Scanning*

Leaders must have a highly developed profiling competency, they must be informed about the environment they operate in and the people they deal with. Profiling requires the ability (skills, experience, expertise and beliefs) to scan the environment for intelligence (appropriate information) to identify critical issues and make relevant strategic decisions both on the individual and organisational levels. Profiling is the ability to quickly detect and understand important issues or factors in situations or people. This involves information scanning, collection, analysis, evaluation and assessment activities.

Psychometric testing and assessment, leadership and cultural survey, leadership competency assessment, organisational profiling and a leadership development plan are all a part of this profiling activity. A major purpose of the individual profiling is to make the participant aware of their own leadership style and associated behaviour and the gaps the individual should address during the duration of the programme and, of course afterwards as well.

Mentoring – *Personal Growth*

Leaders must be good mentors, directly involved in the personal growth of future leaders. Mentoring is a critical component in knowledge transfer and succession planning. Mentoring skills include empathetic listening, giving and receiving feedback, nurturing and patience, encouraging and inspiring and not criticising in public.

The mentoring competency requires the capability to influence others in their personal growth and professional development. It is a supportive learning relationship between a caring individual who shares his/her knowledge, experience and wisdom with another individual who his willing and ready to benefit from this exchange to enrich his/ her professional journey.

It requires guiding without leading, teaching by example, willing to let the one being mentored experience the bumps needed for learning and growth to take a place, genuinely caring for the well-being of others. The altruistic leadership also carries over to the organisational culture. Organisations must be socially responsible and caring members of the communities in which they exist. In turn, a caring society consistently institutionally provides support for all who are in need.

Coaching – *Developing Professionals*

Leaders must be coaches; they must help develop competent professionals. Coaching requires the capability to help develop competent professionals. Coaching is the process of equipping people with the tools, knowledge and opportunities they need to fully develop themselves to be effective in their commitment to themselves, their company and their work. Coaching requires performing as a resource person willing to share expertise to successfully guide projects. Coaching should help develop successful teams and team leaders. Coaching requires continuous feedback.

Leading – *Creating the future*

Leaders must lead; they must be capable to create a future, so others can follow. A leader must have the ability to get followers inspired about a vision of the future, to develop the necessary capability (infrastructure) to achieve the desired outcomes. More than any other competency, leading demands learning, hence the solution leader is also a learning leader in the real sense of charting the course of an organisation in the turbulent waters of the global information environment. The solution leader must possess transformation and change skills.

Solutions must incorporate adaptive complex thinking and strategic management skills: seeing the 'big picture', envisioning the future, and being capable of functioning in the one-world information environment. Leading skills include effectively influencing people; accepting responsibility, motivating others, listening, acting decisively, understanding others needs, and possessing multi-cultural skills. Leaders possess learning skills including being flexible and adapting to change, being open-minded, and have a willingness to take risks, experimenting and being innovative; questioning and being critical, creative and entrepreneurial. The solution leader must be able to solve problems and make decisions, manage conflict and negotiate.

Competing – *Developing Expertise.*

Leaders must be fierce competitors; they must compete on the basis knowledge or expertise. Competing as a competency requires expert knowledge. This expert knowledge depends on the type of organisation and its competitive environment. It can run the gamut from cultural to technical, from business to government. These expert-led sessions are geared for the specific global knowledge for the organisation; they deal with specific topics directly applicable to the performance of the industry and their relations to the organisation. The knowledge transfer here will serve as a platform for attaining global standards. A solution leader's competing skill must involve multicultural skills, and should possess some expertise in international finance, international marketing, international trade and international law.

Managing – *Executing Strategic and Operational*

Leaders must be competent managers; as managers they must focus on execution and immediate implementation. Strictly speaking, to manage is to get things done with existing organisational and operational systems. Good management maximises the capacity of an organisation to control its resources in order to meet current customer demands; being efficient as well as effective in producing goods and services to improve the quality life of its 'customers'.

Functional managerial expertise may be in several areas: global business management skills; information systems and technology management skills; human resource management skills; operations management skills; market management skills; finance management skills and project management skills. Additional characteristics include getting results through planning, organising, actuating (empowering, motivating, influencing), controlling (monitoring) processes, system and people; exercising performance awareness in terms of efficiency (time and cost) and effectiveness (goals and results); and understanding enterprise performance management.

Teams – *Leading, Managing and Participating in Projects*

Leaders must have a strongly developed teaming competency; they must be effective project leaders. Teaming competency project requires the capability to function in a team, as a 'co-operating' group or as 'community of interests'. Each individual team member must share/contribute expertise for the benefit of the 'common good'. Communication and collaboration skills are essential in teamwork. Further, management skills include skills include effectively working in teams (especially project work). The individual co-operates and values others' opinions, shares their work and vision, works toward fostering acceptance of ideas and ideally relates well to others, and has a positive attitude.

Public and private enterprises face different performance challenges in developing countries than in developed countries. A project management approach allows organisations to be more flexible, and affords quicker adaptation to a customer driven global environment. A modern organisation is 'a community of stakeholders', of cooperating interests working together to assure beneficial outcomes for its stakeholders. Many organisations have become project oriented organisations and project management has become a recognised discipline. Projects are a way of life for organisations. However, challenges beyond the specific knowledge of project management as a formal discipline are in the context of the following: the dynamics of a global market, the state of development of the society, country or region, organissational behaviour and performance, leadership and management, and projects and teamwork.

A typical project team has four components: management, knowledge, performance and marketing. The decision team, comprised of executives, listens to and evaluates team presentations on a regular basis, and is comprised of two members from each of the three other teams on a rotating basis. The decision team has key executives, the coach from each team and the chief executive. This mechanism will help participants to acquire executive and strategic decision-making skills, in addition to presentation skills.

Leading Strategic Interventions

Today's Frontier Information Space requires a complex adaptive system framework in order survive, thrive, and sustain growth.

The High Performance Enterprise
The High Performance Enterprise proposed is a complex adaptive system made up of interrelated, interconnected, interactive, and

integrated subsystems. This enterprise operates in the present one-world information environment, is open and dynamic, and transforms energy and information into value for its participating sub-systems. It has multiple purposes, objectives, and functions; some of which may be in conflict. It seeks to maintain stability and order while continuously adapting to the changing environment. If it does not adapt to changing circumstances, it will experience entropy. All life on this planet is a complex adaptive system including the emerging global civilisation, existing societies, and organisations of all types as well as individuals.

Of course, the ultimate purpose of any healthy human system is to survive, thrive, and sustain itself its environment. As a complex adaptive system, it self-organises its environments, unfolding both stability (order) and growth (instability) creating a range of stable patterns, at the edge of chaos (disorder). The system's dynamic movements unfold a range of remarkably stable patterns, which reflect its core organising behaviour (its attractor). The following is a brief outline of such a complex adaptive system and its environment.

The Actuality – Real World

The Actuality of the system is the Real World of global change. It requires complex thinking to understand the dynamics of the one-world interdependent network of human relations and communities. Every human system (Adaptive Complex Enterprise) operates in this turbulent global information environment seeking information to survive, thrive and sustain itself. This one-world information environment is 'filled' with co-evolving and self-organising systems competing for information space. The High Performance Enterprise involves the selecting and interpreting of information, which includes the following phases: Acquiring and identifying, modelling, actioning, and feeding back loops (Performance Consequences).

The Scan – Information Filter

The *Enterprise* uses its perception of the real world as the central reference and scans selected information (Intelligence). Scanning involves finding regularity in information that the system can use to adjust its performance. It acquires information about its environment and its own interaction with that environment. Furthermore, information scanning requires a filter; for example, the 'filter' of a business system is its formal or informal direction (vision, mission, shared values and others) provided by leadership. We continuously receive information from our environment. However, most of the information is not deliberately scanned, it is not consciously acquired. Formal scanning involves conscious, deliberate, systematic acquisition and interpretation of information. How we perceive and interpret this scanned information depends on our internal model, our internalised construct of perceived reality. The information is acquired; regularities are identified, and evaluated by our internal model, in terms of the things that make sense.

The Model – *Perception of Reality*

The Model is the system's perception of reality which may not necessarily be aligned with what actually occurs in its environment. In a business system, it is the 'business model'. The organised system identifies regularities in the scanned information and condenses those regularities into a kind of 'schema' or internal model. There will always be tension between the 'actual or real world' and the perceived world of the organised system. This primary gap is healthy as long as it does not become too wide.

The information is acquired; regularities are identified and evaluated by this internal model. We combine new information with existing data to form a model of our reality. While our brain does this most of the time automatically, we also need to learn to do this scanning consciously. The scanned information provides intelligence that fits the model it uses to operate. It also allows the system to consider a number of competing models, and even create a new model that provides a better 'fit' or alignment with the environment of which it is a part. A learning system acts in relation to other systems in its environment based on the model it has developed.

The Action – *Operational Activities*

The information once scanned into the system drives the system's actions to create value. The enterprise takes action in the real world based on its model, on its perception of reality embedded in its model. The system action is its process activities, its operation. In a business system, these internal processes create and maintain the system value production.

The Consequences – *Feedback Loops*

Operational actions have consequences in the form of performance feedback loops. The high performance enterprise adapts through its feedback loops. It learns to survive, thrive and sustain itself in turbulent environments by maintaining itself and growing at the same time – by aligning and adjusting at the same time.

The human system scans the external environment and receives volumes of information. The enterprise can respond in two ways. This can be represented by two loops, the closed and the open systems. The closed system operates totally within its own environment with little connection to the outside world for adjustment. The changes and adjustments that are made are provisional (relations, structures, competencies, processes). This *adjustment loop* maintains the internal stability and order of the system by continuously looping and feeding back through the internal scan into the model.

The other loop – the open system – connects and engages the model with the outside environment. Constant growth, adaptation and alignment processes define the open loop. This *Alignment Loop* drives the systems growth but also creates continuous instability by scanning the external chaotic environment. This growth loop involves holistic change. These two aspects of behaviour work concurrently. The system can adjust its existing processes and operations, that is, improve or do a maintenance check-up while at the same time it can anticipate the future changes in the environment and align itself to that assessment by transforming its present paradigm of functioning. After examining its complex environment, the system can be reactive or proactive to its changing stakeholder environment.

In summary, as a result of the feedback loops, a healthy system sustains and grows itself. Scanned intelligence is used by the system to take action, which in turn has consequences for the system within its external environments. These consequences are then fed back into the system.

Consequently, scanning and feedback processes are part of the same interdependent activities that sustain and grow the system. Feedback is a looping process, and scanning is part of the loop that keeps the system internally adjusted and externally aligned. Self-generating behaviour emerges from the feedback structure of the system itself, it generates in form of patterns of behaviour.

Managing Organisational Transformation

The major challenge society's public and private enterprises is to align with the continuously changing global information environment. Unfortunately, for most traditional organisations this means a significant change effort. The solution leader has to lead these deep change interventions to create a future for the organisation. It requires risk-taking, foresight, timely decisions and actions all in an uncertain environment. The solution leader must take the organisation into unchartered territories and use a different approach; the solution leader must learn to ride the waves of change in a turbulent environment to achieve high performance and sustainable change.

The most dramatic of these deep change interventions involves managing organisational transformation. These transformative interventions must change the organisational culture and behaviour to meet the customer-driven globally competitive market demands.

As Figure 4.1 indicates, there is a strong relationship between a leader's mindset and the selected performance solutions. The performance matrix has four quadrants. In quadrant A, the traditional leader uses traditional performance solutions, resulting in the same traditional performance with the same systems. In quadrant B, traditional performance solutions are used to improve performance through process improvement of the same system.

Figure 4.1: Leadership Solution Matrix

The leader's mindset may be new but the system is old, consequently it is fixed rather than transformed. In quadrant C, the traditional leader employs high performance solutions resulting in circumstantial and temporary high performance solutions but which the traditional systems cannot sustain. Finally, in quadrant D, the leader generates high performance solutions resulting in sustainable high performance by transforming the traditional systems into market/customer driven processes.

Executing Transformational Change – *Transformational Leadership Challenge*

In today's highly dynamic global information environment, the solution leader must learn to manage organisational transformations to achieve high performance and to sustain growth. The solution leader must strategically understand how to ride the waves of change to high performance. One of the most challenging interventions is Managing Organisational Transformation. It requires making critical strategic decisions to achieving sustainable growth by riding waves of change and restructuring the organisational space.

There are a few critical characteristics in managing organisational transformations.

The high performance enterprise, in order to stay healthy, must, at critical times, significantly change and realign itself, and if necessary, reinvent itself. It does so by riding the waves of change, exploring and exploiting the high performance ranges of each such wave before jumping to the next wave. Failure to do so, results in dysfunctional performance and alignment gaps.

Transformational change demands strategic leadership combined with execution management. It requires a leader willing to take risk and explore the opportunities emerging from major organisational change. It requires tough decisions, timely and effective execution and genuine managerial teamwork.

The Wave Model

The wave model helps us to understand what is involved in a major significant change episode. The solution leader must learn to understand the nature of change and strategies to achieve sustainable development. Transforming organisational performance requires an understanding of organisational structures; changing behaviour requires

changing structure. Changing structure   iour means
changing organisational culture. Howe   re becomes
a major obstacle to realigning organisati   nd a major
challenge to the solution leader.

Can a crises ridden enterprise transform itself from its own inner
resources or does it require outside help? Does it have the capacity,
the leadership, and the relevant management to transform itself?
In this crisis situation, the poor performance culture, the neglected
development of infrastructure, the lack of visionary leadership and
competent management and professionals all are formidable obstacles
to the necessary change. Can the organisation become performance
driven, value obsessed, knowledge invested, innovation propelled and
environment conscious? Can it achieve sustainable performance?

To ride waves of change means paradigm shifting. An essential
aspect of paradigm shifting is transformation. This involves the question
"where would I want to be on the wave of performance?"

An organisation always wants to be on a high performance range
of the wave but to do so it must constantly develop strategies to enable
transformation.

The front of the wave is the area of self-directed change; the back
part of the wave is environment-directed change. Being on the front
means that the organisation is in control of its own transformation,

Figure 4.2 Sustainable Change – Riding Waves

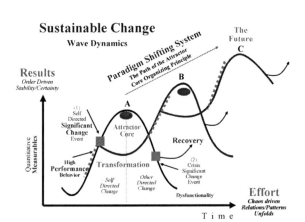

being on the back means that the organisation is reactive. The distinction between the front of the wave and the back of the wave is results; the back part of the wave is the area of low results. Paradigm shifting is absolutely necessary; but sustaining high performance cannot be done by simply improving the old way of doing things. In fact, a sure way to fail in our turbulent environment is to keep doing the same.

Riding from success into more success

If the organisation pushes the high performance habits too far without change, it can 'overstay its success' and end up in the low performance area. Success often prevents change, because it is hard to let go of the old ways. Organisations do not let go because habit changing or paradigm shifting is not conscious. This usually happens only when there is a crisis. The paradigm shifting should occur in the high range but unfortunately it happens more frequently in the crisis change range.

The attractor is in every one of the waves, it is the organising principle that pulls the system through the wave until it loses its attraction. Then when new change occurs, a new attractor is operational. The attractor pulls the system into the future. In business terms, the organising principle is most like the organisation's business model.

When the organisation gets off the wave there is a lag effect that needs to be managed. Lag affords time to learn and relearn. When the system introduces change, a period is necessary to adjust and align itself and discover its new path. It is the period where the risk of stepping off the former wave and transferring to the new model must be managed. It is a time to refocus, regroup and mobilise oneself. Demands on leadership increase during this stage; in particular, for the articulation of a clearer vision, leading in the new and inspiring direction. It may be an unsettling period but it also offers an exciting time of discovery and exploring the new introductions.

Solution Execution Approach

A leader must have an approach to solving strategic problems and should apply a 'solution execution approach', which is based on the complex adaptive systems as previously discussed. This approach, as

Figure 4.3 shows, consists of seven phases: identify strategic issues, understand them, develop a strategic plan, implement a solution/ action plan, and evaluate the execution and its consequences. At the same time, a leader must create information feedback for each phase and communicate with participants of the intervention. Finally, institutionalise the long-term strategic intervention as a permanent part of the organisational behaviour.

This 'solution execution approach' emphasises that the traditional outputs of the systems are aligned and measured in terms of the performance outcomes as desired by the customer.

Identify and Understand the Issues – Build a model

The leader examines the critical issues that must be addressed and the resulting implications for marketing, finance, human resources, information technology, operations, and other areas. This requires a strategic review including an assessment and understanding of the current model used to achieve the solutions and identifying what performance gaps exist.

Develop Solutions and Strategies

Having identified and understood the issues, the leader must develop a plan to achieve the desired solution. Leaders, particularly in developing nations, with poor organisational infrastructure and industrial-age cultures, need to consider the strategies and the conditions that must be in place for a strategy or project to be successful. Bearing in mind that there is no direct

Figure 4.3 Solution Execution Approach

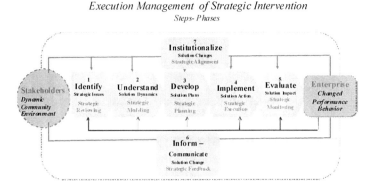

POWER, POLITICS AND PERFORMANCE

control over conditions, leaders must them stack the odds in their favour by influencing, not controlling, critical success factors.

Implement Solutions

The implementation approach needs to be considered along with the general sequence of execution. The major pitfalls need to need to be identified and avoided; and the required resources identified.

Inform and Institutionalise

Two feedback loops are essential for any intervention to work and have the desired outcome. The first one is to inform. All activities require information and constant communication with the participants so that the solution will be achieved. The second one is to institutionalise. The ultimate purpose for any intervention is to have a permanent, long-term impact.

Insights into Strategic Realignment

The actual transformation activity is equal to entrepreneurship; requiring an entrepreneurial approach during the transformative phase and the development a new business model adapting to the changing global information environment. Managing strategic lags means managing performance delays. The following are some of the reasons for such delays.

Initiating significant organisational change causes a decline in performance results

The momentum of the old performance behaviour continues. In addition, of course, there is also the well-known 'learning curve' effect.

Success becomes the enemy of change

Organisational success itself, using a 'winning formula' of performance and repetitively applying, creates habits, which ultimately are translated into automatic, unconscious work behaviour.

Most organisations change only in crises. Ideally, when an organisation is most successful it should be preparing for change. Unfortunately most organisation and its people identify change with the past experience of crisis and therefore will resist change.

...ust become part of Organisation's culture

Organisational alignments requiring transformative change must be embedded in the organisation's performance culture that appreciates 'periodic' change and equates it with opportunity.

In the discovery range performance declines before it rises

Before things get better, they get worse. When a system lets go of the old it enters a 'discovery', experimentation, and entrepreneurial range. Not all take-offs into the discovery range are successful, many systems fail at their first attempt.

Key Transformation Strategies

Partial transformation involves selection of critical areas. Most successful transformation efforts carefully choose and focus on critical organisational areas, functions, and activities that must be aligned with the global market realities. Total Organisational Transformation (TOT) is difficult to achieve. Even the most high performance organisations tend to have 'dysfunctional pockets'. Sometimes TOT is achieved through bankruptcy, dissolution of current business and then starting a new business. Transformation always involves a dual strategy: keep the old going while starting and driving the new. The old culture of success has its own momentum (the old habits die slowly); the new performance has yet to be established.

All organisational change is based on feedback loops

The solution leader must be capable of complex thinking by having a process view of the organisation, consisting of feedback loops. Feedback loops drive organisational change. It is a figure-eight process simultaneously adjusting the activities internally and aligning the organisation with the external, customer driven information environment.

Complexity science teaches us that out of simplicity unfolds complexity. A few simple organisational performance rules can create complex system behaviour. Just as DNA molecules provide the complex blueprint of life and through replication ensure reproduction and survival, so too can a few simple DNA-like performance rules guide the business system. A few simple performance rules can engender complex and adaptive business behaviour.

To create and maintain stability, the system repeats and reiterates by feeding back the performance rules into the system, forming a closed loop. This maintenance loop provides the necessary 'ordered structures' for work to get done in an efficient manner. Efficiency depends on performance loops that are 'controlled' by few simple performance rules. Performance stability rests on these closed system loops.

Change not only requires closed maintenance loops but also 'open feedback loops' interactive with other systems

Sustainable performance and growth requires cooperation and co-evolution with other system in our *glocalised* environment. Open system loops create instability and involve risk-taking and direct learning from the behaviour of other systems. Open loops demand adaptation and redesign of structured stability, the above-mentioned closed performance loops. For example, the impact of a *glocalised* recession on local businesses demands changing the business model and the performance rules. Vision, mission, core strategies, and desired measurable performance results are nothing other than 'simple performance rules' that guide enterprise behaviour, its current and future direction - they guide the alignment, while organisational core processes, relations, competence, and structures drive the internal performance and adjust the system to the desired alignment priorities.

Particularly in recessionary times, the organisation must enforce a dual strategy to attain and sustain high performance and global competitiveness. The solution leader must actively engage in *a survival – maintenance strategy* that focuses on customer retention, improved efficiency of processes and a favourable cash position; *a growth – alignment strategy* that concentrates on internal growth, development of organisational and employee competency preparing for the future. What must we do now to survive and at the same time what must we do now to emerge tomorrow as a high performance, globally competitive enterprise?

The one-world information environment has created a profound challenge for all of us. This paradigm shift is forcing us to be both responsible and accountable for our actions and behaviour. We think and learn, lead and manage in an interrelated, interconnected, interactive and integrated information space in which there are no local problems and solutions that do not have global roots and consequences. What is needed is a new breed of leaders who understand that a new manual of operation and new codes of behaviour are now necessary.

Notes

1. The section on Politics and Leadership is an excerpt from the *Prospectus, The Foundation for Politics and Leadership, A New Direction,* Directors: Winston Dookeran, Dr. Manfred Jantzen, Timothy Hamel-Smith, The Foundation for Politics and Leadership http://www.fplcaribbean.com

2. The section on Innovative Governance is based on an earlier proposal by Dr Alvin Curling for a Centre for International Governance Innovation participation Work plan and conversations between Winston Dookeran, Manfred Jantzen, and Alvin Curling for a work plan with excerpts taken from Winston Dookeran & Akhil Malaki, *Leadership and Governance in Small States, Getting Development Right* (Saarbrücken: VDM Verlag Dr. Muller, 2008; *Prospectus, The Foundation for Politics and Leadership, A New Direction.* http://www.fplcaribbean.com.

3. The section on Developing Leadership, which is part of the agenda of the Foundation, is based on a Leadership Programme that was actually executed at Ansa McAl, Trinidad; and is the basis for a Master's Programme at the University of the West Indies, Trinidad, and part of the *Solution Leadership* by Manfred D. Jantzen, unpublished manuscript. Solution Leadership provides a guide to strategic change and execution management.

4. Adapted from Winston Dookeran, *Uncertainty, Stability and Challenges. Economic and Monetary Policy, A Small State Perspective* (Port of Spain: Lexicon Trinidad, 2006). An earlier proposal by Dr Alvin Curling for a Centre for International Governance Innovation participation Work plan and conversations between Winston Dookeran, Manfred Jantzen, and Alvin Curling for a work plan with excerpts taken from Winston Dookeran & Akhil Malaki, *Leadership and Governance in Small States, Getting Development Right* (Saarbrücken: VDM Verlag Dr. Muller, 2008); *Prospectus, The Foundation for Politics and Leadership, A New Direction.* http://www.fplcaribbean.com.

5. See Winston Dookeran and Akhil Malaki, *Leadership and Governance in Small States, Getting Development Right.* (Saarbrücken:Verlag Dr.Muller, 2008), chapter 2, introduction, 'Getting Development Right'.

6. This is an excerpt from *Prospectus, The Foundation for Politics and Leadership, A New Direction, The Foundation for Politics and Leadership* http://www. fplcaribbean.com

7. The excerpts in this section are from Winston Dookeran and Akhil Malaki, *Leadership and Governance in Small States, Getting Development Right* (Saarbrücken: Verlag Dr Muller, 2008; Winston Dookeran, *Uncertainty, Stability and Challenges. Economic and Monetary Policy, A Small State Perspective* (Port of Spain: Lexicon Trinidad, 2006). See also The World Bank, *The Growth Report: Strategies for Sustained Growth and Inclusive Development*, 2008. Commission on Growth and Development, Conference Edition, 2008.

8. See *'Politics and Development: A strategic conversation on the missing politics in development'* in chapter two, 'Getting Development Right, Leadership and Governance in Small States'.

9. The above outline is based on an earlier proposal by Dr Alvin Curling for a Centre for International Governance Innovation participation Work plan.

10. Robert O. Brinkerhoff, *The Learning Alliance: Systems Thinking in Human Resource Development* (San Francisco: Pfeiffer) 1994; Linda Ellinor, *Dialogue: Rediscover the Transforming Power of Conversation* (New York: Wiley) 1998; Roger Fisher, William L. Ury, Bruce Patton, eds, *Getting to Yes: Negotiating Agreement Without Giving In* (city of publication: Penguin) 1991; Robert Hargrove, *Masterful Coaching: Extraordinary Results by Impacting People and the Way they think and work together* (San Francisco, CA: Jossey-Bass/Pfeiffer) 1999 ; Harvard Business Essentials, *Coaching and Mentoring, How to Develop Top Talent and Achieve Stronger Performance* (Boston: HBS) 2004; Jon R. Katzenbach, *The Wisdom of Teams: Creating the High-Performance Organization* (New York, NY: Harper Business) 1994; Bernard Mayer, *The Dynamics of Conflict Resolution: A Practitioner's Guide* (San Fancisco: Jossey-Bass) 2000; Raymond Noe, *Employee Training and Development*, 4th edn (city of publication: McGraw-Hill/Irwin) 2009; Mary Beth O'Neill, *Executive Coaching with Backbone and Heart: A Systems Approach to engaging Leaders with their Challenges* (San Francisco: John Wiley & Sons) 2007; C. Shelton 'From Chaos to Order: Exploring New Frontiers in Conflict Management'. Paper submitted to the Midwest Academy of Management, Original paper for the Organisation Development Track Conference, presented by Charlotte D. Shelton and John R. Darling; Melvin L. Silberman *Active Training: A Handbook of Techniques, Designs, Case Examples, and Tips* (New York: Lexington Books) 2006; Florence M. Stone, *Coaching, Counseling & Mentoring: How to choose & use the right Techniques to boost Employee Performance* (New York: AMACOM)

2007; David A. Whetten and S. Kim, *Developing Management Skills*, 7th Edn (New Jersey: Prentice Hall) 2006; William Knowlton Zinsser, *On Writing Well, 30th Anniversary Edition: The Classic Guide to Writing* (New York: Collins) 2006.

11. Ansa McAl. '*A Public Dynamic Conglomerate.*' Retrieved December 20, 2005 from http://www.ansamcal.com/index.php?option=com_co ntent&task=section&id=14&Itemid=52; Ansa McAl. '*Vision 2006.*' Retrieved December 20, 2005 from http://www.ansamcal.com/ index.php?option=com_content&task=section&id=20&Itemid=85; University of the West Indies (UWI), '*Mission Statement.*' Retrieved December 20, 2005 from http://www.uwi.tt/missionStatement.asp; UWI, '*Our Vision.*' Retrieved December 20, 2005 from http://www. uwi.tt/vision.asp; UWI, '*Seven Strategic Objectives.*' Retrieved December 20, 2005 from http://www.uwi.tt/strategicObjectives.asp; UWI, '*The Business Development Office.*' Retrieved December 20, 2005 from http:// www.uwi.tt/BusinessDevelopmentOffice.asp

12. See Heisenberg Principle, http://en.wikipedia.org/wiki/Uncertainty_ principle

13. Ralph D. Stacey, *Strategic Management & Organizational Dynamics,* 2nd edition (London: Pitman Publishing) 1996. This work is still the best that this author has found that explains and applies in a clear manner the difficult concepts of complex system behaviour; Margaret J. Wheatley, *Leadership and the New Science, Discovering Order in a Chaotic World* (San Francisco: Barrett-Koehler) 1992; Peter M. Senge, *The Fifth Discipline: The Art and Practice of the Learning Organization* (N.Y.: Doubleday) 2006.

14. See the introduction to his book, *The Age of Turbulence, Adventures in a New World.* (New York: Penguin Press) 2007, 18, summarises the challenges that individuals and societies are facing.

15. Complexity thinking is in terms of network of relationships. This is a shift from the traditional architectural thinking – basic building blocks, foundations, fundamentals etc. The metaphor of knowledge as a building is being replaced by that of the network. System theory perceives reality as network of relationships, interconnected network of concepts and models in which there are no foundations in which one part is any more fundamental than the other. Complexity thinking advocates a view of reality as an inseparable network of relationships. The material universe is seen as a dynamic web of interrelated events. None of the properties of any part of this web is fundamental; they all follow from the properties

of the other parts, and the overall consistency of their interrelations determines the structure of the entire web.

16. In the Cartesian paradigm, scientific descriptions are believed to be objective; that is independent of the human observer and the process of knowing. The new paradigm implies that epistemology – understanding of the process of knowing – has to be included explicitly in the description of natural phenomena. This recognition entered into science with W. Heisenberg and is closely related to the view of physical reality as a web of relationships. 'What we observe is not nature itself, but nature exposed to our method of questioning.' In the QM world, we must choose and because of this, we may actually create reality. In short, nature depends on our perception, and it depends on our methods of observation and measurement. Thus, complex thinking involves a shift from objective to epistemic science, to a framework in which epistemology – the method of questioning – becomes an integral part of scientific theories. Complex thinking shifts the scientific paradigm of scientific objectivity to include the process of knowing. In the QM world, not only do we influence our reality, but also, in some degree, we actually create reality. Because it is the nature of things that we can know either the momentum of a particle or its position, but not both, we must choose which of these properties we want to determine (Copenhagen Convention of 1927). There is no 'certainty' of scientific knowledge in the old paradigm sense, but rather a belief that scientific concepts and theories will always be limited and approximate. Uncertainty is the challenge and risk that life takes. (Note: Heisenberg's Uncertainty principle.) The more we know about a component of a system the less we will understand the whole of the system. The more we define or structure a system and consequently the more we define and understand the component parts, the less we know about the nature of the system as a whole, its dynamics and the more the part becomes alienated from the whole "real" system. The more we structure, the less we know about the active inter-relationships that make up the whole.

17. Malcolm Gladwell, *The Tiping Point: How Little Things Can Make a Big Difference*. (New York: Back Bay Books) 2002.

CHAPTER 5
POLITICS AND THE CULTURE OF CORRUPTION:
CULTURE MATTERS IN PERFORMANCE, THE GOLD POT ECONOMY*

The Case of Trinidad and Tobago
1972 -2010

Culture, as another critical dimension of the Partnership Approach, in its most practical and applied form is both dynamic and important in the performance of organisations, but also in the behaviour and performance of a small developing state. The case of Trinidad and Tobago illustrates the deep relationship between culture and a distorted political economy.

In Trinidad and Tobago, a culture of corruption and institutionalisation of crime is distorting the political economy. The dynamics of the 'Gold Pot' Economy resting on unearned transfer payments from the energy sector and the illicit drug trade need to be explored along with their influence on the national psyche, party politics, and socio-economic development of this country.[1]

A government is challenged to reclaim the country through national teams, boards or advisory councils to promote recovery and strategic re-alignment.

Power of Societal Culture
Bureaucratic State Culture and Development

Culture is both an obstacle and a driver of national and organisational development. The importance of culture cannot be overlooked in the emerging global network of communities. In the context of the global information environment, a society's culture is best understood as a complex adaptive system and is important to ensuring survival and health in a turbulent environment.

We live in a world of growing social, political and economic interdependence. All parts of a society are related to each other and to the rest of the world. Any change in any part of one society is felt in the entire world. A society is a complex adaptive system; it consists of a community of participants. It is a web of formal and informal groups and organisations, private and public institutions. Society is a conscious and unconscious network of individual relationships. Its participating stakeholders interact with each other according to set rules and deep paradigms to improve their behaviour and thus the behaviour of the society, which they comprise.

Culture, the deeply embedded behaviour patterns of how things get done, is critical to understanding the challenges that leadership faces. Increasingly, local problems require global solutions and conversely, global problems demand local solutions, both problems and solutions are in the context of culture. Culture influences the way we think and learn, lead and manage; the way we understand issues and execute solutions. Culture is the most powerful prism through which we view the world around us. Our culture shapes our perception of reality; it filters our perception of 'the way things are'. Culture contains our hidden assumption of 'how things work'. It is our 'implicit' theory of reality. It profoundly contributes to an individual's identity. It shapes our mindset.

Culture is the most powerful paradigm that guides and affects our behaviour and actions. It is a distinctly human capacity adaptable to circumstances and transmitting this coping skill and knowledge to subsequent generations. Culture gives people a sense of who they are, of belonging, of how they should behave, and of what they should be doing. While there are essential similarities, every culture is unique.

In operational terms, culture can be defined as simply the way people live, work, enjoy themselves, and relate to their community and share their expectations of the future. On another level, the culture of a people forms a collective mindset. Culture is a storehouse of accumulated communal experience of success, failure and knowledge that has allowed the community to survive, thrive and sustain itself in changing environments. Culture is deeply embedded in organisational, community and societal behaviour.

Societal culture can be viewed as comprising of three levels. It is the sum total of all the shared, taken-for-granted societal assumptions; espoused or declared values; and artefacts, that is, visible structures. The majority of the society's culture is taken for granted; its assumptions, its beliefs, perceptions, thought, and feelings. At this basic level, culture is mostly unconscious, yet these underlying beliefs that, never actually articulated, are always present to colour the perception of actions and communications. These beliefs are transmitted through everyday language and actions.

Cultures are inherently logical. They are logical systems with developed integrity at their core. An absolute logic prevails over the system of values, beliefs, and norms that constitute culture. A critical challenge in the workplace is to learn to accept the logic of other cultures without judging them according to the very different logic of one's own culture.

Culture is visible through practices and behaviour seen by outsiders, but they are only the tip of the iceberg. The meaning behind or underneath the outward symbols, behaviour, and practices is incomprehensible unless we understand the culture's inherent logic. What seems to be universal is that each culture has a reasoning process, but then each manifests the mental and learning process in its own distinct way.

Cultures can and do adapt when major outside forces demand changes in belief and behaviour. Most cultures show their greatest adaptability in times of crisis. Cultures change at different rates. Corporate cultures can adapt fairly quickly, professional cultures less quickly, and primary social cultures only adapt slowly.

Each culture validates self in a unique way. From an individual's perspective, culture provides the basis of self-identity and community. Culture is the answer to the universal human demand for self-identity, that is, how we communicate to the world who we are and what we believe. Communication can be deeply coloured by relationships, history and status of the persons involved. Even language consists of culturally agreed upon structure, vocabulary, and meanings of written or oral communication.

The culture of a country can be a driver of, as well as an obstacle to global competitiveness and economic development. Mindsets are difficult to change. For example, the mindset of poverty vs. a mindset of wealth. Culture itself determines the perception of scarcity. A culture of poverty has as its core a 'cannot do' attitude as a powerful mindset. On the other hand, a culture of wealth is driven by a positive 'can do' mindset. The power of the cultural paradigm, its role as driver and obstacle to development, must be clearly understood in any local transformation effort. Culture, the behaviour of people at work and important human activities, has increasingly become the most significant variable in change equations.

Culture is always order driven; it changes slowly and sporadically only in crises. Yet local transformation demands that culture must also change. A critical goal of changing local culture is to develop a learning society. It must realistically reflect the changing needs of society and its organised systems. Culture is powerful and is important in national development.

Culture is of particular significance in the development of small nations in their drive toward development status. The 'developed' and 'developing' world each have distinctly different cultures. Developed countries, while having different cultures, share certain characteristics. The most important being the very fact that they have successfully undergone the painful and in most cases lengthy process of development. This process took several hundreds of years of 'industrialisation', urbanisation and for the most part, eliminated poverty.

A second shared characteristic of developed countries is that they have a strong 'identity' of who they are and what their place is in the 'scheme of things'. Most importantly, they determine the pace, nature and direction of change in the rest of world. As a result, their affect, if not outright, determines the course of 'cultural change' in the developing world and its economies. While the developing world, including its 'diverging economies' also has distinctly different cultures, in most cases they also share certain characteristics. The most important shared characteristic is that they have been impacted by the now developed world in the process of development. In some cases, this uneven, lopsided, relationship lasted for several hundred years.

Society, through its culture, has a powerful habituating influence on the way individuals, organisations, and institutions conduct themselves. The power of order and continuity is an important aspect of cultural behaviour and action, and is a strong force that ensures the way things will occur, the method and manner that life will go on. Any culture has a significant impact on how we behave as individuals, as well as organisations. Our business practices are, for the most part, culturally driven and have become unconscious acquired habits – mental models.

The National Power of a Hybrid Society

We living in an increasingly cosmopolitan world in which everyone is attached to a home of his/her own, with its own cultural particularities, but takes pleasure from the presence of other, different, places that are home to other different people. Not only are we becoming a more cosmopolitan culture but many societies are increasingly become a hybrid culture. The Caribbean is dominated by hybrid cultures.

Under the right conditions, hybrid societies are more desirable than monocultures. Hybrid refers here to 'the evolution of new, dynamic, mixed cultures'.[2] Hybridity flourishes in an environment of social cohesion. But this cohesion does not arise from an absence of conflict, but rather, from the capacity to learn and grow through peaceful conflict. This cohesion arises from treating unavoidable conflicts as beneficial tensions rather than destructive ones. This cohesion arises from the recognition that a conflict-free society is impossible and that to deny conflicts over values and between groups, robs a society of its energy and dynamism. Coupled with hybridity, this kind of cohesion increases national power by strengthening economic competitiveness and social capital.

This model has the power to change the way we view individuals, communities, and nations. It is a new standard for human development, a fresh measurement for social capital. Positive conflict tensions and resolutions drive social cohesion. Hybridity and social cohesion develop social capital. Hybridity brings innovation; homogeneity brings stagnation. Wealthy nations, or, aspiring wealthy nations, have no choice but to face three interrelated challenges: diversity, social harmony, and hybridity choice and challenge. Societies must choose which kind of diversity they want, they must create a new basis for social harmony, and they must achieve high levels of hybridity without jeopardizing social cohesion.

Development Challenge for Leadership

Global change powerfully influences local change and forces all public and private enterprises to become high performance enterprises. The leadership must focus on high performance solutions: infrastructure capacity and global competitiveness. In a developing country and in developing organisations, a solution leader substitutes insufficient infrastructure with their own capabilities in order to compete globally. A solution leader in a developing country and developing organisation has two primary strategic tasks: to build local capacity by developing the necessary physical and non-physical infrastructure, and to compete globally by aligning with global markets and meeting global performance standards.

Shortage of Knowledge Professionals

A major constraint to local transformation is the lack of knowledge, or more specifically, the lack of competent knowledge professionals. Knowledge is the real driver of change; and the most critical knowledge for strategic change resides in people. In small developing countries, there is a lack of competent knowledge professionals, those that use knowledge to create value for the stakeholders in public or private enterprise.

The learning organisation and the learning society is knowledge based. The developing country's public and private enterprises must become knowledge based and managed by competent knowledge professionals. The shortage of competent professionals in all disciplines must be taken into consideration in strategic planning and implementation of the high performance organisation. Managing knowledge, the infrastructure of information, and value creating activities, must start with an honest acknowledgment of the scarce intellectual capital in not only our organisation and society, but the Caribbean as a whole.

Scarcity of intellectual capital, specifically scarcity of competent professionals, is a reality we must address as a strategic priority. While a shortage of competent professionals is nothing new, this shortage is now critical. More and more organisations, public and private, are hitting the proverbial wall. The world we operate in has become much more complex and requires a new level of sophistication that was not needed just a few years ago. The new information network economy is global and a successful local organisation is forced to deal with sophisticated regional and global competition. The current global economic reality has intensified the need for more sophisticated and competent professionals.

The Caribbean has far more formally educated individuals,

(sometimes referred to as 'certified intelligent persons'), than it has competent knowledge professionals and it is this imbalance that needs to be addressed for the region to compete in the global information driven market environment.

Bureaucratic State Culture[3]
Dysfunctional Behaviour

Nearly all traditional societies and developing nations have developed both public and private bureaucracies. When a state dominates societal development, its bureaucratic behaviour is transferred to society. Even the private enterprises take on bureaucratic control features. Conversely, the behaviour of both the bureaucratic public and private enterprises is reinforced by the behaviour of the traditional society. A change in societal behaviour requires first, the transformation of the behaviour of the bureaucratic state.

Tension arises between bureaucracies and people in them. Bureaucracies, through their control systems, achieve goals by maintaining order and stability at all costs. Yet, the bureaucratic control systems are operated by people who also have a need to create to achieve goals and risk change and instability in order to grow. Control systems inevitably foster the emergence of shadow or informal systems that make the bureaucracies ultimately ineffective and a burden to future growth.

Traditional bureaucratic control systems are operation and function driven, and assume a stable and predictable environment; they are industrial and mechanical in nature. In such systems, humans are subordinated to the system, and are treated in terms of job functions and tasks as part of the overall operation.

Human beings are treated as 'labour units' and elements in the production function. Human beings have not only a need for order, but also for growth and self-fulfilment. Bureaucracy, as a control system, has a negative impact on human behaviour. The following are seven critical behaviour traits of traditional state bureaucracies: culture of alienation, servitude behaviour, valueless performance, incompetent professionals, subversive behaviour, bureaucratic inadaptability, and shadow network.[4]

Political Economy & Leadership
Leadership, Political Economy and Real Economy

Leadership Challenge

Trinidad and Tobago is a victim of the resource curse. Transfer payments create and circulate within a distorted 'Gold Pot' economy fuelled by energy sector transfer payments (mainly from oil and gas revenues). This creates a mentality of dependency driven by the state and breeds endemic corruption.

A penchant for populist politics over sound economics created the 'Gold Pots' of energy, the government, drugs, the private sector and society. These transfer payments are unearned and do not result from actual local productivity. There is therefore little psychological imperative to save the funds or wean off the payments. Short term consumption spending becomes the norm, alongside waste, corruption and violent crime. Crime is a product of the illegal drugs trade festering within the system. The spending fuels inflation, crowds out private investment, dampens competitiveness, and suppresses entrepreneurship. Politically, a ruling political party, whose primary purpose is mainly to redistribute energy revenues indiscriminately to 'buy' short-term election votes, usually controls the Government 'Pot of Gold'; eroding democracy and good governance. The challenge is to unite in partnership, and throw off the yokes of dependency and corruption to build a knowledge based, service economy. The partnership approach requires exercising power to the long-term benefit of citizens. There must therefore be a system which would allow for a just distribution of responsible use of power by key societal stakeholders, especially the state and the political parties in power.[5]

Trinidad and Tobago needs to transform the severely distorted 'Gold Pot' economy into a knowledge-based service economy. This new economy must adapt to an information-driven, open-market environment to achieve equitable and sustainable development. Any such societal transformation requires a collaborative effort involving all sectors of the economy, interest groups, and citizens. It demands national dialogue. An enlightened and patriotic leadership, that places country over political party and all other self-serving interests, should guide this effort at societal change. The structures and incentives, which have bred the current leadership culture need to be examined to determine the means of engendering good governance and practices.

Instead of transforming society and the system of governance, political leadership usually focuses on maintaining political power at the cost of society's benefit. The leadership of political parties, both in power and in opposition, develops and executes misguided policies that encourage underdevelopment, leading to a regressive state. The politics of underdevelopment and particularly its socio-economic dynamics and its impact on the well-being of society and its citizens need to be addressed.

Political Economy Perspective

Historically, in the classical tradition, economics was not separated from politics and therefore continued emphasis was placed on the important role of the state. In North America, particularly in the US, economics as taught in universities, assumes that economics is a science and must be separated from the study of politics. As a result, important institutions such as the Central Bank and its governance were to be insulated from any political interference.[6]

It is debateable whether economics, particularly at the macro level, will ever be or even should be free from politics. It can be argued that economic development will always involve the role of the state – the government and political parties in power. It simply requires enlightened political leadership that puts country above party as a prerequisite for contemporary economic development. The point here is that for most of the world, including in Trinidad and Tobago, macroeconomics and politics have never been separated. Consequently, politicians must be knowledgeable about economics or otherwise they will make purely populist political decisions that can have devastating economic consequences.

The Real Economy's Dynamics

Trinidad and Tobago's real economy consists of three major transactional sectors, each with its own dynamics but heavily influenced, dependent and driven by the 'Gold Pot' economy. The largest sector is the state dependent economy. There is also the traditional, formal taxpaying private enterprise driven economy; and the informal, non-tax-paying economy.

In the traditional economy, the government's duty is to provide public goods and services. The Government's macroeconomic role is to steer the economy and government policies to achieve sustainable development. Taxation is the major source of government revenue. Whilst the government may encourage savings and investment, it is for the most part left to the private sector. Similarly, the government may encourage global competitiveness and efficiency by the private sector through various policies, including subsidies. In a traditional economy, there is an emphasis on the accumulation of wealth and not just the redistribution of wealth.

In the 'Gold Pot' economy, the major factors in the economy and sources of wealth are the transfer payments from each 'Gold Pot.' The Government 'Gold Pot' is derived mostly from energy dollar transfers and it dominates the 'Gold Pot' economy and Trinidad and Tobago's real economy. In this 'Gold Pot' economy, greed and fear can tip either side of the equation. Bribery, lack of transparency, corruption, secretiveness, theft and a culture in which everyone and everything has a price are the by-products of this distorted economy. Everything is state dependent, the only ideology is statism. Those involved in all 'Pots of Gold' have personal relationships within the government, which they can influence; none of them want strong government institutions. As a result, there is low national productivity.

Politics and Power of the 'Gold-Pot' Economy
Political Power and Economic Distortion

Political decisions created the current distorted 'Gold Pot' economy, but they can and should correct it. The current distorted economy cannot achieve sustainable development and achieve the desired quality life demanded by this country's citizens.[7] Populist politics, more so than economics, created the current 'Gold Pot' economy. Politically motivated decisions rather than economics-based decisions maintain the distorted economy. Whilst key economic variables such as the availability of natural resources, world scarcity and temporary demand for energy resources have tended to support this politics at least in the short term, these resources distort the economy. They also obstruct traditional economic analysis and colour economic indicators that measure economic performance.[8]

Figure 5.1 The Gold Pot Economy

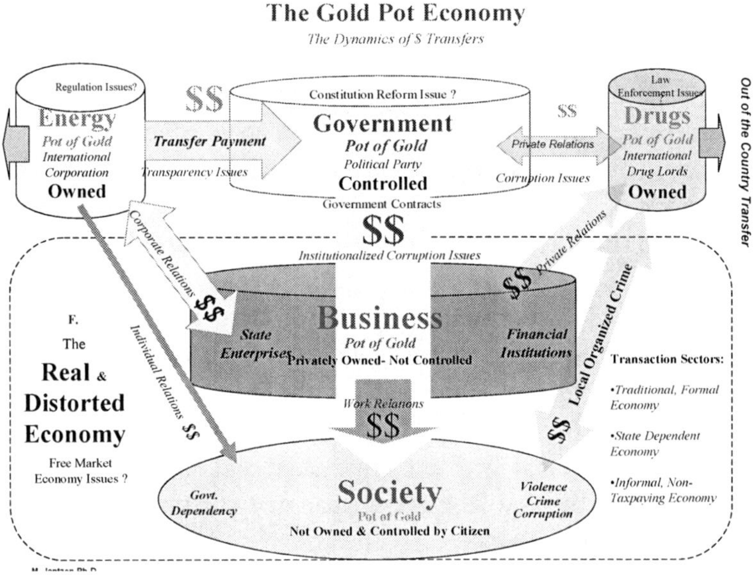

The Gold Pot Economy
The Dynamics of $ Transfers

In such a political economy all major economic decisions are guided by the politically motivated decisions of the political party in power. In such a case, economic considerations will always be secondary to political considerations. Politics is about securing and maintaining power and economics only serves as a tool to do so.

Fear and Greed drives the 'Gold Pot' Economy

The 'Gold Pot' economy discussed in Trinidad and Tobago consists of six powerfully attractive elements each with its own dynamics: energy, drugs, government, private sector, and society 'Pots of Gold' and the 'Distorted Real Economy'. Together these elements explain the distorted economy and the destructive greed and fear they unleash on society.

Traditionally, greed and fear are the powerful drivers of the open market economy. Greed drives the accumulation of wealth, and fear drives the institutionalisation and preservation of ownership of that wealth, as well as the limitation of risk and a desire for stability. Of course, unbridled and unregulated greed and fear can lead to violent swings, destruction and redistribution of wealth in the economies. In the case of the 'Gold Pot' economy, individual and collective greed and fear become unrestrained by traditional ethical and legal boundaries.

Such unbridled greed and fear can permeate the entire society, because society and its critical institutions are directly affected by the dynamics of the various 'Pots of Gold'. The 'Pots of Gold' distort the real economy to such an extent that traditional economics no longer provide an adequate explanation of economic behaviour at both the macro and micro levels.

'Gold Pots' as 'Unearned' Transfer Payments

All of the 'Pots of Gold' always involve a transfer of dollars. More precisely, a 'Gold Pot' involves a transfer of legal or illegal payments between two or more co-operating economic entities in the 'Gold Pot' economy. On the macroeconomic level, this transfer of dollars is perceived as the real 'Pot of Gold'. It is simply a monetary flow to the rest of the economy without any associated actual production of goods and services (in the case of energy, this is merely the extraction of natural resources). The major direct sources of the 'Gold Pot' transfer are the energy sector, drugs, the government, state-owned enterprises and indirectly the highly dependent private sector.

On the micro economic level, a 'Gold Pot' is perceived as unearned income in terms of the traditional economic performance criteria. Finite resources are extracted in the Energy 'Gold Pot', but this is done by foreign firms and is not a result of actual national production (although it is reflected in the GDP). The money is not associated with real performance. Therefore, these transfer payments are not associated with production, and so there is little will to save them. Short-term profligate spending by the government becomes the norm, as does equally profligate consumption (mainly through imports) in private society. They are perceived in the traditional economic sense as being risk free although they certainly may involve violent crime, waste and corruption.

The rest of the economy is critically dependent on these 'Pots of Gold' and their transfer flows. In fact, many in the economy often develop a dependency syndrome and have a short-sighted perception centred on consumption and receiving risk free government payments. It has the consequences of causing insufficient savings; crowding out private investment, fuelling inflation, dampening competitiveness and suppressing entrepreneurial vim and activity.

Societal Distortions of 'Gold Pot' Economics

The 'Gold Pot' economy distorts the culture and behaviour of the entire society; it affects every citizen, organisation, and institution of the country.[9] It has a corruptive influence on economic, social, and political activities. It may inflict long-term damage on the culture and values of the country. As mentioned before, whilst greed and fear are accepted motives in the free market economy, unbridled and unchecked they undermine traditional societal values and begin to change individual and collective behaviour.

The 'Gold Pot' Economy distorts the dynamics of the economy; it diverts critical resources and economic activity to unproductive use. It shifts the focus from hard work, productivity, wealth creation and long-term sustainable development to short-term gains and sustaining political power. A misguided industrialisation policy results in mostly large, unproductive buildings, white elephants and financially non-viable, unsustainable industrial plants. The 'Gold Pot' economy destabilises society and its major institutions. With regard to governance, a ruling political party whose primary purpose is mainly to redistribute energy revenues indiscriminately to 'buy' short-term election votes usually controls the Government 'Pot of Gold'.

The Energy 'Pot of Gold'
Is it a threat to sovereignty?

The Energy 'Pot of Gold' is owned and controlled by large foreign corporations, which are contractually joined with the government. There are two types of Energy 'Pot of Gold' dollar transfers. The first type is the foreign, energy-dollar transfer and the second is the local, energy-dollar transfer. The first includes the transfers to the government, transfers by international corporations to the local business partners, and transfers to domestic labour.

The second involves the transfers of the bulk of foreign dollars to the local economy, mainly through government largesse. Both foreign and local energy transfer payments represent a permanent loss of natural resources to the country and both severely distort the economy. Whilst the international corporations control the real, physical Energy 'Pot of Gold', the local dollar transfer is the perceived and practical source of the

Energy 'Pot of Gold'.

The Energy 'Pot of Gold' is contractually linked to the government. The government enjoys the largest share of the energy transfer payments and it forms the largest part of the Government 'Pot of Gold'. The government accepts little risk in exploration, development and production. Yet, it receives continuous transfer payments on behalf of the state of Trinidad and Tobago as national revenue.

To hedge any potential losses and protect their 'risk investment', the foreign corporations demand and receive government backed production sharing contracts. These contracts distort the control and ownership of Trinidad and Tobago's resources in favour of the corporations. For instance, a weak, cash-strapped government, a corrupt one, or one seeking to quickly ramp up spending to engage in populist 'vote buying', may negotiate for short-term gains; which may be detrimental to the long-term development and revenues of the country. As a result, these powerful international energy corporations may practically have both ownership and control over the Energy 'Pot of Gold' with the blessings of the government. The international energy companies prefer a weak government, or at least one that is easily satisfied with contractual dollar transfer payments.

Finally, the energy sector becomes a permanent offshore sector of the economy that is predominantly controlled and owned by foreign interests. Hence, it gives credence to the perception of a new form of a plantation economy with the added dimension of the permanent depletion of the natural resources of oil and gas.

The Drug 'Pot of Gold'
Is the drug trade destroying the fabric of Society?

The Drug 'Pot of Gold' is mostly owned and controlled by international drug lords with local transfer payments. Unlike the energy sector where the actual source of energy (oil and gas) is local, the source of drugs is external and the country is used as a trans-shipment point in the global drug trade. There are at least two types of drug dollar transfers. One is the dollar transfer derived from drug transfer shipments and the other is dollar transfer from local drug sales from the relatively small Trinidad and Tobago drug market.

Unlike the Energy Pot, this Drug 'Pot of Gold' is informally linked to the economy. It officially and legally has no source and cannot be declared. Consequently, the drug lords would prefer a weak and corrupt government with weak and ineffective law enforcement and judicial system. There is an infusion of cash into the economy through money laundering in this informal economy. This informal and illegal process corrupts and distorts the economy. This infusion of liquidity contributes to increases in prices.

The inflow of drug money has a multiplier effect on the economy, affecting all sectors and economic activities of the economy. The drug money may also taint the practices of financial institutions. Money laundering and drug money are not recorded in national accounts, consequently, the Central Bank has no control over the drug economy. The drug economy is a major driver of the informal economy and corruption feeds this informal economy. Both the Energy and Drug 'Pots of Gold' inflate property prices and consumer prices.

The Drug 'Pot of Gold' is the major source of violent crime; and it is estimated that approximately 80 per cent of all major crimes can be traced to drugs from gang formation, murder, and robbery to corruption in all aspects of society. The profitability of drugs is significant. This high rate of profitability leads to violence within the drug organisation. The drug sector is informal and cannot rely on the formal legal system. Consequently, violence is part if the enforcement of order in the drug economy. This raises the question as to whether the local drug lords become so powerful that they have become immune from prosecution and justice.

The Government 'Pot of Gold'
Does the Government Pot of Gold pave the way for Dictatorship?

The Government 'Pot of Gold' is derived mainly from transfers from the Energy 'Pot of Gold'. To a smaller extent, the Drug 'Pot of Gold' adds to the Government 'Pot of Gold' through corrupt transfers from the drug industry attempting to influence the government. Due to the constitutional and political framework, the political party in power is *de facto* also the government, hence the political party owns and controls this Government 'Pot of Gold' and has control over internal transfer payments. There is lack

NB

of transparency in the transfers within the Government 'Pot of Gold'.

It uses the transfer payments from the energy sector to stay in power by promoting dependency on the party. Since there are no traditional left-right party ideologies in Trinidad and Tobago, only a form of authoritarianism, the prize for political party to win government is to gain the Government 'Pot of Gold' for itself. Since the political party is all-powerful, it will not promote strong governmental institutions, and ultimately will not tolerate any social, economic or political opposition.

When the government increases its economic sphere and its state ownership, it automatically increases the power of the political party. Trinidad and Tobago is one of a few countries in the world which did increase the number of state owned and controlled enterprises. The new government is reversing this trend and is concerned with innovation, value to the customer-citizen and efficiency of operation, not only the political party's power.

The Private Enterprise 'Pot of Gold'
Does the Private Enterprise 'Pot of Gold' destroy Entrepreneurship and Ownership?

The Private Enterprise 'Pot of Gold' is privately owned but not necessarily controlled. In the 'Gold Pot' economy, control is exercised through transfer payments. The Domestic Business 'Pot of Gold' is derived from dollar transfer payments from the Energy, Drugs, and Government 'Pots of Gold'. Local businesses are for the most part dependent on energy, government or drugs dollar transfers. As a result, there is only very little independent private enterprise or an independent business community.

Clearly, the current economy of Trinidad and Tobago is dominated by the government sector. In many instances, private enterprise survives solely on government contracts. Only a few local conglomerates have been able to expand into the larger region of the Caribbean and beyond. These entities are less vulnerable to the political relationships of the party in power. Yet, even these conglomerates would not be profitable without the government.

The bedrock of democracy is property ownership. The 'Pot of Gold' erodes the concept of ownership, as many private sector entities are made dependent on the government. This, of course, translates into the political realm, as property and enterprise ownership precedes democratic independence.

The Societal 'Pot of Gold'

Citizens are dependent on internal transfer payments but do not control the Societal 'Pot of Gold'. The Societal 'Pot of Gold' is citizen owned but it is mostly filled with unfulfilled expectations, fool's gold if you will. Ideally, this 'Pot of Gold' represents the Quality of Life 'Pot of Gold,' but as a real 'Pot of Gold', it does not exist. High expectations of easy wealth engendered in the good times of high resource revenues and government spending (with revenues distributed by the ruling party to attract and retain more voters) distort and degenerate any culture of hard work and disciplined productivity. Instead, a dependency syndrome develops with much of society dependent on the government. Fewer people want to work for treasure as they have come to expect government handouts, entitlements and preferred contracts.

Political Action Agenda

The national strategy for societal transformation driven by a knowledge-based service economy is to reclaim the country from past misguided policies by transforming the 'Gold Pots' into long term national wealth-generation and equitable distribution structures. This requires the involvement of the national community in a dialogue facilitated by enlightened leadership and a new government.

The challenge is to find ways of reclaiming the nation's natural resources, national and local government, personal and property security, private enterprise economy, and the quality of life for citizens and society. For each critical national issue, an appropriate national advisory council, board or teams should be formed to develop the corresponding national strategy and advice on its implementation. The national advisory council should consist of the following strategic teams:

- resource and energy team
- national security and crime team
- national and local government team
- private economy and enterprise team
- societal quality of life team
- recovery and sustainable development team

Figure 5.2 Reclaiming the Country Strategy View

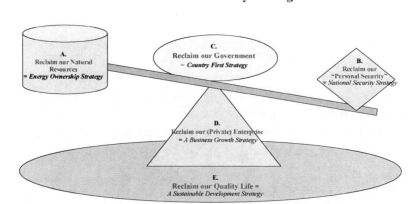

Strategic Change Framework
Reclaim Our Country Strategies

Resource and Energy Team

The challenge for this resource and energy team is to reclaim ownership and control of national resources. Since the Energy 'Pot of Gold' is predominantly foreign owned and controlled, any societal transformation must reclaim control and ownership of the national resources. The membership of this team should reflect the actual interests of the national community.

The task is to develop a national sustainable resource and energy strategy that is aligned with and directly supportive of a knowledge-based service economy. The team should develop a national resource and energy strategy with attainable solutions that benefit all.

The strategy of this team should address foreign ownership and/or control of the energy sector. The possibility and feasibility of local ownership and control of natural resources should also be addressed.

This is not to suggest that the potentially disastrous option of nationalisation or Venezuelan or Zimbabwean style expropriation would occur in the energy industry. The policy should simply aim to increase local private sector ownership and participation in the energy sector through incentives and regulation, whilst re-negotiating energy sector contracts on terms more favourable to the government, keeping in mind free market principles. Government transparency and accountability in the energy sector; the development of alternative sustainable energy sources, and alignment with a knowledge-based service economy are all important initiatives.

National Security and Crime Team

The challenge for this team is to reclaim personal and property safety and national security. Room must be made for the development and implementation of a comprehensive national security and crime strategy aligned with a restructured economy. This new strategy should address the illicit economy including money laundering and the drug trade; as well as the reform of national security and intelligence administration and the supporting infrastructure such as the Police Service and Defence Force.

National and Local Governance Team

The imperative is to reclaim national and local government. This team must promote constitutional reform and develop a governance strategy that assures constitutional reform. The new government must emphasise good governance with public sector reform (to create an efficient and effective public service), and a government aligned with an information-based service economy. The new government is reclaiming a more inclusive government that puts the country first.

Private Economy and Enterprise Team

An independent private enterprise economy must be reclaimed. This team should develop an independent private enterprise and business sector strategy that is the foundation of a genuine middle class. Since the Private Enterprise 'Pot of Gold' is owned but not controlled by private enterprise, the task of the team is to develop a strategy to reclaim the private sector economy by promoting business growth and fostering an independent business sector. The foundation of a sustainable economy is an independent business community and the growth of a genuinely prosperous middle class.

This strategy must address the over-dependence on the government (contracts) and act to minimise government's distorting impact on the private sector. Entrepreneurship needs to be promoted and incentives offered for innovation and research as well as for increased private saving and investment. Employment incentives in risky ventures and other facilitating and supporting government activities also need to be offered. The private sector must be independent, free-market driven and based on knowledge-driven service industries to create sustainable and growing wealth.

Societal Quality of Life Team

There must be a guaranteed basic living standard for all members of society. The strategy must be to reduce poverty; enlarge the extent of the social safety net, as well as health care and employment opportunities; the setting of the minimum wage; entrenching worker safety; ensuring the availability of affordable housing and basic utilities; and the alignment with a knowledge-based service economy.

The Societal 'Pot of Gold' is neither owned nor controlled by citizens but always promised by the political party in power. It is a perceived 'Pot of Gold' that every citizen desires to benefit from. It builds powerful expectations that all will benefit from the Government 'Pot of Gold' of transfer payments, whilst promoting dependency.

Recovery and Sustainable Development Team

The challenge is to develop a strategy of sustainable growth with an emphasis on building a knowledge-based service economy. The task of this team should be to develop immediate and short-term as well as long-term sustainable development strategies with an immediate focus on economic recovery, employment, and long-term sustainable growth incentives. Long-term sustainable development will require an alignment with a knowledge-based service economy.

Since the Government 'Gold Pot' has caused the major distortion in the economy, the government must also redirect its spending and industrialisation priorities. The government must break the cycle of profligate spending during booms and painful cuts during recessions, and reorient priorities toward the long term. In the context of the current global and local recession, the government has a critical role to play.

This team ought to develop strategies in several areas. The first is in fostering creativity with an emphasis on training and development in critical growth sectors of the economy by transforming the entire education system. The second is diversification of the economy to counter-balance the distorting impact of the offshore sector on the economy. This includes identifying and fostering growth sectors such as the downstream energy sector, specialised manufacturing, financial services, tourism, shipping and specialised agriculture. The third is the national communication infrastructure with an emphasis on information communication technology, supporting critical sectors of the economy. The fourth is traditional infrastructure with an emphasis on a national transportation system. The final area is a state-centred foreign policy that puts national interests first and fosters sustainable development.

Conclusion

Politics distorted the economy of Trinidad and Tobago and must now also reclaim and redirect the economy. The challenge for political leaders and a new government is to set a new direction, align the economy with the turbulent one-world information environment, and transform it into a knowledge-based economy. The political leadership must entrench good governance and equity for all citizens. Some of the strategies and tasks have been absorbed by newly created boards.

Notes

*Contributed by Manfred D. Jantzen
1. Winston Dookeran and Bridget Brereton eds, *East Indians in the Caribbean: Colonialism and the Struggle for Identity* (London: Kraus International Publications) 1982.
2. Thomas L. Friedman, *The Lexus and the Olive Tree: Understanding Globalization* (New York: Anchor) 2002.
3. Manfred Jantzen, *Solution Leadership: A Guide to Strategic Change*, unpublished manuscript.
4. Robert K. Merton, *Social Theory and Social Structure*, Revised edition (Glencoe.IL: Free Press) 1957.
5. The author developed the first draft in late 2006. Some additions were made up to May 24, 2010 when Trinidad and Tobago had a regime changing election. The author's assessment of the political economy has not changed as of May 2010. The new People's Partnership government is introducing a new direction similarly to the Political Action Agenda suggested. Manfred Jantzen *Solution Leadership: A Guide to Strategic Change*. Forthcoming.
6. Political economy emerged from moral philosophy. In the 18th century, it began as the study of states' economies and polities, where the term was

coined political economy. Contemporary political economy most often refers to interdisciplinary studies drawing from economics, law, and political science to explain how political institutions, a political environment, and an economic system influence each other. Historians have employed political economy to explore the ways that people and groups with common economic interests, in the past, have used politics to further their interests.

7. Hans C. Blomqvist and Mats Lundahl, *The Distorted Economy* (New York: Palgrave Macmillan) 2003. The authors offer an important and timely analysis of the cause, effect and resolution of distortions in the economy and apply their analytical framework to several case studies such as the trade policy of developing countries, apartheid in South Africa and socialist planned economies.

8. For example, real employment statistics are difficult to get.

9. For example, in Menno Vellinga, *The Political Economy of the Drug Industry: Latin America and the International System* (Gainesville, FL: University Press of Florida) 2004. Stemming from an international conference held in Utrecht, this collection encompasses the political, economic, social, and legal aspects of the illegal drug industry. The introduction provides an overview of the political economy of the drug industry followed by discussions of the impact of the drug industry on the Latin American source countries; drug trafficking and money laundering ; the war on drugs, trans-national crime, and international security; and current options for intervention and control. Pierre Kopp, *Political Economy of Illegal Drugs* (New York:Taylor and Francis) 2007; Ivelaw L. Griffith, ed, *The Political Economy of Drugs in the Caribbean* (New York: Palgrave Macmillan) 2000.

CHAPTER 6
Coalition Politics & Good Governance

Political Parties and the Partnership Approach:
The Case of Trinidad and Tobago

The Partnership Approach

Coalition politics is the politics of today. In the past it has been argued that only a two party system with one winning party and one opposition party will provide the desired national stability. The new political paradigm of political coalition reasons that the coalition unity, considering the increasing diversity of interest in a society, is the best way of offering the necessary governmental stability and the best way to deliver performance to the people.

The promises of a new Coalition Partnership provide a healthy foundation for nation development and a better government by putting country first above party politics.

Coalition politics is based on inclusion. Today the whole world is under the challenge of the politics of inclusion – include everyone, include the poor, include the dispossessed. This became the foundation for the new Coalition Partnership.

Getting the political philosophy, party politics, exercise of power, shared principles and values right is essential for achieving the ultimate goal of one nation, one people, one government, and one future. To be successful in this quest in today's complex and dynamic information environment requires a Coalition Partnership Approach to good governance.

This chapter should be treated as a case study of the emergence of a third party in a traditional two-party state. The Congress of the People (COP) became a political party and national movement between 2006 and 2010 and a pivotal partner in the *Peoples Partnership Party* and government on May 24, 2010. What follows is a brief account of the major ideas and programmes developed by the COP movement to incorporate as part of the new Partnership Approach.

Getting the Political Philosophy Right is a critical dimension of the Partnership Approach.

Three traditional central concerns of political philosophy are the political economy by which property rights are defined and access to capital is regulated; the demands of justice in distribution and punishment; and the rules of truth and evidence that determine judgments in the law. Figure 6.1 provides a conceptual framework and road map for the realignment of society and economy and ultimate destination of One Nation, One People, One Government with One Future.

To achieve the destination of One Nation requires a New Economy with the goal of inclusive development and an emphasis on equity, poverty reduction and sustainable growth-development. To achieve the destination of One People requires a New Social Order with the goal of nurturing harmonious society from cultural diversity. This new social order emerges out of racial harmony, social balance, religious tolerance, and geographic integration.

One Government requires a New Politics with the goal of good governance – a democratic government with citizen and community participation, national and individual security, law and order, and competence. To achieve the ultimate destination of One Future requires a New Direction guided by core principles and shared values of truth, justice, and freedom.

Getting the Politics Right is another critical dimension of the new Partnership Approach

The goal of politics and political parties is to get power, state power. In turn, this state power should be used to supply good governance. In the case of a small developing state, this state power should guide the national sustainable development. Getting the politics right so that the power of the state is used for the benefit of society – that is good governance.

Figure 6.1 The Ultimate Destination – Alignment[1]

The Ultimate Destination
Realignment of Society and Economy

Realignment of society and economy requires a road map with goals, critical markers along the path guided by principles to the ultimate destination of :

One Nation	**A new Economy** **Inclusive Development**	**Equity** Growth Poverty Eradication
One People	**A New Social Order** **Harmonious Society**	**Cultural Diversity** Racial Harmony Social Balance Religious Tolerance Geographic Integration
One Government	**A New Politics** **Democratic Governance**	**Community Participation** Law & Order Competence
One Future	**A New Direction** **Shared Values**	**Truth** Justice Freedom

Our political-party partnership or coalition approach is designed to achieve good governance. This approach should include critical steps with actions. The first step is to identify and understand the critical societal and political issues and arrive at an agreement on a political coalition philosophy, synthesised from the party philosophies of the leading partners in the coalition.

The development of a formal coalition model involves political dialogue with all segments of society resulting in a social contract and a protocol for politics and government, expressed in a formal 'People's Charter'. The coalition methodology also includes implementation and execution of the coalition model. These action plans outline the mechanics of political change and are executed by engaging relevant processes and action groups, *circles of hope,* to gain government. Finally, the success of the partnership approach is evaluated both by actually getting into a coalition government and achieving and sustaining good governance. While our partnership or coalition approach emerges from the political environment of Trinidad and Tobago, it can provide a guide for reorienting politics in other small states.

The third dimension of the Partnership Approach is getting the Exercise of Power Right

Getting the economy right requires political power, using state power for sustainable national development. Development in the Caribbean shows an unequal distribution of power with little middle class based power. This leads to slow development. The Epilogue discusses the challenges and solutions for Caribbean development.

Politics in Trinidad and Tobago created the distorted economy and politics will have to change it. A dysfunctional system is one where results are not proportional to the effort spent, but even more importantly, one that will develop dysfunctional behaviour. People will gradually align with the requirements of the dysfunctional system and in the process will become dysfunctional. Similarly, a dysfunctional political system will yield the same or similar results. If we want different results and achieve a new nation, we must not only get the politics right, but also the exercise of power.

Power without principles becomes personal power forming the basis for authoritarian behaviour. In a political context, it is a much more dangerous state when politics is without principles because it can easily lead to dictatorship. Personal power ignores principles and operates on the individual's own perception and own actions of what is good for him/her.

The distribution of power directly affects sustainable development. Aligning the distribution of power in society is critical to its development. This is particularly so in the case of small states where an unequal distribution of power can derail sustainable development. The following sources of power, when unequally distributed, will result in distorted national development: state based power; political party (process) power, market (economic) based power, money (wealth) based power, media (public relations) based power, and individual (personal) power.

Getting Principles and Shared Values Right is the final dimension of the Partnership Approach

Politics without power describes a political party out of government. The challenge of any political party 'out of office' is to promote 'noble purposes' with shared values and core organising principles. These principles provide the glue that holds the party together, and form the basis for an attractive ideology. Politics without power relies on principles and noble purpose.

Party politics must be guided by core principles and shared values. A principle is a fundamental truth, law, doctrine, or motivating force. Principles are obvious ideas that are often accepted as a matter of faith. A principle is also considered an essential element or constituent of a process. Thus, principles of a process are key characteristics that separate the process from other approaches. A principle is a positive attribute that serves as the foundation for the conduct of behaviour. Principles are qualities that most people support because they are viewed as socially appropriate and inherently valuable. Principles must be embedded in a political philosophy of good governance.

Politics without power relies on principles. When a political party is without power, i.e. without seats in government it relies on noble purpose and shared values and core organising principles. When the party enters government, it is has access to power and may very well exercise 'power without principles' and replace the party and government derived power with personal power. Power with principles is, of course, the ideal state. A party in power is challenged to maintain its guiding principles. If the party in power loses its principles, it degenerates quickly into the personal power syndrome. Politics with power, guided by principles and a noble purpose is necessary for sustainable development.

Party politics is guided by core principles. Politics with principles and the Partnership Approach as applied to the political environment of Trinidad and Tobago will be the focus. Next we outline the political-party Partnership Approach as applied at an organisational level and transferred into effective polices and processes for good governance.[2]

Political Context:
Perspectives on National Movements

'Two defining features of democracy are the periodic renewal of the mandates of leaders through free, fair, and competitive elections: and a set of basic rights of expression and an organization that facilitates the exercise of political choice and for holding leaders to account.'[3]

Trinidad and Tobago is still on the journey from a colonial democracy to a choice less democracy to a genuine independence and a democracy with direct citizen participation. We are still fighting for our own identity and the right to shape our future, the democratic values of the society and the workings of our political institutions. Competitive elections and holding leaders to account could be the missing link in our political system. Are our politicians able to behave the way they do because of this missing link? Is this missing link the reason why some have described us as a 'choice less democracy?'

There are two competing groups in our polity. Votes are not easily transferable, which leads to the lack of 'electoral competitiveness' in our political system. Citizens have one instrument to influence the decisions that governments make on their behalf - the vote. Our national challenge is to improve the effectiveness of the vote; otherwise we will have to settle for a 'choice less democracy' where office holders are not held accountable.

The key to making our electoral system more competitive is through the creation of a 'new media'. Political leaders and media power players enjoy enormous power – including the power to withhold information from the public and the power to distort information. This obstacle becomes even more pronounced when leadership at all levels – business, faith based institutions/bodies, labour, civil society and intellectual – become hostile to changing the structure of power. Such leadership operates on the principle of enlightened self-interest, not in the interest of the public good. Liberation through education is the best platform to challenge the workings of a failed political system. The challenge to fix politics is to engage in the process of political change and seize the emerging opportunities.

The COP movement has emphasised building the unity process, and this was not by the unity of the political leaders, but the unity of the people across ethnic, social, and political corridors. There was a need for a movement to stop the drive in that dangerous direction and for the expansion of the role of citizens in governance and decision-making, for the resolution of problems left by history in the nation-building project: the Tobago-Trinidad relationship; establishing the identity of a Trinbagonian personality and culture using what is best from its main pillars of the children of slavery and indenture; deepening the governance process to reflect community rights; and other unresolved issues.

This movement for the deepening of democracy seeks a renewal of society in the face of its rapid degeneration and chronic all-round crisis including the crisis of legitimacy of the existing governance structures. The goals of the COP movement are inclusive development, harmonious society, democratic government, and shared values. There have been several such progressive national movements in the past. The drive for legalised representation of the labouring people's interest was first witnessed in the dockworkers' strike of 1919 and continued to the anti-colonial uprising of 1937. The drive for people's participation in the developing governance structures continued with the 1946 success in the demand for universal adult suffrage.

The independence movement began in the 1930s up to the period led by the Peoples National Movement (PNM) in the 1950s, to formal independence in 1962. The movement for real benefit of the fruits of independence for the ordinary man and for sovereignty of the nation was the 'Black Power Movement' of 1970 led by the youth only eight years after independence. The movement for workers' participation in governance in the economic and political spheres started with the post-Black Power period in 1970 to 1975 culminating in the oil and sugar strike and the creation of the United Labour Front.

Trinidad and Tobago have now arrived at a historical stage in which the opportunity arises to lay a new foundation for the transformation of the country; a foundation established on the footing of good governance and shared values so as to create a harmonious society in which all persons will have an opportunity to achieve their full potential.

Despite the promise of our Independence in 1962, we have failed as a Country to forge a Nation united by a single vision in pursuit of our goal to create a secure and vibrant participatory democracy. Instead, we have allowed the creation of a dependency syndrome as a tool of patronage and mobilisation and the creation of divisions among the different races in our plural society. This sense of division has been exacerbated by the manner in which politicians have implemented the winner-take-all electoral system in which large sections of communities, not aligned to the ruling party, are disempowered and relegated to second-class status. This is the challenge we now face in the movement towards fixing the fragmented politics of our time.

In addition, we face the threat of neo-colonialism posed by big money that seeks to influence the development of the country to achieve their own narrow self-interests through financial manipulation of our political parties. The people need a government they can trust, a government that will look out for all and particularly the poor and the marginalised, and not simply be at the service of party financiers.

To meet this challenge, the country needs to align itself to a political platform in which those who offer themselves up to the electorate do so based on a desire to serve, putting country before allegiance to personalities and party. If we are to successfully meet this challenge, it is essential that we embrace the politics of principle and establish a framework for good governance to which all parties aspiring to form the next government will subscribe.

COP Movement
Principles and Values Guiding Political Action

The politics of value advocated by the COP movement focuses on nationhood, good governance, security and direct people participation. Without such guiding principles the power hungry politics of personality and 'dog eat dog' threaten to cause disintegration and dissension among the leaders. For any unified political vehicle to emerge there must be consensus on the principles and codes of political and electoral conduct by which the parties will be guided. 'The People's Charter: Principles and Codes of Political Conduct'[4] will be the foundation on which a sustainable and lifelong union can be formed so as to act as the vehicle for the transformation of our country. Principles and values guiding political action.

If we are to achieve a true sense of nationhood, it is essential that we forge a common vision for the country, identifying the areas of national life which will be given pride of place so as to ensure the quality of life of each individual is improved; particularly the lives of the poor, the disabled and the marginalised. Regrettably, our current political system is all about divide and rule in the quest to gain political power. It is the disharmony, the suspicion and the greed which such a system breeds which today epitomises life in Trinidad and Tobago.

A small country cannot afford to leave any person behind. Everyone has unique strengths, which, working together will allow us to prosper in harmony and peace. The old political paradigm must be broken and united.

We can create a nation in which all people are cherished and can benefit from a shared prosperity.

We will not achieve this nationhood to which we aspire, unless we put in place and uphold systems of good governance in which we hold ourselves accountable for achieving our goals and we do so in a transparent and fair manner at all times seeking the common good of our country. It is the job within the Coalition Partnerhsip Approach to transform the country from lawlessness and apathy to one in which peace and justice prevails. The needs of the people are the first priority. In this context, the COP movement created a platform for governance which raises politics to a higher level – recognising that no maximum leader or party can ever have all the answers and the consequent need to listen and benefit from the creative spirit, energy and ingenuity of the widest cross section of our People. In this way we will build a nation embracing the wonder, beauty and imagination of the multi-cultural elements and diversity of races and religions in the country.

The values guiding the political actions of the COP movement are compressed into the three powerful ideas of truth, justice and freedom. They are the core organising principles without which the Movement would fragment into incoherent political factions. They are the 'glue' that holds the natural differences together and binds us into a national political movement with a common good, purpose and direction. They are essential guides to our political actions; they keep us on the 'right path', assured of being on course. They provide the standards to judge and live by, and to act on.

Truth is a core value of the COP movement and its political action and we expect government to be truthful, and elected leaders to act with integrity when exercising the legitimate power citizens have entrusted to them. The caring citizen relies, depends and expects the government and politicians to work for the common good of all. The political action of the COP movement will always be guided by responsible and transparent behaviour and genuine caring for the welfare of all citizens. One Nation, One People, One Government and One Future must be enshrined as the guiding truth.

Freedom and Justice are also ideas of the COP movement. The political actions must always be in defence of political freedom and the embedded constitutional rights associated, especially guarding the right of free speech. The primary responsibility of the state is to provide safety for its citizens. On the national level the government is guided by the right of self-determination, independence and sovereignty. The government must always be the defender of justice. In all political actions it practices fairness, impartiality and even-handedness. Equality and social justice are at the core of practicing parity, fairness, equal opportunity, and the avoidance of any form of discrimination and inequity.

The People's Charter is a Declaration of Principles of the COP movement
Government should:

1. Partner with the people in establishing the conditions in which everyone can fulfil his/her true potential so that the country can flourish on the basis of sustainable development - everyone counts and everyone is needed.

2. Provide a safe, secure and sustainable environment where all people can live, work and play without fear and in which their quality of life is optimised. Crime must not be tolerated and measures must be taken to end the lawlessness and disorder that contribute to the atmosphere in which criminal activity thrives.

3. Ensure that the disadvantaged in our society are provided with the tools to enable them to become productive and make reasonable provisions for those persons who by reason of illness, old age or disability cannot work.

4. Provide the framework for education and training which is relevant to the needs of the modern world, with particular emphasis on the need to become a knowledge-based economy and to introduce a platform for young people to engage in entrepreneurial activity.

5. Build a diverse and democratic society that respects human rights, in which all people live in dignity and security, free of all forms of discrimination on the basis of religion, colour or gender.

6. Not tolerate any form of corruption nor politicise the civil service, commissions or state enterprises.

7. Promote legislation for the registration of political parties and their funding, subject to review of an independent body, to be established based on the guidelines promoted by the 'UN Convention against Corruption' (UNCAC), which reports annually to a 'Joint Select Committee of Parliament'.

8. Support a system of governance under which all major sectors of the population are represented; and encourage the participation of women at all levels of governance.

9. Invite international observers to oversee every general election in accordance with the 'Declaration of Principles for International Election Observation' and 'Code of Conduct for International Election Observers' whose report is promptly laid in Parliament.

Responsible members of Government should uphold the following principles of personal conduct:

1. Selflessness: Decisions should be based solely in terms of the public interest, not personal financial gain or other material benefits for themselves, their family, or their friends.

2. Integrity: Holders of public office should not place themselves under any financial or other obligation to outside individuals or organisations that might influence them in the performance of their official duties.

3. Objectivity: In carrying out public business, including making public appointments, awarding contracts, or recommending individuals for rewards and benefits, holders of public office should make choices based on merit.

4. Accountability: Holders of public office are accountable for their decisions and actions to the public and must submit themselves to whatever scrutiny is appropriate to their office.

5. Openness: Holders of public office should be as open as possible about all the decisions and actions that they take. They should give reasons for their decisions and restrict information only when the wider public interest clearly demands so.

6. Honesty: Holders of public office have a duty to declare any private interests relating to their public duties and to take steps to resolve any conflicts arising in a way that protects the public interest.

7. Leadership: Holders of public office should promote and support these principles by leadership and example.

Political Process of Change:
Dialogue & Mechanics

As part of the Coalition Partnership Approach, a new social contract between the government and the people is required. A contract under which the government covenants to govern in a fair and transparent manner and which holds itself accountable for delivering a better quality of life for all. The government must undertake the transformation of the country, encouraging the diversification of our economy and creating an entrepreneurial knowledge driven, service oriented economy in which meaningful jobs are created to achieve sustainable development for the long term.

The political vehicle forming the government is based on the mandate of the people and is a solid foundation where the interests of each sector have a voice. Solutions embracing the concerns of all and producing a just and fair outcome sometimes require compromise of our positions but never of principles.

The Coalition Partnership Approach as advocated by the COP movement requires the establishment of a Protocol for Politics and Governance setting out the principles of governance to which all parties will adhere whether or not they form the government of the day. Such a protocol will create institutions and mechanisms which will enable the government to listen and take account of the voice of the people. This protocol promotes open and transparent government and holds the government accountable for achieving the goals established in collaboration with the people.

Figure 6.2 Political Action for a Better Tomorrow[5]

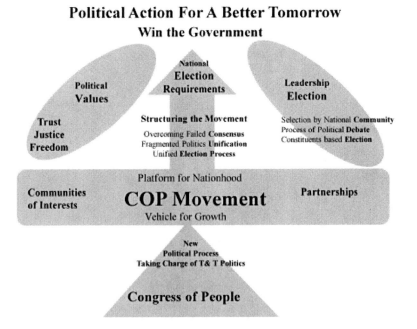

Political Action For A Better Tomorrow
Win the Government

National
Election
Requirements

Political
Values

Leadership
Election

Trust
Justice
Freedom

Structuring the Movement
Overcoming Failed Consensus
Fragmented Politics Unification
Unified Election Process

Selection by National Community
Process of Political Debate
Constituents based Election

Platform for Nationhood

Communities
of Interests

COP Movement
Vehicle for Growth

Partnerships

New
Political Process
Taking Charge of T& T Politics

Congress of People

The Coalition Partnership Approach encourages a platform for governance for the engagement of society by establishing three channels through which the views and opinions of the People can be taken into account: direct citizen participation, a civil society board, and community government. The protocol establishes a number of mechanisms and institutions to ensure good governance including: a financial and fiscal commission, cabinet and parliamentary matters, special issues regarding Tobago, legislative priorities, and the constitution.

The drive to nationhood places societal development of Trinidad and Tobago centrestage and requires a changing of priorities for development of the economy. A major national challenge for Trinidad and Tobago is to restructure the society and economy from a severely distorted economy, into a human-centred, knowledge-driven service economy. Achieving this restructuring requires a genuine collaborative and unifying national effort involving all sectors of the society and economy, all communities of interests, all citizens of the country. It demands a national dialogue, a national discussion on this new human centred, knowledge-driven service economy.

Nationhood is the glue that holds the core values of the nation together and starts with understanding the workings of the political system. The politics must change and opportunities for changing the politics are emerging and must be grasped to change the paradigm of politics and alter the behaviour of the political system in Trinidad and Tobago. Both the electoral agenda and government agenda need to work in tandem. Sometimes, political ideas are way ahead of the political consciousness.

The transformation of the electoral and political systems requires a convergence of all the different political currents throughout the country and all the different political ideas, to establish that there is more in common than there is in division. That is the first step in the process of engineering a solution: to create a political environment where the entire country will benefit.

The COP movement created the foundation for a new Coalition Partnership Approach toward unification, together with the United National Congress (UNC), the Movement for Social Justice (MSJ), the Tobago Organisation of the People (TOP) and the National Joint Action Congress (NJAC).

As part of the Coalition Partnership Approach, the seven *Circles of Hope* were introduced to map out joint proposals on: security and justice; quality of life: health, education and infrastructure; employment; poverty reduction and the economy; competitiveness and equity; corruption and integrity; and people issues – community, aging, youth and children.

Figure 6.3 Political Movement toward Nationhood[6]

Movement toward Nationhood

In the Case of T&T, there is a Failed Consensus to build Nationhood. There is a real distinction between Statehood and Victimhood and our future driven concept of Nationhood.
Nationhood trumps the complimentarity of Statehood & Victimhood.

Statehood Politics
Political Party and State Power over Nationhood - Aborted Nationhood
Failure to achieve:
Discipline – Production – Tolerance

Victimhood Politics
Leadership loyalty over State and Nationhood – Permanent Opposition
Misguided values
Bad Experience, Discrimination, Personal Loyalty

Nationhood Politics
People (Citizen) participation in governance – National Patriotism
Shared values
Truth, Justice and Freedom

Each *Circle of Hope* would be a driver of the plan for the transformation of the country and form the basis on which the government pushes forward inclusive development of the country, so that everyone can participate in a shared prosperity and enjoy a high quality of life.

As the political representatives focus on the issues and not on personalities and power, the goals are to serve the people; and to transform the country into one in which 'every creed and race can find an equal place'. The aim is to constantly strive to energise the economy so that all people experience a shared prosperity. How can we improve the quality of life for each individual and in particular the poor and the disadvantaged? The solutions proposed by the *Circles of Hope* encourage input from the populace so that the wisdom and ingenuity of the people can be tapped and a unified reconstruction plan formulated.

This unity of action creates the platform for dialogue and collaboration among political leaders to transform the politics in Trinidad and Tobago.

ENGAGING SOCIETY:
Citizen Participation

An electoral agenda gets a party into power, but the political agenda sustains the party in power. It is the government's agenda that gives credibility.

It is this dialogue that enables our society to experience and be involved in a real participatory democracy.

Having laid the groundwork of a platform for governance, the imperative of winning demands that electoral consensus among UNC, MSJ, TOP, NJAC and COP was achieved. Furthermore, the trust of the people was earned by engaging them in the process, including the Circles of Hope, the People's Charter, the Principles and Codes of Political Contest and the Protocol for Politics and Governance, and in dialogue and debate.

As a result, the COP movement has led and facilitated a One-Party Solution and became a unifying force guided by clarity of values, passionate commitment to nationhood and unwavering belief in building a better future for the country. The government will engage society by establishing three channels through which the views and opinions of the people can be taken into account: direct citizen participation; a civil society board; and community government.

The COP movement as part of the new Coalition Partnership Approach proposes the creation of an internet portal 'E-view', which will be accessible to all so that the people have a voice in governance. Every individual and group will be able to express views, opinions and ideas on the development of our communities and the country as a whole through this internet portal. In order to ensure that this facility is accessible by every sector, the government will take steps to ensure that broadband service is available everywhere and that internet cafés are established in every community throughout Trinidad and Tobago. On a scheduled basis, the monitoring council will publish a report incorporating the views, ideas and opinions expressed through E-view for consideration and implementation by the government where feasible.

The COP movement as part of the new Coalition Partnership Approach proposes that all civil society organisations will be invited to register in a Civil Society Register and to appoint two representatives to represent each of their organisations. Every two years these representatives will vote for the civil society representatives who will be appointed to the Board subject to a maximum of 24 board members. This Board will establish Stakeholder Advisory Councils from among its members and such experts in their respective fields as the board members consider are representative of various civil society associations. An amendment to the constitution will be proposed under which the President will be required to consult with, and choose independent senators from among the persons recommended by the Civil Society Board.

The COP movement as part of the Coalition Partnership Approach proposes a system of community government to empower communities by giving them a voice in defining community problems and solutions. Each Community Government Assembly is required to consult with and take into account in their strategic plan and budget the facilities and services which such community considers desirable. In addition to direct contact with the members of the community every person will be able to present their views through the E-view internet portal which the Community Government Assembly will review and adopt where feasible for purposes of developing its community government plan. Each Community Government Assembly is required to prepare a community government plan and budget for accomplishing the goals and objectives for their communities which includes the ideas and opinions of the members of the community, and to report to Cabinet on a regular basis as to performance and implementation of the Community Government Plan. These reports will be submitted to the appropriate Parliamentary Committee for consideration.

Notes

1. Adapted from a Powerpoint presentation by Dr Manfred Jantzen to members of the COP, COP Operations Centre, Charlieville, May 2007.
2. Winston Dookeran and Akhil Malakai *Leadership and Governance in Small States. Getting Development Right.* (Saarbrücken: VDM Verlag) 2008.
3. Yusuf Bangura, ed. *Democracy and Social Policy.* (Basingstoke: Palgrave) 2007.
4. Mr Timothy Hamel-Smith was a major contributor to the formulation of the People's Charter.
5. Adapted from a Powerpoint presentation by Dr Manfred Jantzen to members of the COP, COP Operations Centre, Charlieville, May 2007.
6. Ibid.

CHAPTER 7
ENTREPRENEURIAL ECONOMY & HUMAN POTENTIAL: A NEW PATH FOR ECONOMIC DEVELOPMENT

New Space for Growth and Development
- **Entrepreneurship**
- **Public Private Partnerships**
- **Higher Education**

Growth is the key contributor to national development. The government, through its fiscal policies, as reflected in its budget, is fostering entrepreneurship, public private partnerships and education as drivers of growth.

Entrepreneurship is the clearest and most effective development path. Stoking entrepreneurship will require developing human capital and the willingness of all citizens and stakeholders to take risks and assume responsibility as they contribute to development. This requires building a knowledge economy. The three fundamental pillars of development in this context are competitiveness, inclusiveness, and expansionism.[1]

Building a Culture of Entrepreneurship

The world is rich with opportunity and our perspective of this frontier world is in the context of a one-world information environment. This new powerful paradigm shifts the rules by which human systems survive, thrive, and sustain life on this planet. Individuals and organisations including private and public enterprises, and entire societies have to adapt if they want to stay healthy and be a player in this new frontier space. In the early 1490s, the explorers of two small nations claimed the new world and influenced the course of history. Brazil speaks Portuguese and a large part of the Americas speaks Spanish. Europe viewed the rest of the world as a frontier space to be claimed and the rules of colonisation laid the future for a new world order.

Five hundred years later, a new frontier came into existence with the advent of the WWW and phenomenal growth of internet applications. This frontier operates on the science-based ICT platform. The ICT platform allows information to become the dominant wealth and value creating resource, surpassing traditional land, labour and capital. Information as a resource moves near the speed of light and changes all existing rules of value and wealth generation. The information dynamics is evolving a one-world information environment and the ICT platform interrelates, interconnects, interacts, and integrates information into value, and potentially, wealth.

This global information and communications platform opened up a new frontier space to be explored by those willing to take risks as explorers, discoverers and entrepreneurs. These frontier individuals and their organisations make up the new rules of the game and lay claim to territories in form of markets. In the information environment there are few formal and institutional rules and regulations. It brings to mind the 'robber barons' of unbridled capitalism in late 19th and early 20th century in America. Anything is permissible as long it makes money. Similarly, the great global financial crisis and its accompanying global recessions reflect the unregulated wild frontier behaviour of the new age of information.

It is in this turbulent frontier environment, with fierce competition for market territories and unbridled greed for accumulation of wealth by individuals, organisations and nation states that the traditional Third World countries have to navigate a path for development.

The information resource driven frontier world changes the relationship between the state, citizen and private enterprises. The emergence of the entrepreneurial economy as the driver of national growth and sustainable development depends on this new breed of information and knowledge entrepreneurs. These risk-taking entrepreneurs are the first wave of explorers, innovators, and discoverers that a society must encourage and support to actively participate and claim a share of the Frontier Economic Space. The role of the state and government must shift from owner and controller of resources to genuine facilitator and catalyst of this frontier entrepreneurial economy. It is this new information and knowledge driven entrepreneurial economy that will be the driver of growth and sustainable long-term development.

Any approach to fostering greater entrepreneurship must involve direct engagement with the business community, labour, other interest groups, and stakeholders. When these stakeholders in business are engaged, it soon becomes clear that these different groups are not exclusively concerned with their short term self-interest or with extracting as much out of government as possible. In fact, these citizens are greatly interested in creating an environment allowing individuals to grow and realise their full potential.

Within this context, the methodology for fostering entrepreneurship must be grounded in the four premises of removing uncertainties, setting conditions for growth, building a culture of entrepreneurship, and redirecting people-centred social programmes. Let us look at these premises and some critical aspects of the development path for Trinidad and Tobago as outlined in the 2011 and 2012 budget statements.

The most relevant programmes come under the headings of building a culture of entrepreneurship; revitalising underdeveloped areas; developing the domestic capital market; new entrepreneurial industries; development owned by the people; and setting conditions for growth.[2]

As the world is revolutionised by the prevalence, power and speed of information and technology, we are being thrust into a new frontier, ungoverned by many of the institutions, both formal and informal, that have traditionally upheld much of the economy. We are headed into a new environment comparable to the Wild West of the past. The methodology for development therefore places a powerful emphasis on entrepreneurship.

To be flexible and in touch with reality, citizen participation through a multi-stakeholder approach becomes even more of a priority in developing a practicable strategy. Development must be centred in building a culture of entrepreneurship, even if it challenges an entrenched, dependent, and risk-averse outlook in business. It should involve changing and limiting the role of the state to that of a catalyst for growth.

This includes bolstering infrastructure through a public sector investment programme, and increasing ownership in state enterprises by members of the public; whilst winding down state involvement. Domestic capital markets and investments would be further bolstered by listing state firms on the market. Underprivileged areas should be revitalised, helped along by small business incubators and other incentives to boost entrepreneurship on all levels, even as businesses collaborate more to reduce costly corruption and enable more meritocratic procurement and corporate governance. This method sets the stage for private-sector led development.[3]

Sustainable growth needs a deep foundation for a culture of entrepreneurship. In the past, by not developing the entrepreneurial capability in the society at large, far too much reliance was placed on a state directed development strategy. Trinidad and Tobago is now moving towards a people directed development strategy. To do that however, people must be equipped to handle the job.

The traditional business class of the private sector must now become more entrepreneurial and risk taking and the economic environment must be set for them to do so. This environment was set on two grounds. There is indeed credit capacity in the banking system and we a supportive environment has been created through the interest rate policy as well as incentive programmes to encourage the use of that credit facility. The private sector now has the opportunity to take more risk without compromising their stability in the financing.

Beside the continued emphasis on energy production and food production, sustaining growth will take place by the identification of new areas of economic activity. Five growth poles[4] have been identified in Trinidad and Tobago for expansion in the medium term using a cluster development approach creating opportunities for areas with special economic needs. These growth poles will form the basis for a new incentive programme and can develop the entrepreneurial potential of Trinidad and Tobago.

One of the projects identified is the revitalisation of the East Port of Spain region which has remained underdeveloped for far too long. New initiatives have been identified and they will call upon the universities of Trinidad and Tobago, along with civil society and the government and indeed, the community that is affected, to design an entrepreneurial plan. The aim is to resuscitate interest and activity in the oldest part of the city much like old Havana in Cuba and older parts of other big cities of the world. The aim is to create opportunities in arts, culture, music and in sports; and in so doing, to establish a framework of 'business incubators'.

This incubator approach is a technique that has been used very effectively in both South Africa and also in India. A large part of the recent economic success in India has been attributed to this approach. India has developed a very vibrant small businesses sector that has been promoted and anchored by the business incubator system.

The following areas have the foundation to become viable industries and will be supported by the government growth initiative. They include the fashion industry, the design industry, the waste management industry, and the ship building industry.

Development and Public and Private Partnerships

The Government will also increase energy production in the country sustained by the new impetus of developing an onshore economy as opposed to the enclave economy. In the past, instead of becoming more resilient, the economy became less resilient. Instead of becoming less exposed to the international financial system, it became more exposed.

To build resilience requires fostering development owned by the people. As a consequence, the programmes of public offerings of some state enterprises have been introduced. The state has a substantial investment in the Public Sector Investment Programme (PSIP) directed at triggering growth in the economy. In preparation of the PSIP, projects were chosen to generate construction activity. Seventy per cent of the PSIP is generated towards construction activity and was the basis for triggering some element of growth in this economy. This effort will be supported by other initiatives such as tax measures to create an environment where the business sector will get sufficient incentives from the public authorities.

Two areas for immediate action were the energy and agricultural sectors. Apart from some of the other measures that were put into place the government has taken the bold step of reducing the interest rate available to farmers through the Agricultural Development Bank.

In the future, this bank or any other development financial institutions must not rely on the Treasury for support. Initially, they must at least break-even while at the same time their social purpose is directed to increase production in the country.

All the various measures with respect to the free trade zone including a 90 per cent accelerated allowance were at increasing activity in these free trade zones. Within that context the anti-export bias will be removed in favour of the creation of a pro-export bias. This will also induce larger foreign investment.

The fiscal framework must support investments in sectors other than the energy sector. The government places an emphasis on providing a framework for the manufacturing and services sectors to restore the confidence of work prospects.

In those sectors there is still the need for public direction because the role of the state has now changed from becoming the director of development and owner of the development process to being a catalyst[5] for development. In so doing, the government will improve the stock market performance in the country and build a domestic capital market by having more shares being placed in the market for more activity.

To this end, collaborative governance is the key platform for success. A multi-stakeholder governance approach is based on transparent and meritocratic procurement, effective and accountable corporate governance, and responsible business ethics to make markets more effective. Collaboration means that business and equity are not mutually exclusive. Poverty can be eradicated through profits as opportunities are created in low-income markets. Platforms must be created for increased dialogue and action on good business governance and anti-corruption; and business associations should be strengthened. Ultimately, this will reduce the costs of a corrupt network of personal connections, and enable business to work on a more level playing field and to increase efficiency.

Development is future focused and must not necessarily be built on existing configurations but should build on 'new' value adding activities. The focus is on process design for development; development is an increase in the diversity of a country's products using existing and potential capabilities. In such a new development approach[6] the traditional business organisation has to be re-defined.

The firm is viewed as a network community of enterprising stakeholders. The product is the solution to the customer's perception of their own needs. New products can and should be derived from existing capabilities of production. These capabilities are the competencies of individuals, organisations, and of society. Their use reveals the potential for future product creation. Consider Ricardo Hausmann's [7] example of the progression in Finland from the resource of wood, which requires the capability of wood cutting machines, moving to general cutting machines, toward the new definition for automated machines that cut, toward general automated machines resulting in a firm like Nokia assisting in the transformation of Finland from a natural resource-based economy into a knowledge-based economy and eventually shooting to first in the World Economic Forum's competitive index.[8]

The stakeholder here is the entrepreneur or private owner, working in the information environment of an ICT platform.

The key attributes of the complex dynamic system approach surround the idea of consensus and flexibility. An approach originating on the ground and moving up would generate new ideas and processes to foster the emergence of ideas. This would be within a self-organising system which trusts stakeholders to organise themselves according to their own self-interest. The aim of this is to foster creativity with an emphasis on building capabilities (competences) for development. Inclusiveness is encouraged for the fair inclusion of interest groups. Integrating, coordinating, and cooperating among all stakeholders would build up to an overall attribute of systemic integration. Information flow must involve dialogue between stakeholders for emergence of solutions to take place. The state's role is a catalyst in the development processes and provides critical capabilities that cannot be bought and the private sector's role is demarked as the executing agent.

With regard to the latter, a clear relationship between the state and private sectors must be established within an open architecture. This architecture has some key features. It involves dialogue and consensus building in a self-organizing community of interests. There must be the existence and promotion of appropriate legislation for development. The government in partnership with public and private enterprises must work together to achieve solutions. This may require appropriate incentives for public involvement (though these need not be financial).

Key Recommendations for Development
Action must be taken on initiatives focusing on new growth with commissions and the like set up. Business zones must be established and made examples of the new development path. They would best be private sector

run with strong and special input and investment from the government. Such zones would incorporate an effective infrastructure to make it easy to do business, including: urban transport systems, logistic systems, day-care, healthcare, labour training, permits and certifications (in a one stop shop). Such infrastructures would be complemented by a pioneer fund which would provide incentives for new entrepreneurial efforts and gain information about successful business plans from lenders.

Foreign direct investment would be sought through vehicles such as Senior Advisory Councils (to attract global executives) and direct firm searching and enticing. To gain experience from relevant successes elsewhere, initiatives and institutions such as Infotel, which trains for the needs of new industries; Comfama, which provides social services; Sergio Fajardo, a successful Colombian reformist mayor; Zonamerica Montevideo, which is a private sector built and run business zone; Petrobras as an example of successful privatisation; Monterey Tech, where students and staff start and run businesses in a business park; and Mexico, where citizens are rewarded with prizes for identifying useless government red tape, should be explored. Such initiatives can only be kept accountable with strict rules of transparency which create a public record, using new media amongst other means. Immigration must be loosened and talent brought in. Flexible labour training for new capabilities is also necessary; possibly funded by a levy on wages. Process building must take place. This will spur a general strategy of competitiveness which will involve the reduction of red tape, and the streamlining of regulations to increase development.

Taking Ownership[9]

Based on past budget expectations a change in perspective is required. In the past, people often asked 'What can I get from this budget?' Now, people are asking what they can be. The answer to this question depends largely on a change in attitude and changing role of government in Trinidad and Tobago. Consequently, the appropriate question about any future budget should be viewed by the citizen in terms of 'what I can be' not 'what I can get'.

The underlying assumption in the 2011 and 2012 budgets is a groundbreaking shift in terms of the new role for entrepreneurship and ownership. The new entrepreneurship requires the business sector to become more prone to taking risks. Unfortunately, the current private business sector tends to be risk adverse and has little interest to move into the development path given the choice between commercial profitability and development dividends. Calling upon the creation of a new entrepreneurial class will require a helping hand to move towards growth on a more sustained basis.

This new entrepreneurship calls upon the private sector to change its own perspective towards this country from not 'what I can get' but to 'what I can be'. This new entrepreneurship resides in the small business sector and the creative industry in Trinidad and Tobago. The creative industry is reflected in art, in culture, and in so many areas in which the country has a natural talent. The government, through its budget, places a fair amount of emphasis on creating the conditions for that new entrepreneurship among the small business groupings in the country; linking education to business opportunities to form development clusters and using the Public and Private Partnership Approach, the incubator system, and the creation of opportunities for the small business sector.[10]

Currently, there is excess liquidity and the banking sector is looking for projects that can work. The fiscal regime is providing all the elbow room for action to take place, and there is a change in the perspective of the country moving from 'what I can get' to 'what I can be.'

Sustaining this growth however, is also important. Triggering it is important, to get the process restarted. Sustaining it requires a three to five year frame and it is in that context that the 2012 budget is a multi-year budget. Given the current situation in the global arena as well as in terms of our lack of confidence in Trinidad and Tobago; the government must take some bold risks. Since the perspective of this country is moving from 'what I can get' to 'what I can be', then this risk is less than we might expect. The government is building insulation against the negative impact of a double dip recession which the world may be facing. The government has instituted a Tax Collection Amnesty and Taxpayer Covenant[11] to counteract possible unsustainable tax revenue risks and the impact of the recession revenue.

We are in charge of change and execution is a major challenge

In the past, many governmental institutions were allowed to not take responsibility for their actions. Many state institutions have lost their social focus and their leadership does not feel compelled to be accountable and responsible for ensuring that their mission is achieved. Whether it is in the development finance institutions, the small business development companies, wherever it is, there is a tendency that 'government must do it for us.' What the government is in fact accountable for, is delivering the goods and services for which the institution was set up – that is execution.

The fundamental philosophy the government has embarked on, is to get a new direction, to trigger growth, to sustain growth, and to increase efficiencies in the public institutions. This cannot be achieved in the short term. To implement government's growth initiatives requires another philosophical shift, a public-private partnership approach, for example, the Artists Coalition of Trinidad and Tobago and the Association of Psychologists were encouraged to partner in the establishment of trauma centres with the state as catalyst. Another Public and Private Partnership Initiative is the design industry. The government is hoping to explore this untouched market and supports those in the garment industry who can exploit a growing world market. The government is also implementing measures to tap into the world's outsourcing industry. Outsourcing is growing at a rapid rate and we, as a small economy, should tap into this industry whether it is in the field of ICT, Education, or Medical Services. These are the kinds of directional changes that the government proposes to achieve, the national potential 'what we can be.'

Knowledge Economy and Education

A knowledge economy is crucial to competitiveness in small island states. Higher education demands partnership to be effective. The government should provide the framework for partnership and higher education reform.

When the state cannot provide free tertiary education, building financial incentives and a suitable regulatory regime that can remain flexible and impose reform into higher education must be the centre of any strategy. It is simplistic to view reform as a choice between a highly centralised system and completely autonomous institutions. There are many more stakeholders and forces involved that must be brought together. Whilst acknowledging that higher tuition fees are necessary in order to reduce overall costs and spur equity, any move to place more of the burden of financing on the student, ought to be concurrent with increased means tested bursaries. These loans are most efficiently delivered by commercial banks with government oversight. Along with privately sponsored students, commercialisation of service units, the institutionalisation of consultancies, and especially higher tuition fees, this is part of a necessary move toward adopting free market principles to spur quality. Any reform must be specific to the small island state.

The network university, targeted courses based on different states' development requirements, and distance education are all important to this context and must be explored. Implementing alternative financing strategies, installing new management structures (that are participatory and consensus oriented), and introducing demand driven courses are necessary. Fee increases must be linked to productive infrastructure development or proceed in an extremely gradual way in order to gain necessary public assent. The major challenges are infrastructures, the degree of market orientation, enrolment, and maintaining quality whilst increasing size and accountability. We must face them to build a performing knowledge economy.

Knowledge is a major driving force in development, fuelled by changes in the globalised economy and the new information era. The building of a knowledge economy has become possible due to the creation of knowledge through research and advances in technology, investments in education, and an openness to innovation. At the heart of this impetus is the search for competitiveness and sustainable development. Investment in knowledge infrastructure, including human capital offers a new wave in economic restructuring, with 'higher value added products with closer customer linkages.'[12]

Finland was able to transform from a natural-based economy into a knowledge-based economy in a short period, ranking recently as number one in the World Economic Forum's competitive index.[13] Investments in education and information systems have been credited with this progress.

Higher education is now at the centre of strategies for sustained growth and inclusive development. Coupled with a regime for innovation and ICT infrastructure, investment in human capital has high development dividends as it prepares an economy to meet the challenges of competition in today's integrated global economy. In an aggregate sense, education influences the macro economy through its impact on productivity and technical change as it affects economic growth. Changes in the competitive structure increases the development's potential, while the adaptation to an innovative system advances social cohesion in inclusiveness in the well-being of society.

A recent World Bank publication[14] argues that a country's competitive advantage in the global economy is linked to the converging impacts of globalisation, knowledge as a main driver of growth, and the information revolution. Opportunities are emerging from these challenges. Knowledge has become a primary factor of production. Building knowledge societies requires a sound incentive-based macroeconomic regime, a modern ICT infrastructure, a competitive innovation system, and a high quality of its human resources. The contribution of tertiary education is vital to the emergence of innovation systems and to the development of human resources.

One of the main messages of the World Bank report cited above is that 'the state has a responsibility to put in place an enabling framework that encourages tertiary institutions to be more innovative and more responsive to the needs of a globally competitive knowledge economy and the changing labour market requirements for advanced human capital.' Three arguments that justify governments' support for funding universities are the existence of externalities from tertiary education, equity issues, and the connective role of tertiary education in the education system as a whole.

While education does confer private gains to individuals, education can be considered a public or quasi-public good. Education is a significant generator of external benefits; and individuals do not capture all the rewards of education. Indeed, there are significant externalities in the production of education as the overall contribution of tertiary education to economic growth goes beyond the income and employment gains accruing to individuals. These are crucial to a knowledge-driven economic and social development, and permit workers to use the new technology and boost productivity.

Apart from its contribution to economic growth, higher education has broad economic, fiscal and labour market effects. There are linkages and spill over effects by the clustering of human capital alongside leading technology firms as exemplified by technology intensive poles in Silicon Valley in California, US; Bangalore in India; Shanghai in China; Campinas in São Paulo, Brazil, and in similar poles in East Asia and Finland. There are various studies that have measured the positive correlation between increases in educational levels and consumption, tax base and the reduced dependence on medical and social welfare services. There are also non-economic externalities in promoting greater social cohesion, and appreciation of diversity in societies. *Higher Education in Developing Countries: Peril and Promise* concluded that 'tertiary education is important in building capacity and reducing poverty.'[15]

According to Nobel Laureate Joseph E Stiglitz,[16]

> there are no prescriptions for how a country creates such a culture 'of knowledge'…but government does have a role – a role in education, in encouraging the kind of creativity and risk that the scientific entrepreneurship requires, in creating the institutions that facilitate ideas being brought into fruition, and a regulatory and tax environment that rewards this kind of activity.

This is a new challenge – a challenge of offering financial incentives in higher education – and this goes hand in hand with the old challenges of promoting quality, efficiency, and equity. The rise of market forces and the recurring fiscal austerity facing governments have reduced the reliance of the traditional state control model to impose reforms and have introduced a flexibility that relies on regulations and incentives.

In the past, the dominant role of governments in the financing and provision of higher education was easily translated into a relationship characterised by a high degree of centralised control or by a great deal of institutional autonomy. Today, there is much more complex interplay of forces that rely on state regulations and financial incentives; participation and partnerships with industry, civil society and professional associations; and competition between higher education providers.

An initial step is to define a reform programme within a coherent policy framework. Such a higher education development strategy should comprise answers to what type of system will contribute to growth in a knowledge-based economy, and what are the roles of the institutions within the higher education system, and how could the new technologies be harnessed by individuals and enterprises? Several countries have attempted this exercise including New Zealand (The Tertiary Education Green Paper - 1998); France (Plan for the University of the Third Millennium – 2000); South Africa (Report on the Council of Higher Education – 2001) and India (India as a Knowledge Superpower: Strategy for Transformation – 2001).

Steps to design enabling regulatory frameworks, in most cases, will require legislative measures, consensus building mechanisms on cost sharing, quality assurance mechanisms, and financial rules and controls. In this context, government funding will remain the major source of financing for higher education in developing countries. 'Negotiated' budgets based on historical trends may now be replaced with financial incentive formulae that steer higher education institutions toward compliance with quality, cutting edge research, and efficiency and equity goals. Funding may be linked to performance, but it may also be linked to the mobilisation of additional resources through increased cost sharing.[17]

Some universities have established competitive funds to promote quality improvements. Under such systems, institutions bid for extra budgetary financial resources that are linked to proposals aimed at specific internal policy changes. Such policy changes may be within the faculties to help define their missions, market niches, development objectives, and action plans to achieve these objectives. The process must be transparent. Successful organisations, even in the academic world are those that challenge and re-invent themselves 'in the pursuit of more effective ways of responding to the needs of their clients and stakeholders.'[18]

There is a growing recognition that the cost of higher education must be shared in a more equitable way among the various stakeholders. Higher education opportunities should be accessible to all qualified persons and the state must play a crucial role in ensuring that no one is prevented from studying by lack of financial resources. As such, any shifting of costs to students must include parallel programmes of scholarship and loan programmes that cover both direct and indirect costs (foregone earnings). This raises key issues of equity and management.

The World Bank conducted an international review of student loan programmes which highlighted serious shortcomings on the long-term viability of these programmes. The World Bank report concluded that student loan schemes should meet the following conditions: an appropriate marketing strategy; transparent targeting to most deserving students (academic and social criteria); close supervision of academic performance of the student; interest rate and subsidy rate to protect financial sustainability of the scheme; and efficient management of the scheme. Better results may be achieved when the programmes are financed and administered (with enforceable guidelines) by the commercial banks. The challenges of 'borderless' education across institutions and programme types – lifelong and part-time – requires a flexible management approach.

Funding Mass Education

The Organisation for Economic Co-operation and Development (OECD)–UNESCO report[19] provides an analysis of the World Education Indicators programme (WEI) that was launched by the UNESCO, the OECD and the World Bank in 1997. The countries in the programme were Argentina, Brazil, Chile, Egypt, Jamaica, India, Indonesia, Jordan, Malaysia, Paraguay, Peru, the Philippines, the Russian Federation, Tunisia, Thailand, Uruguay, and Zimbabwe. In its introduction, the report affirms that 'education is an investment in the collective future of societies and nations, rather than simply the future success of individuals'.[20] Comparing the growth patterns between WEI and OECD countries, the findings support the hypothesis that in the early stages of industrialisation, investment in capital is important, but as development deepens, the role of human capital as a strong driver of economic growth, takes over.

Whilst investment in education promotes sustainable economic growth, it can help equalise social disparities. One of the key findings of this study was that 'the goals of expanding educational systems and maintaining [sustainable] equity are inextricably linked to questions of educational finance'. Demands on education and demands for educational opportunities are growing in WEI countries. The resources required to meet these demands are highly dependent on macroeconomic stability.

Apart from the issue of downturns, whether cyclical or contagious, the share of tax-based revenue, as a percentage of GDP is also significant. In China this ratio is merely six per cent while it is 40 per cent in the Netherlands. This restricts the public sector capacity to fund education expenditure in many WEI countries. Combining public and private expenditure may help, but it may still be too small. In Indonesia this amounts to 1.8 per cent of GDP compared to 9.9 per cent of GDP in Jamaica. The World Bank estimates that an appropriate range of investment in education as a percentage of GDP is between 4 and 6 per cent, of which higher education would generally be between 15 and 20 per cent.

There is a wide array of mechanisms used in WEI countries for financing education. Small states warrant different priorities. Partnerships with neighbouring small states have seen the establishment of a 'network' university. Strategic choices as to offerings are influenced by the countries' critical human skill requirements. Partnerships with external providers of tertiary education, including distance education, have been the traditional model. This approach is being overtaken by market developments, as cost incentives push foreign universities to locate special faculties in distant places that could be attractive to students and faculty. At the same time, franchise partnerships are being developed between local private providers of university training and marketing arms of established institutions.

Bruce Johnstone[21] discusses the finance and management agenda of tertiary education in the context of five themes: expansion and diversification of enrolments, participation rates and number and types of institutions; fiscal pressure as reflected in overcrowding, poorly paid faculty, and major deficiencies in the university's hardware and software installations; the orientation towards the market in search for non-governmental revenues; the demand for greater accountability by all stakeholders; and the demand for greater quality and efficiency — more rigour, more relevance and more learning.

The issue of 'commoditization' refers to the conversion of education outputs into market products. It is argued that the production of high quality learning materials at low unit costs will bring education to all.[22]

These issues provide a framework that can be used to do empirical work for educational planning.

In a keynote address at the Seminar in Salzburg, Austria in November 2002, on 'The Funding of Higher Education', Johnstone elaborated on trends in higher education worldwide: rising costs, institutional austerity, overcrowding, rising tuition fees, deterioration of quality, limitations on capacity and on accessibility, deterioration of faculty morale, and diminished confidence in government by the public. The cost per student of higher education increases in response to high enrolment pressures, the move towards mass education and the surge in faculty ambition. This means that there will be higher frontiers in the production possibility curve in education. Is there any innovation that will lower production costs in higher education? Information technology, yet to be fully explored may have the potential. For now, higher education costs are to be met by revenue increases from taxpayers, parents, students, donors (philanthropists), clients, entrepreneurs, business interests and consumers.

Technological change has posed a real danger of a growing digital gap between nations. This new 'divide' was clearly illustrated in the World Bank study[23] which stated that 'Sub Saharan African countries together have one internet user per 5,000 populations; in Europe and North America this proportion is one user for every six inhabitants'. Within countries, access to the Internet is heavily skewed in favour of high-income families and there may even be a 'digital gender gap'. A well functioning ICT system could reduce administrative and management cost, improve the quality of instruction and learning, and reap the economic gains to better access information cross-campus and across the globe. This is an opportunity for future funding by forging new university partnerships with business, manufacturing and the extractive industries.

In striving for financial viability, policy strategies are required. For instance, we must either work towards greater efficiency and/or supplement public revenue with non-governmental revenues. The introduction of revenue supplementation, also known as 'cost sharing' can take a variety of forms such as charging/raising tuition fees, increasing other fees, and freeze grants and other subsidies. Scotland has replaced tuition with loans to be repaid after graduation as a contribution to an endowment fund. Australia has adopted a higher education contribution scheme to be repaid after graduation (students may get 25 per cent reduction if they pay upfront - which gives the appearance of giving a discount to those who can pay - or it may be seen as an incentive).

Makerere University in Uganda has been heralded as witnessing a 'quiet revolution' where student enrolment expanded, quality standards prevail and tuition fees have been systematically introduced. Restructuring at Makerere had three central and interrelated elements: implementing alternative financing strategies, installing new management structures, and introducing demand driven courses. The University encouraged privately sponsored students, commercialising service units, and institutionalising consultancy arrangements. David Court[24] describes the results as dramatic. In the space of five years, tuition fees were raised from zero to 70 per cent, and 30 per cent of the running costs of the university were internally generated. Much of this achievement can be attributed to steady improvement in the country's macroeconomic performance and 'government's willingness to respect university autonomy'. Within the institution, there was imaginative leadership that had 'faith in the benefits of a market orientation and professional and participatory management, and their unambiguous sense of ownership of the reform process.'

The issue of tuition fees and cost sharing is not value free or politically neutral; those promoting it claim equity or fairness, (with parallel loans and grants), greater capacity, hence more equity, improved quality of teaching and sustainability of finances. Finances will be volatile during public finance cycles. Those in opposition argue a loss of equality, the absence of a level playing field (some students have to earn incomes while studying), loss of public control, and a sub-ideal state. In order to be acceptable, tuition fees must supplement, not supplant, public revenue or the increase in enrolments may not happen, and financial assistance programmes must run parallel.

Also, increases in fees should be modest and regular. Some institutions have linked increases in fees to productivity expenditure, like better-equipped classrooms and laboratories, Internet access, new programmes and courses and savings. The design of a tuition fee policy is an inexact science. Should students bear the cost of research or only teaching? What proportion of one's income (or foregone income) should be spent on fees?

The OECD report states, 'in a majority of countries, the minimum tuition fee falls below ten per cent per capita, although it reaches one quarter in Chile and Uruguay and about half of GDP per capita in Thailand.' How are selections for grants and loans to be made and are they portable in today's multi-institution scenario (private, public, corporate, levels of higher education institutions)? What are the goals of tuition fee policy: to increase university budgets, increase educational opportunities, widen the participation, improve accountability and quality of institutions, promote responsibility of students, and build closer links between the universities and the labour market? Is tuition fee a tax deduction and/or public support? Must tuition fee be abolished at all levels?

Endowment and pension funds provide financial resources that need to be managed. Foundations and university endowments have traditionally been invested in government securities and equity holdings. In the US, investment portfolios aim to 'shoot for profits even in bad times' by investing in hedge funds. Universities appoint fund managers to implement a strategy for investment. Such managers determine the level of exposure and risk profile of the portfolio of investments. The returns to these investments represent an income stream, and the university must have the expertise to assess performance and decide on a preferred investment strategy.

Most universities set themselves an entrepreneurial mandate. Consulting firms spin off university academics,[25] sometimes with profit sharing arrangements between faculty and university, at other times on a purely private basis. In a period of rapid change, new training opportunities emerge as in the transition economies or in the information industry. Decision-making at universities is not geared to respond timely to these rapid changes in the market, so an entrepreneurial mandate emerges. In discharging this mandate, universities get opportunities to increase and diversify their sources of income, to explore new forms of thought and training, and to take on an entrepreneurial outlook. There is also a downside as all departments may not have the same market power and there could be a diversion from the traditional canons of academic responsibility and integrity.

Philanthropy is big business in the US, prompting higher education leaders to emulate the US experience which provides another avenue to supplement public funds. Such contributions have thrived on favourable tax treatment but the driving force is the existence of a culture of philanthropy. In many cases alumni associations provide the organisational platform for university fund raising activities. Such activities help in the expansion of capital programmes, although there has been a recent trend to fund major areas of socially desirable research in areas like medicine, genetic engineering, and biotechnology.

The reform of higher education financing was alluded to earlier in this chapter. Such reforms would include performance and incentive budgeting, expenditure reforms that include outsourcing of non-academic services, compensation reforms that include manpower planning systems, and devolution in spending authorities. Such a reform exercise may include radical restructuring of the system of higher education that may yield lay-offs, early retirements and reassignments. Universities are known to resist change, and more so radical change. It is an exercise in political economy, where the constituencies of 'winners' in the change process must gain influence over the 'losers'. A major change agent in the university setting lies in the information revolution, as scholars have instant access to other scholars thus widening opportunities and competition at the same time.

Political Governance and Commercialisation of Education

The political governance of higher education 'has become an important issue as systems and institutions struggle to deal with new external and internal demands.' These demands are reflected in changes in management and administrative structures for higher education as well as in changes in performance that aligns education with national development, and in new models of public accountability, resulting from rising demand for new and better education.

In addressing these issues, the distribution of power and the equilibrium between 'winners and losers' among the stakeholders come to the fore. The forces for change in tertiary education describe the links between regulations and incentives, participation and partnership, and societal pressures. At the centre, is the issue of political governance the core process that shapes the environment. Economic growth and development are structurally linked to the knowledge economy, as merit-based, equitable, and efficient educations are essential to economic transformation. Inevitably, decisions on these matters are made in the political process that has become more complex in today's world.[26]

Derek Bok, former President of Harvard University, has suggested that 'universities show signs of excessive commercialism in every aspect of their work' but he was hopeful that the trend was not yet irreversible.[27] He was probably right when he stated: 'In higher education, the cards are stacked against any institution that lacks an established reputation and a lot of money.' Bok sees a major conflict between the commercialisation of higher education and protecting the integrity of research and preserving educational values. Several scholars, he claims, have linked 'the recent growth of moneymaking activity to a lack of purpose in the university.' Bok does not agree, rather he argues 'that a university must have a clear sense of values needed to pursue its goals with a high degree of quality and integrity'.

The rise of market forces in higher education has opened up the doors for additional cost sharing avenues, but at the cost of turning universities into 'knowledge factories'. According to Stanley Aronowitz,[28] 'the learning enterprise has become subject to the growing power of administration, which more and more responds not to faculty and students, except at the margin, but to political and market forces that claim sovereignty over higher education.' The marketplace is now encroaching on the work of the universities, as it has done in hospitals, and cultural institutions that have been thought to serve other values. These are bold assertions and 'a mute reminder that something of irreplaceable value may get lost in the relentless growth of commercialization.' The values of the university, reform in social justice, social equity, preservation and promotion of cultural values, and the generation of new knowledge must not falter on the mantra of commercialisation.

Derek Bok argues that commercialisation may undermine academic standards by encouraging appointments of professors who can bring corporate funding, or restricting the full sharing of knowledge, reducing adherence to ethical behaviours, and introduce opportunities for private gains. In this environment, new challenges emerge for preserving educational and academic values, and new conflicts of interest will arise in protecting the integrity of research.

Trinidad and Tobago

Trinidad and Tobago's *Fast forward Agenda* is all about transforming the country into a knowledge-based society. Government, working with the public and private sectors has produced an exciting roadmap that charts a clear and determined course to a society virtually connected and a knowledge-based economy. *Fast forward* provides far-reaching strategies for the development of a connected country that will adapt, flourish, and prosper in the new global information society.

Trinidad and Tobago is in a prominent position in the global information society through real and lasting improvements in social, economic and cultural development caused by deployment and usage of information and communication technology. Our Connectivity Agenda is to provide all citizens in our country with affordable Internet access, focus on the development of our children, and adult skills to ensure a sustainable solution and a vibrant future, promote citizen trust, access, and interaction through good governance, maximise the potential within all of our citizens, and accelerate innovation, to develop a knowledge-based society that is: Connected. Committed. Competitive. Creative. Caring. Community.

The new development direction for our economy requires that our goal must include sustaining strong economic growth, creating a competent, productive and sophisticated workforce, improving efficiencies and service quality in public sector agencies, improving education at all levels and increasing science and technology literacy through cutting-edge information and knowledge, improving social equity, and helping people become information sensitive.

Notes

1. From a speech by Winston Dookeran 'The State of the Economy, May 21, 2010 on Competitiveness, Inclusiveness and Expansionism (Moving from Promises to Performance, The Underpinnings of the 2011 Budget', Minister of Finance, September 30, 2010).
2. From a speech by Winston Dookeran, 'A Development Approach, Entrepreneurial Economy', Post Budget Forum September 9, 2010 *(Moving from Promises to Performance, The Underpinnings of the 2011*

Budget, Minister of Finance, September 30, 2010). This speech summarises developmental aspects of the budget.

3. Foreign *Direct Investment: Policy issues and Recommendations for Caribbean Development:* Article published in No Island is an Island: The Impact of Globalization on the Commonwealth Caribbean, Gordon Baker (editor), published by Brookings Institution, 2007.

4. The first pole includes the 4 Cs, covering Couva, Charlieville, Carapichaima, and Chaguanas. This project will be primarily private-sector driven with Government acting as a catalyst. The second pole will focus on developing the South Western Peninsula of Trinidad, constructing a new Industrial Estate which will create jobs in the area. The third growth pole will be the East Port of Spain Area. The fourth growth pole involves developing the North-Coast. We will do a business plan for a new 'Connective Development Project', which would create an underground tunnel from Maracas Valley to Maracas Bay. The fifth growth pole is in the North East region of Tobago where we will provide incentives for persons who are prepared to establish business enterprises with preference given to persons who will be establishing businesses in the services sector.

5. There is an interesting historical perspective on the shift of the role of the state from strong control to a more catalyst promoting private enterprise and an entrepreneurial economy, this author in his earlier studies including his doctoral dissertation focused on the early phases. During the hundred years from 1766 to 1865 the Ruhr mining region, the modern heart of the Rhenish-Westphalian industrial region in Germany expanded with development of the coal field. In the same period, public policy in the form of Prussian and French state intervention had a significant impact on the direction and speed of the region's economic growth. Specifically, changes in mining and other laws and their administration affected the Ruhr region and its mining industry. In turn, changes in the regional economy, transportation, technology, business organisation, and entrepreneurial activities affected law and state policy. During the century under discussion state policy moved from one of strong state control over mining and related industries with severely restricted private enterprise, called the *Direktionsprinzip,* to one of free enterprise with a minimum state regulations. Manfred D. Jantzen Ph.D. *Law, Economic Policy, and Private Enterprise:* The Case of the Early Ruhr Region, 1766-1865, The *Journal of European Economic History,* Vol. 2, No.3 1973. *Public Policy in Industrial Growth, The Case of Mining Region, 1766-1865* (New York: Arno Press) 1977.

6. Modified Suggestions and Concepts of Dr Ricardo Hausmann based on *Complex Dynamic System Behaviour Business*; delivered July 2010 at a workshop facilitated by the Minister of Finance, Trinidad and Tobago.
7. See Dan Steinbock, 'Finland's Innovative Capacity', Regional Development 13/2006, 19–26, Ministry of the Interior, Finland, www.intermin.fi/julkaisut.
8. "Between the late 1960s and late 1990s, the innovative capacity of Finland rose drastically. The most dramatic shift occurred in the early 1980sm largely due to Nokia's bold technology strategy, which went hand in hand with its international growth strategy, under the leadership of Kari. H. Kairamo."
9. This section is based on a speech by the author, in his capacity as Minister of Finance, on the 2011 budget given to a business audience. It is a plea for developing the human potential. He makes an emotional appeal to the citizen not 'what I can get', but 'what I can be'. His speech calls for the new entrepreneurship, sustainable growth, and a new partnership between the citizen, the business community, and the government He expresses hope for the country's future development through the implementation of the budget proclaiming we are in charge of change. Speech given by Winston Dookeran as Minister of Finance 'Not what I can get but what I can be' on September 9, 2010 at the Trinidad and Tobago Chamber of Industry and Commerce.
10. For the concept on Business incubator, see http://en.wikipedia.org/wiki/Business_incubator
11. Tax Collection & Amnesty: The budget arithmetic is proposed to be a 5.5 per cent deficit. We do believe that we must move back to a balanced budget but this will take this sometime hence most of what we've done in this year's budget is really predicated on a medium term range and we shall move in that direction. The tax amnesty in my view is a very important measure. It is true that we have had two or three such amnesties before but we believe at this time that this was a very important source of revenue. The tax arrears figures amount to about thirteen billion dollars. Now that's a very large number but what is active, amount to about seven billion dollars. If everyone paid their taxes then we would have no deficit in Trinidad and Tobago. Let us make the call for compliance and let us take it seriously.
12. Taxpayers Covenant: We are introducing a new covenant between the taxpayers and the government with very basic principles where we can have what is normally required in a normal tax system – including no harassment but also including enforcement if in fact there are those who

do not wish to pay. And in that context I want to suggest that this is a part of not what I can get but what I can be. Because in the final analysis what I can be depends on the wider environment and what I can get depends largely on me. And therefore we now have to realise that the fortunes of the wider environment are indeed going to be more important to who I am than the fortunes of my individual situation. It is in that kind of context therefore that the risk that we are taking is based on the presumption that the people will now engage in a new beginning, in a new perspective and in so doing people can change the economic fortunes.

13. See, Carl J Dahlman, Jorma Routti, and Pekka Ylä-Anttilaeds, *Finland as a Knowledge Economy. Elements of Success and Lessons Learnt (Washington, DC: The* World Bank) 2007, 1–4.

14. Finland placed first place in the World Economic Forum's Global Competitiveness Index, which ranks 117 countries. See Tom Wright, 'Finland again ranks First among Global Competitors' *International Herald Tribune*, September 29, 2005.

15. See *Constructing Knowledge Societies: New Challenges for Tertiary Education* (Washington, DC: The World Bank) 2002. The proportion of goods in international trade with a medium-high or high level of technology content rose from 33 per cent in 1976 to 54 per cent in 1996.

16. See Growth Commission, *The Growth Report: Strategies for Sustained Growth and Inclusive Development.* http:/www.growthcommission.org. (Washington, DC: World Bank Publications), 2010.

17. Joseph E Stiglitz, Nobel Prize lecture, 2001. http://nobelprize.org/nobel_prizes/ecomonics/laureates/2001/stiglitz-lecture.html

18. The 2008 World Bank Report argues: 'A critical feature of any policy design to encourage funding diversification is to allow incremental resources to remain available for use within the institutions that generate them….Positive government incentives for income generation can take the form of, for example, matching funds linked to income generated from outside sources in some ratio, or even of a multiplier coefficient with a funding formula, as practiced in Singapore and in the US state of Kentucky.' See The World Bank Annual Report 2008 (Washington, DC: The World Bank – Office of the Publisher).

19. Dr David Kemp, Minister of Education of Australia in a 1995 speech to the OECD thematic review of tertiary education entitled 'Strategic Developments in Higher Education', stated: 'The uncertainty of the future underlines the importance of a policy framework which gives as much flexibility as possible

to universities and students, and highlights the importance of building institutions that are responsive to change.'

20. OECD, UNESCO, *Financing Education – Investment and Returns, Analysis of the World Education Indicators.* (Paris: UNESCO Publishing; OECD Publications), 2002.View Executive Summary at http://www. oecd.org/dataoecd/27/8/2494749.pdf

21. Ibid. Introduction, 7.

22. See Bruce D. Johnstone, Alka Arora and William Experton. *The Financing and Management of Higher Education: A Status Report on World Wide Reforms.* (Washington, DC: The World Bank), 1998; and Bruce D. Johnstone 'Worldwide Trends in the Financing and Management of Higher Education'. Keynote address, Salzburg Seminar, Salzburg Global Seminar November 20–24, 2002, Salzburg, Austria.

23. Anne Muller and Teresa Murtagh, eds, 'Higher Education for Sale' in *Education Today,* the Newsletter of UNESCO's Education Sector, Oct–Dec 2002. Muller and Murtagh stated: 'In this way, teachers all over the world can be freed from the chore of reinventing the wheel. The Massachusetts Institute of Technology has shown the way by making its own web material available free. Let's hope this heralds a worldwide movement to commoditize education for the common good.' Another sign of the way things are going is that Apollo and Sylvan learning (firms that sell higher education) are quoted on the US stock exchange.

24. The World Bank, *Construction Knowledge Societies: New Challenges for Tertiary Education.* (Washington, DC: The World Bank) 2002, 14.

25. See David Court. *Financing Higher Education in Africa: Makarere, the Quiet Revolution.'* (Washington, DC: The World Bank) 1999.

26. This may apply more readily to programmes with a high 'technical' component, such as engineering, science, economics, medicine, management etc, the humanities do not easily offer themselves to market-based solutions in attracting new funding.

27. Yin Cheong Cheng. 'Beyond Economics', *The UNESCO Courier* 2002, 37, in a comment 'Beyond Economics' stated that the 'foremost challenge is to manage commercialization, to rise above short-term pressures and to take a more ethical stance towards education, a long-term strategic view.'

28. See Derek Bok *Universities in the Marketplace: The Commercialization of Higher Education.* (Princeton: Princeton University Press) 2003. And the Preview of Alberto Amaral, Glen A. Jones, and Berti Karseth, Governing Higher Education: National Perspectives on Institutional Governance, (Dordrecht: Springer – Kluwer Academic Publishers) 2002.

29. See Stanley Aronowitz. *The Knowledge Factory: Dismantling the Corporate University and Creating the Higher Learning* (Boston: Beacon Press) 2000, 164. For a full discussion on the issue see Winston Dookeran and Akhil Malaki. *Leadership and Governance in Small States, Getting Development Right.* (Saarbrücken: Verlag Dr. Muller) 2008, chapter 3, 'Politics and Development: A Strategic Conversation'.

CHAPTER 8
Finance & Development:

Power of Financial Markets

Financial markets and monetary instruments have an undue influence on world economies, as evidenced by recent crises. The International Monetary Fund and the World Bank seem destined to have a much smaller role. Financial liberalisation and the growing use of electronic money, along with increasing financial sophistication, have stymied central banks.[1]

The system in Trinidad and Tobago must become more dynamic and less concentrated to spur growth, whilst keeping regulations relevant and consistent for the whole Caribbean. Any Caribbean-wide strategy must acknowledge that the Caribbean Community has reached its limits and more radical reforms are needed for economic integration. Currency unions in developing countries provide the right mix between flexibility and stability of exchange rates. Partnership may yet engender solutions for monetary stability. Inflation targeting – simple, transparent and effective – seems the way forward for many developing countries. Strategic policies must be made to combat discriminatory tariffs, especially in light of an economic geography that places economic blocks often with little regard for national boundaries. To build competitiveness, price and non-price monetary factors must find more common ground.

What is the central bank's role in development? Often, the hardest thing for a governor of a central bank to grasp is the gap between theory and practice. As the world economy staggers from crisis to crisis, financial markets that punish countries, whose policies they judge inadequate, are blamed. Each new scene of financial turbulence brings forth more demands for governments to subdue markets. Does this suggest that financial markets have become too powerful?

If so, then money does matter. The next questions are: How does it affect our lives? What must we do to steer the economies in the right direction? The world of money today is filled with uncertainties; the toolkits available to us to tinker with and shape the economy are still being tested. Some of these uncertainties are derived from strong free market behaviour that promotes a single global finance system. Rapid change and advances in information technology have made designing tools even more difficult.

This era of uncertainty has created new rigidities, 'money illusions' and expectations that lie at the heart of the debate on money's impact. Effective monetary policy is nowadays primarily concerned with addressing short-run disequilibrium situations. The classical position is that relative prices are determined by real forces of demand and supply. The absolute price level is determined by the quantity of money and its velocity of circulation. This position has much less practical relevance than it once did and has little bearing on policy.

The shift of power from policymakers to financial markets has aroused three main concerns. One is that the sheer size of foreign exchange and bond markets can overwhelm monetary and fiscal policy, wresting influence over interest and exchange rates from the state. Daily turnover on the currency markets now exceeds the global stock of official foreign exchange reserves. Financial markets have become the oft-capricious and powerful judges of economic policymaking. Secondly, central banks and governments are accused of responding more to financial markets rather than altering the market forces to benefit their countries. Their obsession with price stability, it is argued, could impose excessive deflation on economies.

Finally, global financial liberalisation and a vast array of new financial instruments may have dulled the effectiveness of monetary and fiscal tools, so that changes in interest rates or government borrowing have a smaller impact on an economy. There has been the growing use of electronic money, which may further reduce central banks' control over the money supply, and an expansion in derivative activity, which allows firms to insulate themselves from changes in interest rates. Liberalisation and innovation have made financial markets far more volatile and more vulnerable to financial meltdown, prompting increasing financial instability.[2]

As economies produce and grow, the spectre of inflation is rising once again. Inflation is not dead, and risks remain asymmetrical; concurrent with the admittedly encouraging global growth, inflation risks could intensify.

Apart from that inflationary risk, there are welcome signs of safety and stability in emerging markets. International investors appear increasingly willing to reward countries that show greater commitment to economic reform and transparency. More and more countries, including emerging market economies, have now subscribed to the IMF's Special Data Dissemination Standard. This standard, which promotes the availability of accurate and timely financial statistics, was first established in April 1996, but assumed greater significance with the onset of the Asian crisis.

Recognising the greater transparency prompted by the Special Data Dissemination Standard and other measures fuelling the progress that emerging markets have been making in lowering risks; investors have rewarded them by improving their risk ratings.

The International Financial Architecture is reflective of the new political order. The countries of the G20 have assumed position at centre stage and have come to replace many of the institutions that wielded political power in the past. There is clearly a shift in global economic and political power and those in the region must be very adaptive to that global political change.

The Caribbean in the past has had to face some of the negative consequences of these architectural changes and now they are once more on the national agenda. It is in that context that Trinidad and Tobago took that initiative very recently to currently chair the Small States Forum at the World Bank and began talks in that forum with both the IMF and the World Bank to find a voice in the G20. Small states cannot sit back and allow these deliberations that would have affected people in this part of the world without becoming an active party in that regard.

So, Trinidad and Tobago, representing small states, has made substantial diplomatic moves at IMF meetings to seek a voice for small economies and countries in the G20 deliberations. The response, at least from international financial institutions has been quite encouraging. But there is much to be done, and Trinidad and Tobago will be approaching other Caribbean countries to join together with those from all sorts of economies to secure that voice.

The Case for Small Economies

Some critical issues impacting small economies must be part of shaping the manifesto for the leadership of the IMF. In particular there is concern that changes to the international architecture, in which the IMF and G20 sit, lends themselves to a potential contravention of natural justice where clubs of large countries sit and develop rules for smaller states to follow without adequate consultation, consideration, and engagement.

Development of international financial regulation, supervision, risk management, and the assessment of financial sectors does not support a level playing field between small and large states. Preferential treatment given to areas important in some large states, from mortgages, regional banks to hybrid capital, treatment that proved so dangerous in the financial crisis, also penalises institutions in small states beyond economic justification. Small, open economies such as St Lucia and Tonga proved particularly vulnerable to this preferential treatment. For example, in the wake of the 2008 financial crisis, tourist-dependent St Lucia's hotels were 80 per cent empty during its peak tourist period in late 2008 and early 2009, while remittances to Tonga dropped by 15 per cent from June 2008 to June 2009 (te Welde 2009).[3] Additionally, Cambodia witnessed a 50 per cent decline in FDI in 2009. This has contributed to the loss of approximately 102,527 jobs in the country since September 2009 (either permanently or temporarily) due to the closure of 93 garment and shoe factories in the first eleven months of that year. This is a significant development when one considers that the country's garment sector accounts for 83.2 per cent of its total exports (ODI 2009b).[4]

Furthermore, there is concern that, while small states particularly need help in the financing infrastructure, the criteria of lending by the multinational institutions is better suited to larger states with capital markets, credit ratings and diversified private-sector players. The criteria used for long-term and short-term support pays too much attention to the level of GDP per capita, and does not sufficiently account for higher levels of fragility and vulnerability to natural and economic shocks. Finally, in order to address these issues, a new leadership position in the IMF focusing on the challenges of small economies may be required.

Liberalisation of Financial Services

There is a trend towards the integration of banking and insurance services. If there are two industries that fit the requirements of the global market, these would be them. There is a new urgency in the world of financial services liberalisation. Our immediate response in the Caribbean should be to establish a Caribbean-wide regulatory system as the first step in coping with the demands of liberalisation. This proposal needs to be fast-tracked alongside the WTO process on the liberalisation of financial services. This will require enormous professional effort and political determination for execution.

One strand of economic literature argues that finance is unimportant; it is simply the handmaiden to real production. However, in recent years, there has been increasing evidence that financial systems do play an essential role in economic development. Hence, the financial system must be linked to growth. As the effect of the global financial crisis shows, even relatively strong economies may collapse when the foundations underlying their financial systems are weak.

One of the important challenges of development in small states such as Trinidad and Tobago is to identify the best financial system that will promote fast, yet sustainable economic growth. Evidence from richer countries has shown that as economies mature, capital markets become more effective at intermediation than banks. One simple truth was first expressed in what is called 'Say's Identity'[5] and argues: regardless of the prices and interest with which they are confronted – individuals always prefer to use all of their proceeds from the sale of commodities and bonds for the purpose of purchasing other commodities and bonds. People sell goods only for the purpose of buying more. Supply creates its own demand. This basic identity has helped us to understand the workings of our foreign exchange market and suggests a need for a more diversified structure in financial intermediation.

What is the business of financial intermediaries? They lend at one level of interest rate and borrow at a lower level. They purchase primary securities from the market and substitute indirect securities and financial assets at higher prices. The margin between these prices is the intermediary's profit. Financial intermediation has grown significantly, globally and regionally. The banking sector, however, continues to dominate the financial landscape, accounting for as much as 80 per cent of all financial assets in some regional economies. Thus, financial sector diversification must push forward. Banking crises have been found to be far more devastating in countries where banking constitutes a relatively large share of the financial sector.

Trinidad and Tobago has a relatively modern and sophisticated financial structure, both in terms of the variety of institutions and the range of financial instruments available. Its financial system is today comprised of a range of finance institutions, including commercial banks, merchant banks, trust companies, mortgage finance companies, thrift institutions, development banks, mutual funds, credit unions, insurance firms, and other institutions. Today, more than ever, the system needs to become less concentrated and more dynamic. As our economy develops, we must ensure that financial decision-making is not concentrated in the hands of a few gatekeepers at banks and similar institutions. Richard C. Breeden, former Chairman of the Securities and Exchange Commission (SEC), was quoted in the *Wall Street Journal*[6] as saying:

> In countries where financial markets do not work as well as in the United States, investment decision-making is concentrated in the hands of just a few dozen gatekeepers at banks and investment firms. The result is that financing trends to flow primarily to a cadre of established businesses with strong relationships to the old guard. By contrast, the United States has literally thousands of gatekeepers in our increasingly decentralized capital markets, many of them with a much higher appetite for risk...It is not because our scientists are smarter than their scientists. It's because we're creating a system that provides capital more quickly to people willing to take big risks...and our economy is reaping the rewards.

We must ready ourselves to construct a financial system that enables us to compete in an increasingly integrated world market and which helps to insulate us from financial contagion originating in other parts of the world.

Proper banking regulation is crucial to prevent or minimise the cost of banking sector failures, as banks dominate the financial sector. In recent years, some countries in our region have experienced banking system difficulties that have hampered growth and generated fiscal costs as high as 10 to 20 per cent of GDP, sometimes more.

There is a threshold where, when these costs become high enough, the crisis inevitably enters the political arena. Evidence of this can be seen in Indonesia, where the fiscal cost of the Asian financial crisis was calculated to be nearer 80 per cent of GDP and the authoritarian regime of Suharto was toppled.

Many Caribbean states have therefore adopted reforms aimed not just at dealing with high-risk banks but also, more importantly, at strengthening banking supervision to reduce the likelihood of future crises. They have firmed up guidelines on financial prudence, established minimum capital requirements, adopted better systems to monitor asset quality, made provisions for bad loans, and imposed tighter limits on excessive concentration of risk, all factors in past banking crises.

Trinidad and Tobago must quicken the pace of structural finance sector reform as it remains vulnerable to terms of trade and investor sentiment fluctuations; despite having taken the right measures to support financial sector stability. When oil and gas prices were high, Trinidad and Tobago felt it had the attraction and resources to become a financial centre in the region. Today, this idea no longer seems tenable. Indeed, with development of ICT, traders hardly need go to the market. Computers are taking markets to traders, wherever they are.

The future may therefore be hinged on maintaining the soundness and stability of our existing financial system through a proper regulatory framework along with continued deepening and widening of the financial system. This is why Trinidad and Tobago's firm policy at the Central Bank is to comply with the Basel Committee's 'Core Principles for Effective Banking Supervision'.[7] In tandem with this, the establishment of an Integrated Regulatory System that incorporates banking, insurance and pension funds is now being designed for Trinidad and Tobago.

The Monetary and Financial Policy Agenda

There are a number of issues on this agenda for small states. Three issues are key to future policy planning. Competitive and open markets, the rule of law, fiscal discipline and a culture of enterprise that is driven by innovation and productivity are all important factors in sustaining the growth process. Human expectations are always subject to bouts of euphoria and disillusionment, and our system must be strong enough to take such a diversion in stride. At one time, it was felt that stability would come from ensuring strong fundamentals. Today, that is simply not enough.

Is inflation targeting the way forward? Policymakers have traditionally used strategies such as controlling the growth of the money supply or pegging the exchange rate to a stable currency in pursuit of price stability. However, financial liberalisation is leading to a breakdown of the traditional relationship between money and nominal income and may have reduced the ability of central banks to control inflation. With market pressures forcing some countries to abandon their exchange rate bands, monetary policy is losing its nominal price anchor, and is leading many central banks to search for an alternative framework that would engender stability and future growth.

In recent years we have seen a promising approach. This strategy is called inflation targeting. The idea behind inflation targeting is to publicly announce and pursue specific target rates of inflation. Among other things, this approach calls for a central bank to be generally independent of politics, to have a mandate to pursue price stability, and preferably to have an explicit inflation target at which to aim. An excellent model comes from New Zealand, where the Reserve Bank has had full independence over the operation of monetary policy since 1990. The government set an inflation target of zero to 3 per cent. Any governor of the reserve bank who fails to meet this target can be fired and any change in this target must be debated and approved by Parliament.

Inflation targeting provides transparency and accountability. Its simplicity and openness also make it far easier for the public to understand the intent and effects of monetary policy, in addition to holding policymakers accountable for inflation performance. The announced target creates a penalty for failure and reduces the temptation for governments to spring inflationary surprises simply for short-term output boosts. With a credible target, the market is more able to predict how the central bank is likely to respond to internal and external imbalances.

Transparency of the monetary decision-making process is the key. Traditionally, central bankers have been secretive, but the new environment demands that we communicate more clearly with market participants if we wish to influence their behaviour and expectations. In Britain, minutes of the interest rate decisions taken at regular monthly meetings between the Chancellor of the Exchequer and the Governor of the Bank of England are published swiftly. The Bank of England also produces an inflation report, which helps markets understand the factors that guide the interest rate policy. In the US, the Federal Reserve publishes the transcripts of its federal open market committee meetings. It also publicly announces all decisions to change the federal funds rate, rather than leaving it up to the market to work it out.

There is credible evidence that inflation targeting has helped to boost monetary policy credibility in some countries. This could well be a suitable monetary framework for small states, which place a high value on a stable currency.

Ricardo Hausmann, former chief economist at the Inter-American Development Bank, puts the issue[8] of exchange rates this way: every government faces a 'trilemma': (1) if it wants a fixed exchange rate and free movement of capital, it should forget about managing interest rates; (2) if it wants to manage interest rates and keep the exchange rate fixed, it must control capital flows; and (3) if it wants to manage interest rates without affecting capital flows, it cannot have fixed exchange rate. It is impossible to have the three things at the same time; a fixed exchange rate, free movement of capital, and regulated interest rates.

One of the three has to be relinquished and the respective price much be paid. In a world of increasingly mobile capital, countries cannot fix their exchange rate and at the same time maintain an independent monetary policy. A choice must be made between the confidence and stability provided by a fixed exchange rate and the control over policy offered by a floating rate. In the Caribbean, our vulnerability to external shocks such as sudden shifts in commodity prices has been the deciding factor.

History is on the side of greater flexibility. Since the mid-1970s, the number of countries with flexible exchange rates has increased steadily. This suggests that global architects should be promoting and preparing for a world of floating currencies. Floating rates have struck countries with flexible rates instead of fixed exchange rates, though the effect has been more severe for countries with fixed exchange rates. Confronted by sudden market panics, we have seen floating exchange rates overshoot guideposts and become highly unstable, especially if large amounts of capital flow in and out of a country. This instability carries real economic costs.

To get the best of both worlds, some countries have loosely tied their exchange rate to a single foreign currency, such as the United States dollar, or to a basket of currencies. Others are tightly tied through a currency board or, even better, a currency union. Economists are deeply divided about what is the optimal exchange rate regime, but it seems that in the interest of stability, some form of linkage with more established currencies such as the US dollar is only prudent for developing countries in the position of those in the Caribbean.

It is clear that structural adjustment strategies have not met the expectations of rising living standards in an equitable manner when considering the quality of growth. The first generation of reforms adopted by Latin America and the Caribbean has largely failed to alleviate pressing issues of inequality and poverty. Based on a scenario of business as usual with continuing slow growth and recurring crises, the prospects for future reduction in the numbers of the poor do not look bright.

Poverty has always been a controversial, as we have seen through vigorous demonstrations in WTO Ministerial Meetings, at the World Economic Forum Meetings and, more recently, at the IMF/World Bank Meetings. All of these demonstrations were ostensibly mobilised around the theme of poverty and poor nations. According to recent news:

> The International Monetary Fund and the World Bank were set up together to help rebuild a post-World War Two economic system. Both came under fierce fire during the spring meetings of the two institutions when angry demonstrators said that the lenders were not doing enough for debt relief and that their policy prescriptions only deepened poverty in developing countries.[9]

The International Financial System is under great scrutiny. The call for changes in its global agenda is becoming louder. This call, however, is not only for the system to deliver us from poverty, but also a call for changes in our analytical framework and our method of analysis. Some amongst us may argue that 'quality of growth' objectives are utopian with no coherent, rational or analytical grounding. But given the present economic, social and political realities, small states may have little alternative but to face these new challenges.[10]

The Adaptive Response by Small States

Small states are experiencing a turbulent convergence of forces which are redefining their place in the global order. New economic borders are emerging, political options are widening, and new international regimes are redrawing the ties that bind them to the rest of the world. Yet, they still grapple with lingering problems: economic dualism, unemployment, low productivity, inequality, low saving and investment rates, and weak entrepreneurship.

We in small states sometimes believe that our size hinders development. In fact, size need not be an issue. There are many examples of small states that have grown rich and prosperous without significant natural resources or preferential trade accords. They did so by linking their economies with the world economy and by achieving external economies of scale rather than by relying on internal forces. They determined their cultural strengths and built on them. They developed policies and strategies that unleashed the microeconomic forces for growth, and they complemented these with a suitable macroeconomic framework.

All nation states, particularly small states, may be called upon to cede some of their sovereignty in order to develop economically. The challenge is to do so without compromising the core principles of their sovereignty. Within this context, we will focus on some of the challenges facing small states in today's world. There are three broad challenging areas: the first is to tackle volatility, vulnerability and natural disasters. The second is to transition to the changing global trade regime. The third is to strengthen capacities within small states.

How can small states take charge of this dialectic between nation-state and markets? How can the state be transformed into an efficient developmental agent without forsaking its social and political responsibilities? A new worldwide system of economic relations is emerging, in which every nation-state is being incorporated into the global economic system. Nation-states must increasingly share their decision-making space with global corporate interest and civil society. For this reason, the state's role in development must be redefined, though not necessarily reduced. If the foundations of social life are not to be further eroded, this change in economic processes must be countered with 'high-energy politics' involving intensified public participation and democracy.

Caribbean governments appear to be caught in a crosscurrent; stymied by introspection and indecision and unable to articulate viable economic strategies for lifting their countries to a higher equilibrium economic level. We stated in chapter 3 that: 'The growing gap in the Caribbean between expectations and performance and the rising tension between intention and reality, had widened the space between the area of politics and the area of discharge of governance. Not only has this resulted in a deep disillusionment with institutions and politicians, but the role of the state and its ability to govern have come into question.'

Small states are indeed more vulnerable to external events, including natural disasters. Their greater trade openness, concentration of commodity exports and dependence on net capital flows all serve to make them more vulnerable to external shocks. Income is equally vulnerable, and income streams can become very volatile. There is therefore a need to design a mechanism that would act to counter this whilst incorporating differing conditions in states, as both strong and weak states pose threats to global economic security. It is true that cross border private capital flows have grown substantially in recent times. Small economies, however, are still viewed as riskier investments by private capital than larger developing economies are, even if they enact the right policies.

How can small states adapt to the changing international environment? International trading regimes are essentially devices of political economy: they are in place at least as much to protect nations from their own interest groups as they are to protect nations from each other. In this sense, the process of change and adaptation can be best analysed in a framework of political economy.

We must identify the winners and losers in this framework.

Change is normally associated with altering the character of national expenditure to another set of expenditures that will usher in a new matrix of investment and consumption. But how can we do this? Losers are easily identified. They are the participants in the current economic structure and are normally adequately represented in the political system. They make appropriate noises and are satisfied by the status quo.

On the other hand, the winners belong to the next generation and are a product of as yet unrealised opportunities. They therefore cannot be easily identified or mobilised. Change is challenged by finding an appropriate incentive mechanism that would allow the losers to become winners. Caribbean societies can best adapt to their new trading environment if the framework for the political economy of change can be designed and an appropriate strategy marked.

At the international level, strategically targeted policies have been built into the trading framework, despite states attempting to protect their allies and dependents from these trade barriers. These policies and other protectionist sanctions have been used by the United States, amongst others, and are clearly implied in 'social clauses' on environmental and labour issues which have been seen by many to discriminate against exporters from developing countries.

Caribbean states' strategic approach must become more deliberate to adapt to the new trading environment. Such strategic policies will alter the pace, the time and the scope envisaged in the change process. Another aspect of the political economy of change deals with the core-periphery dynamics of the new economic geography. Compact economic units no longer coincide with national boundaries. For example, it is argued that the triangular axis of New York, Washington and Toronto represents one economic unit. So too does the block of California, Texas and New Mexico. The boundaries of the Caribbean economy can no longer exclude Florida. Market forces must therefore work within this new economic geographical arrangement.

There are two distinct and related processes that seem to be taking place: one is the relocation of industries and services in regions that are favoured with an attractive and richly endowed environment. The second is a specialisation of economies that favour regions with established industries and attracts firms away from those with less developed initial conditions. New knowledge and insight into these aspects of the political economy of change - winners and losers, strategic policies and economic geography dynamics - should form part of a scholarship agenda as Caribbean countries adapt to the new trading and financial environment.

CARICOM and Building Competitiveness

Building Competitiveness is an exercise in political economy. We therefore raise two main issues. The first is the reliance on the price factor in the adjustment strategy as opposed to the non-price factor. The price factors are: exchange rates, interest rates, commodity prices and asset prices. Too much emphasis in the typical adjustment programme has been placed on the price factor. It is true that the non-price factor is more of a medium-term goal toward building a competitive economy, but extreme reliance on the price factor can encourage Caribbean underdevelopment.

This is so because markets are imperfect and resource transfers emanating from changes in the price factor can have extremely negative effects. It has already been pointed out that the resource flows between multilateral institutions and Caribbean economies harm the region. The challenge of building a competitive economy cannot rely as heavily as it had done in the past on price adjustments; rather, a better synergy between the price and the non-price factors must be worked into the adjustment matrix.

The second issue can best be described using a World Bank phrase: 'institutions matter'. Many supporting institutions which develop competitiveness may need to be refocused toward understanding the strategy, public policy or regulations. This remains an enormous link with international economy, be it through economic intelligence, market strategy, public policy or regulations. This remains an enormous part of the change ahead. Our preparation to meet these challenges must come to grips with the argument that 'institutions matter'.

The limits of CARICOM must be considered. This is a matter of determining an optimal economic space, keeping in mind the theoretical underpinnings of the debates on regionalism, open regionalism and multilateralism. Integration paradigms of the past are being challenged, as the pace of change of regional integration is outstripped by the rate of change of global integration.

The institutional structure of the integration process is less important than the economic structures that would grasp opportunities and withstand the risks of global integration. So far, much of the preparation in the integration agenda has been institutional with concentration on WTO arrangements, and the CARICOM Single Market and Economy (CSME).

These institutional frameworks are important, but CARICOM may have reached its limit. The CSME is too much a minimalist position. Do we need a new platform on which to negotiate with other sub-regional groups and to expand trade, investment and financial relations throughout the hemisphere?

We have always been in search of a theory of Caribbean development. We have analysed the Caribbean dependency relationship at great length. We have assessed the neoliberal development policy, often with scepticism. William Demas's[11] comment on neo liberalism perhaps makes the point very clear: 'I differ from the new economist only in the speed and scope of the process of the Caribbean Community becoming internationally competitive and of the extent of opening up our other economic transactions with the outside world.'

We have promoted the establishment of more attractive business environments. We have talked about export-led growth. We have warned about our local businesses being out-competed. We have pushed the limits in searching for a theory of Caribbean development. Let not the agenda for scholars reflect a state of under-development. The scholarly agenda is outlined in the epilogue of this book. Many of the issues have also been discussed in the chapter on the new space for growth and development.

In today's global economy, where new global imbalances are emerging, new frontier industrial policies are required. The global imbalances are reflected on three fronts: (1) in the simmering foreign exchange currency wars, visibly noticed in the current 'on and off' tension between the United States and China and the realignment of currencies in the world; (2) the re-emergence of new food crisis resulting from the growing gap between supply and demand and this is transmitted to countries of the world, especially those which are heavily dependent on the importation of food or the raw material needed for the production of such food; and (3) the continued ripples in oil and gas prices, as the politics of the world energy sector shift to changes in technology.

These global imbalances are a reflection of the changing political order and small countries like those in the Caribbean, must be prepared to anticipate and, as far as possible, develop policy actions to protect our economies and the well-being of our people.

The challenge of change requires us to depart from the premises of past development strategies and embrace sustainable programmes. These are the underlying premises upon which the new frontier industrialisation strategy is being constructed. That strategy is premised on four basic points:

(1) Re-invigorate seismic research to identify potential resources of hydro-carbon as we seek to expand private seismic data to an open data room and set the basis for renewed exploration in the hydro-carbon sector;

(2) Develop an aggressive programme based on finance, technology, and management to make Trinidad and Tobago's economy more competitive and, in this regard, the Government has recently established the National Competitiveness Council along with the Economic Development Board to chart the new frontier ahead of us. Implicit here is the need to speed up our decision making and we are already engaged in a programme to improve our ratings and the ease of doing business. Much of these changes require the deep professional bond, strong political commitment and a clear direction which must be embraced by all;

(3) Our international promotional effort for new investment in the on-shore and off-shore development must now expand our global reach to include Indian, Chinese, and Brazilian investment prospects. As such, a new era of economic diplomacy will now inform our efforts to vigorously seek investments to support the new direction in our development strategy; and finally

(4) No longer must we view the energy sector as a privileged enclave of a few but, indeed, we must move to the democratization of this sector in search of opportunities to finance new economic space in our quest for inclusive development.

Finally, let us draw the attention to key obstacles to change in the Caribbean by posing a penetrating question. What is holding back growth and development in the Caribbean? This is the question asked by a Caribbean scholar, Avinash Persaud. He argues that the anti-growth coalition, so deeply embedded in the socio-economic and political culture in the small states of the Caribbean must be 'broken', before any growth and development can take place. The challenge therefore, for policymakers, development takers, practitioners and those engaged in the field of economic change is how to break the anti-growth coalition.

Notes

1. Central Bank of Trinidad and Tobago. 2002. Compilation and speeches delivered by Mr. Winston Dookeran, Governor of the Central Bank of Trinidad and Tobago, 1997-2002. Speech Catalogue: *Issues and Themes.* Port of Spain. (unpublished).
2. Winston Dookeran, 'Money Matters: Emerging Challenges for Small States', Distinguished Lecture Series, Institute of International Relations, The University of the West Indies, St. Augustine 2000.
3. te Welde TW (2009) The global financial crisis and developing countries: taking stock, taking action. Overseas Development Institute Briefing Paper 54. http://www.odi.org.uk/resources/ download/2822.pdf. Accessed 06 November 2011: 2
4. te Welde TW et al (2009) The global financial crisis and developing countries: Phase 2 Synthesis. Overseas Development Institute Working Paper 316. http://www.odi.org.uk/ resources/ download/4784.pdf. Accessed 06 November 2011.
5. See Jean Baptiste Say: *A treatise on political economy; or the production distribution and consumption of wealth.* Translated from the fourth edition of the French. (Kitchener: Batoche Books) 2001; T. Sowell , *Say's Law, An Historical Analysis.* (Princeton, NJ: Princeton University Press) 1972; Steven Kates, *Say's Law and the Keynesian revolution: How macroeconomic theory lost its way.* (Cheltenham: Edward Elgar Publishing Limited) 1998.

6. John R. Wilke, 'Mutual Fund Growth Altering Economy'. The *Wall Street Journal*, June 16, 1996.
7. Basel Committee on Banking Supervision – International Association of Deposit Insurers 'Core Principles for Effective Deposit Insurance Systems. Basel, Switzerland, June 2009.
8. See Barry Julian Eichengreen and Ricardo Hausmann 'Exchange Rates and Financial Fragility'. (Cambridge, MA: National Bureau of Economic Research) November 1999.
9. See 'Fifteen years is enough says new report on IFIs' Halifax Initiative, April 2010. See www.choike.org/2009/eng/informes/1729.html
10. Winton Dookeran, *Uncertainty, Stability and Challenges: Economic and Monetary Policy, Small States Perspective* (San Juan, Trinidad: Lexicon Trinidad) 2006.
11. William G. Demas, *The Economics of Development in Small Countries with Special Reference to the Caribbean* (Montreal: McGill University Press) 1965, xv, 150.

CHAPTER 9
BREAKING THE ANTI GROWTH COALITION*

Solutions for Caribbean and CARICOM Development

Overview

The power-culture is also holding back growth and development in rest of the Caribbean. The anti-growth coalition, so deeply embedded in the socio-economic and political culture in the small states of the Caribbean, it must be 'broken', before any growth and development can take place.

Here, a blueprint is provided for breaking the anti-growth coalition in small developing states and deepening private sector development. The author believes that the Caribbean policymakers have limited choices to guide the development path. The author discusses four such limitations that shape the economic reality of the Caribbean. The economic structure shapes the political structure such that it is hard for Governments to reshape the economic structure. For example, state employment is high and few political parties will risk the electoral wrath of public sector workers to change that. New and radical initiatives to transform the country can find no other sponsors that the old established businesses resistant to disruptive change. The glue that holds this together is the appearance of community and partnership as the enterprises that benefit most from special preferences are major benefactors to social initiatives.

An inefficient public sector benefits the 'insiders' – those middle and upper classes with connections – versus the 'outsiders'. These powerful forces against change are not unique to the Caribbean but they are more entrenched in small or developing states where the middle and upper classes can have a distinctly different existence within their guarded walls and well manicured gardens and well-cared for homes than others. The political economy constraint to the governance and modernisation of small states is perhaps the single most important argument for greater regionalism. The author argues a convincing case for disruptive change. The agents of disruptive change must be prioritised. The author explores these critical instruments of disruptive change which includes technology, finance, business-facilitation and competition policy.

Introduction: The Luxury of Limited Choices[**]

In comparison with many regions of the world, the collection of 26 small states surrounded by, or bordering the Caribbean Sea are blessed with a number of fundamental positives. The region as a whole is juxtaposed between two large, wealthy continental markets with a combined GDP of $21trillion today – significantly greater than the combined GDP of South Asia, East Asia and the Pacific. The region boasts a pleasant climate and a beautiful physical environment, indeed, tourism is the major industry in many of the nations with beaches and hotels that are the most coveted in the world.

In the 18 states of the English-speaking Caribbean, the proportion of the population in abject poverty is modest. Less than 5 per cent of the population in Barbados, for example, live below the poverty line. Poor public health is not a pressing weight on growth and income inequality is not as extreme as in many of continental neighbours to the south. Literacy is close to universal in many countries and very high in most others. One factor behind these positive social fundamentals is that public expenditure on education as a percent of GDP is one of the highest in the developing world - averaging 5 per cent in CARICOM.

The region's track record of creativity is remarkable. Despite its size, the region boasts three Nobel Laureates in just five decades since independence.[1] Major genres of music: Reggae, Dance Hall, Soca, and Calypso began here. The region produces an incredible number of talented superstars in the cultural and sporting arenas including people such as Bob Marley, Rihanna, Usain Bolt and Sir Garfield Sobers. The Caribbean Diaspora maintains strong cultural and financial links with home and contributes hard-currency remittances which, for some countries, are a significant source of balance of payments support. Language is not a hindrance to international trade. Many critical public institutions, from constitutional democracy and judicial independence to sanitation systems and psychiatric hospitals, have a long history. Political change is mostly democratic and peaceful.

The Caribbean should not, however, be viewed as a homogenous region. Even after putting aside Cuba, Puerto Rico, and Haiti, there are enormous differences within the region. The continental countries of Guyana, Suriname, and Belize boast small populations inhabiting large expanses of well-watered and fertile land. Dominica, Grenada, Martinique, St Lucia, and St Vincent - the "more Volcanic" are small and lush, with rivers and mountains. Anguilla, Antigua, Aruba, Bahamas, Barbados, Cayman, Curacao, and Turks and Caicos, the mainly coral islands, are tiny, flat and water-poor but blessed with world-renowned beaches and reefs. The larger islands of Jamaica and Trinidad and Tobago have significant manufacturing employment. Minerals make a substantial contribution to development in Trinidad and Tobago (oil, gas), Guyana (bauxite, gold and diamonds) and Jamaica (bauxite). Fisheries and forestry have special significance for Guyana and Suriname. There are many more differences. Remittances are as much as 15 per cent of Gross National Income in Jamaica and Guyana, but are sub-5 per cent in almost all other CARICOM countries. Per capita income is ten times greater in Trinidad and Tobago than neighbouring Guyana. Eighty per cent of the population live below the poverty line in Haiti and as noted before, just 5 per cent in Barbados.

The region as a whole has deep cultural and economic divisions. Two hundred and sixty years after the first Navigation Act, trade, capital and labour continue to flow along the fault lines of language both at the intra-region level and between the region vis-à-vis the rest of the world. These fault lines ignore geography and instead follow the haphazard settlements of 17th century squabbles among warring European empires.

Given these differences we must be cautious in drawing generalisations across this varied group of small nations and even within language or geographical sub-groups. Yet, with few exceptions, since the end of the Latin American debt crisis the acceleration of emerging market growth around the world has bypassed the Caribbean. From 1972 to 1988, the Caribbean as a group strongly outperformed other emerging markets or small states in terms of GDP per capita. Since then the region has strongly underperformed.[2] This picture of stalling relative growth worsens if Trinidad and Tobago is removed – a reasonable adjustment given that Trinidad's recent economic path has been strongly driven by the favourable development in international prices of their primary export, gas and its derivatives. This woeful trend over the past 22 years continues to this very day. While GDP growth in Latin America is forecast to average above 6 per cent in 2011, it is expected to average just 2.0 per cent in the Caribbean, and this, despite the Caribbean having further to bounce back, having suffered the greater decline during the recession of 2008–2009.

Public debt levels have risen to potentially unsustainable levels. Seven of the ten most indebted countries in the world are in the Caribbean. Not all of this relates to trying to satisfy unrealistic expectations. Public finances in the Caribbean have been disproportionately burdened by new expenditures relating to climate change, post 9/11 physical and financial security and the growing trend towards reductions in customs tariffs. The structural economic outlook is not obviously rosy. Agriculture and manufacturing exports are generally uncompetitive and have declined sharply since the late 1980s. In parts of the region, tourism is threatened by alarmingly high crime rates.[3]

The international financial crisis and its response put at risk the region's international financial centres. Even before the assumption of liabilities following the Clico and Stanford International Bank debacles, debt levels placed tight constrains on governments of the region. With few exceptions, local businesses and citizens complain about a decline in the quality, efficiency and purposefulness of governance.

With the public sector over-burdened by debt and inefficiencies, future growth must be private sector-led. But the private sector appears ill equipped to set a high pace of economic activity or to take advantage of recently negotiated, concessionary, trade agreements such as the EPA with the EU. The world is not waiting for the Caribbean. Many of the concessions granted in the trade agreements yet to be implemented by Caribbean governments, are necessarily temporary in order to fit with global trade rules and are being eroded by new FTAs being implemented by Europe and the US on the one hand and Caribbean competitors on the other. Competitiveness is low with only one Caribbean country making the top 50 in the World Economic Forum's 'Global Competitiveness Report' ranking for 2010-2011. Talent is leaving. Caribbean countries dominate the list of the top 20 countries in the world with the highest tertiary-educated migration rates. Many in the Caribbean Diaspora have found it easier to be successful abroad than at home, further fuelling the brain drain.

The traditional response of Governments in the region has been major tourism-related infrastructure projects, subsidies and initiatives for agriculture and renewable energy, significant expenditures on education and tax regimes to boost the presence of third party international business. Better linking agriculture with the hotel sector has become a policy cliché in the Caribbean. These are typical 'apple pie and ice cream' initiatives that few argue against. Where the public sector is fiscally constrained, donors have often stepped in with similar agendas. But, like Albert Einstein, we need to question if more of the same will lead to a different outcome. While the headings must be right (Education, Tourism, Environment, Energy, Agriculture, International Business, etc.), the manner in which some of these investments are made, organised and linked to the rest of the economy, needs to be examined to ensure they are not at a point of diminishing returns.

Consider briefly the most sacred of cows: public education. The Caribbean is justifiably proud of its investment in free, universal, education amounting to around 5 per cent of GDP per year. There have been very high social and economic returns from free primary and secondary education. But, after receiving a largely tax-payer-funded education, an estimated 50 per cent of local university graduates in the region as a whole, go abroad for work. It is alarmingly worse in the English-speaking Caribbean. Second, the education system is turning out a disproportionate number of doctors and lawyers, who enter protected professions at home and are not a force for entrepreneurial change. Third, research ranking suggest that the incentives to the University and secondary schools may have tilted the balance too far towards quantity over quality. The concept of free education is not in question.

There are few things governments can do that can generate as much social and economic return. The question is whether universal access to education is being delivered in the right and most focused way today. Debate on the subject is largely stifled in the Caribbean, especially when compared with countries many times richer which have already departed from free tertiary education.

The same goes for a range of other initiatives under the skills agenda. There is no shortage of public sector officials with certificates and training courses under their belt. But better skills matched to the same poor incentives or disproportionate interests, will do little to lift public sector productivity. Certification is not education.

Even if we were not in an age of austerity and deficit reduction, there are other popular public investments that deserve more scrutiny. Large subsidies to sick public transport companies sit alongside profitable private transport firms. Despite brand new airports and air-travel subsidies, a number of factors make it hard to extract commercial returns on air transport investments such as legacy labour costs, political demands to serve "social routes" high fuel costs and air-ticket levies.

In the past the region's charismatic, nationalist leaders cited the vulnerabilities of size and the legacy of Empire, as reasons to insulate the regional economy from the cold winds of international competition. These issues have historic legitimacy. But the recent experience of the region and elsewhere suggests that the answer to uncompetitive industries is not to provide long-term pandering to their 'uncompetitiveness' through continued protection, but to expose them to competition. Gradualism can mean the aggressive removal of barriers within the region first and later more globally, but the essential point is that trade policy is the most important policy consideration in the pursuit of increased competitiveness in the Caribbean and lies at the fulcrum of the region's problems and challenges.

In the past, Caribbean countries hoped to establish global competitive industries through import substitution industrialisation. But internationally competitive, yet locally protected industries do not easily coexist. There is an argument over the success of import substitution, but however we interpret economic history, that path is no longer available given the realities of new trade rules that restrict special preferences and hefty public debt levels. Of course these realities do not stop protectionism being touted in the political hustings. As Adam Smith observed a couple hundred years ago, the voice and influence of existing, protected businesses, drowns out the disorganised voices of consumers and the putative voices of the yet to be developed businesses. The political economy of protectionism is not unique to the Caribbean, but it is more acute in small states where everyone personally knows the losers. The lack of fiscal space may be the best driver for getting out of this particular political-economy rut.

The "Luxury" of Limited Choice

While it may not be obvious, we believe that Caribbean policymakers have the luxury of limited choices that should guide the development path. Consider these four economic realities:

1. *Where overseas markets are large, and local markets small, there are few alternatives to an outward orientation, with export-driven growth and fading protectionism. Autarky does not work for small states.*[4]

2. *Where overseas markets are distant and countries are physically small and not well-endowed in energy and water, there is little alternative to the export of 'weightless' products.*

The best examples are professional services exported down a broadband connection. It is politically hard to accept but with the clear exception of Guyana, Suriname and Belize, Caribbean countries cannot easily out-compete the Australians or Brazilians in sugar or many other agricultural exports. While some of the more extreme members of the environmental lobby like the notion of getting back to nature, the Caribbean would be imprisoned in poverty if what it did was to weave baskets for cruise ship passengers or export sugar, bananas and coconuts.

That is not to say there is not potential for better integration between agriculture and the hotel sector regionally, or that there is not a role in small states high-value added 'bespoke' agricultural exports, where a substantial part of the value-added lies in the marketing and packaging. There is plenty of potential in the export of specialty rums, sugars, chocolates, coffees, rare meats or fish.[5] But it is to say that it is unlikely that income growth will be associated with a substantial increase in agricultural employment in the smaller water and energy-short states.

Similarly, Caribbean nations also cannot easily out-compete the Chinese and Indians in manufactures except with subsidised energy and capital, neither of which is sustainable. Caribbean countries cannot produce mobile phones for a few cents and cars for less than a thousand dollars. They can, however, provide a great place for professionals and artisans to live and work. A large proportion of professional services, such as legal, accounting, medical diagnostic, engineering, architectural, design, music production, editorial, and financial services can be digitised and exported down a broadband connection.

A business environment that fosters international professional services, especially those found in financial centres, will also significantly raise the sophistication and linkages of Caribbean exports.[6] But this is not about turning the Caribbean into cookie-cutter Caymans. Creative and Artisan services like high-value watch and jewellery repair, bespoke tailoring or intricate leather/metal craftsmanship are also relatively light per value and can be air-freighted around the world.

3. *Where capital is tightly held coupled with a plantation legacy, there is little alternative but to encourage existing "establishment" businesses to expand regionally and globally, creating economic and political space for entrepreneurs, micro-enterprises and workers co-operatives.*

   The legal arrangements that open overseas markets are already there within CARICOM and with the EU. The Caribbean must make haste to implement these agreements alongside efforts to widen the availability of finance to emerging business through, for example, secure transaction and factoring programmes.

4. *Where countries are physically small and tourism a large component of the economy, it is critical to invest in preserving and enriching the natural, built and social environment.*

   There is no space to waste in a small state. Tourism based islands disregard at their peril issues such as coastal management, water run-offs, waste management as well as social despair that can be a breeding ground for drugs, crime, corruption and general lawlessness.

There are not many viable alternative paths to the ones cited above: outward orientation; weightless exports such as professional and financial services; supporting entrepreneurship partly through wider access to capital; and paths that intertwine economic, social and environmental goals. This does not need to be an expensive agenda or imply 'big government.' What it absolutely must be is an activist agenda in certain critical areas.

Political Economy

The catalyst for change in the Caribbean will not emerge from another discussion of what Caribbean countries should do. Peer on the desks of permanent secretaries and you will find stacks of yellowing consultancy reports. The real question is not the 'what' but the 'why'. Why, in spite of knowing all that we do, change has not materialised? There are physical and financial constraints and implementation deficiencies. But the overriding constraints are matters of political economy.

As mentioned earlier, the economic and political structures are almost inextricably linked. An inefficient public sector benefits the 'insiders'– those middle and upper classes with connections – versus the 'outsiders.'[7] These powerful forces against change are not unique to the Caribbean but they are more entrenched in small or developing states where the middle and upper classes can have a distinctly different existence than others. There are two distinct Kingstons in one physical place. The political economy constraint to the governance and modernisation of small states is perhaps the single most important argument for greater regionalism.

If the 'what' ignores the political economy context; initiatives are likely to become subsumed by the forces of stagnation. Today's new institutions and new investments are destined to become tomorrow's new obstacles. The creation of 'tourism development investment funds.' originally designed as an agent of modernisation, now combine with other incentives to become the subsidy that enables unprofitable and inefficient businesses to cling to positions on precious beach lands thereby impeding development of the industry. With a few exceptions that prove the rule, The University of the West Indies, a beneficiary of substantial Government grants, is no longer a regular source of rich domestic policy analysis, radical reform or internationally renowned research expertise. In some areas it can be a reactionary agent to reform.[8]

In contemplating enduring, sustainable change we need to prioritise those changes that have the potential for disruption, not in a wilful sense, but as a source of innovation. Too many of the existing instruments and strategies – grand construction projects, new University centres and buildings and renewable energy projects with strategic business partners – necessarily favour and reinforce the established order. This means thinking as much about incentives as institutions. It means focusing as much on enabling outcomes that cannot be predicted as easily as betting on single, big, prescriptive, solutions. The critical instruments of disruptive change are technology, finance, business-facilitation and competition.

Critical strategies for Governments include an aggressive stance towards: (a) exploiting technology, (b) nudging new organisations of capital – without providing capital, (c) re-organising the delivery of public services so as to place the citizen-consumer at the centre of decisions on allocation and, (d) taking a more aggressive stance to regional trade and national competition policy. These ideas are often glibly expressed, but seldom translated into practical policy strategy. Therefore in the next Section we will describe what it means and how to do it.

Agents of Disruptive Change
An Aggressive Technology & Research Policy

Large developed countries can afford to allow the market to set the pace of technological change within their countries. Small states do not have this luxury. Without the benefit of economies of scale, technology is often a critical ingredient in remaining competitive.

Where local markets are small and overseas markets are distant, broadband connectivity is as essential to economic development as roads, airports and electricity. In today's world it is a primary factor of development. While we may be reaching diminishing returns from investments in more airports, we are merely at the foothills of the scalable opportunities to be had from increasing access to broadband. Industry incumbents will resist a restructuring of the industry and in small economies their influence through employment and cash flows is considerable. If Caribbean countries are to be successful in the modern age, Government needs to take a proactive stance in the development and promotion of broader, cheaper access to information communication technology (ICT).

Additionally, research into technological innovations should be fostered. The region boasts a long and proud history in the area of regional agricultural research. In the English-speaking Caribbean regional research programmes in soils, banana and cocoa began in 1946/47 at the Imperial College of Tropical Agriculture (ICTA) and by 1960 when the ICTA was merged with the then University College of the West Indies to become the Regional Research Centre (RRC), there were world-renown programmes of research in tropical plant breeding and herbicides. The RRC's heyday was in the 1960s with pioneering work done on pigeon peas and root crops and its research on pest, disease and weed management was internationally highly regarded.

From the 1970s, when other countries and regions were stepping up their efforts in agricultural research, funding in the region became scarcer. The emphasis, as was fashionable at the time, switched from research to 'out-reach' to Government and farmers. Regional research efforts diminished as a driver of innovation and around the same time we witnessed a decline in competitiveness of the region's agricultural products, such as sugar, rice, cocoa, and tropical fruits. Strengthening research and development (R&D) capacity at research institutes and University departments, through research grants, is a critical component in maintaining and deepening competitiveness in these products. R&D is a network activity and is also strongly dependent on investment in ICT capacity.

ICT Infrastructure to Support Export Competitiveness

Local Entrepreneurism and Cost Reduction

Cheap, high bandwidth is a prerequisite for exporting professional services to large, distant markets. Technology overcomes these physical obstacles. Countries that lie on the outskirts of poorly connected areas, in hard to reach regions, can, through broadband, be in the fast lane of the communications super highway. This enables and promotes weightless exports. But the bandwidth must be dependable and high, as that is what is required to download, for instance, the architectural drawings of a hotel, a series of detailed medical scans, tradable financial data, or support high-definition video conference calls. Dial-up can't do it.

Simply being on the communication super highway can also introduce competition into local markets by plugging local consumers into global markets. The local customs office can offer a 'plug-in' to on-line retailers that would allow goods to be taxed on line and so labelled that they can be delivered directly to purchasers thereby eliminating the need to be processed by an already congested customs authority. Land-locked Hungary is an example of a country that, through investments in ICT, has positioned itself at the virtual heart of Europe while remaining geographically on its edge.

E-Government...Again

Technology potentially cuts the distance between citizens and Government. It can dramatically improve how Government serves its citizens in a myriad of ways but most obviously through the licensing and regulatory process. There is no reason why many renewals of licenses and approvals, where the original documentation has already been received, validated and electronically filed, cannot be processed online at 'mygovernment.co.xx.'

While the marginal costs of such services are low, users would be prepared to pay surcharges for the convenience and cost savings of not having to spend time queuing in poorly ventilated government offices. These surcharges could be used to fund both the initial expenditure on e-government as well as a gradual restructuring of public sector employment away from such activities through retraining for other employment or even to pay for attractive redundancy arrangements. Technology can also be used to improve customs logistics and clearing – a key constraint to trade in the wider Caribbean.

The economics of ICT – high fixed costs and low variable costs – lends itself to a 'natural' monopoly. In small states in general and the Caribbean in particular, ICT is often left to a sleepy private sector monopoly for residential fixed-lines and duopolies for mobile and business telephony. Unsurprisingly, this has failed to deliver cheap broadband or promote innovation as compared to the services available in larger or developed markets.

Some maintain that Caribbean markets are too small to sustain a competitive market. However, following liberalisation, Denmark, one of the smallest European countries, with a population similar to the English-speaking Caribbean, now has some 62 different telecom providers proving that geographical size is less of a constraint on competition than often thought. Given the importance of ICT infrastructure there is also scope for some 'pump priming' investments ahead of market development.

Technology Policy.

Apart from the political economy challenges, there are a number of technical ways in which ICT infrastructure can be promoted. Much turns on the commercial viability of a particular market and Governments will have to experiment a little before they find the optimal solution for their circumstances. Where existing arrangements with incumbents impede change Governments could focus instead on new technologies and generations of connectivity such as 3G, 4G and WIMAX.

Offering a degree of free 3G connectivity to the public could be made a condition precedent to being awarded any new 3G or 4G licence. The amount of 'useful' connectivity will change over time. It is critical that governments avoid arrangements with pre-determined technology platforms and firms. Effective regulation, not necessarily controlling ownership, is a minimum requirement. Alternatively, through an annual auction Government can buy a certain amount of free broadband access for any company registered in the country and any citizen, funded either through the proceeds of the sale of licenses or by taxes and charges on service providers. Such an initiative would lead to enormous, positive, disruptive power at a small and falling cost.

Governments could effectively sponsor whole islands (Barbados, Antigua, Aruba) or cities (Kingston, Port of Spain, Georgetown) becoming wireless (or WIMAX) zones, free below a level of bandwidth that would be sufficient for a start up business or for the marketing of local businesses. Nothing would change the business brands of Caribbean islands as much than if businessmen and women on a visit for vacation or work were to discover that as they leave the plane, there is free, island-wide, broadband.

Of course a key constraint for many Caribbean states is their small size and distance. In this regard, there is significant scope for a regional approach to the provision of the hardware connectivity. There are already advances in this area, most notably the Eastern Caribbean Fibre Optic System (ECFS) which was launched as early as 1995, connecting all of the eastern Caribbean. It is owned by France Telecom, Cable & Wireless and AT&T.

Placing the consumer at the heart of decisions on the delivery of public sector services, corporate regulation and trade and competition policy

Public Transport

The public sector in the Caribbean on average represents approximately 30 per cent of employment and GDP. Governments in the Caribbean as elsewhere use expenditure to maximise the power of patronage. But this also constrains consumer choice and production innovation as clearly shown in the public transport sector.

An inexpensive, dependable transport system has substantial positive economic, social and environmental externalities. Yet sitting alongside the heavily subsidised state bus companies (often with expensive, broken down buses parked up in bus depots in the centre of town, employing well-paid drivers to drive buses that are often empty) are profitable, private operators. The revealed preference is that it is an industry that can benefit from greater competitiveness. Governments can instead replace transport corporations with transport authorities that enforce service quality and quantity, health and safety regulations and auctions routes. Bidders could bid on the basis of the quality, frequency and fares they would offer on the basis of a lump sum subsidy for unpopular routes or perhaps a fee to the Government for ownership of popular routes. There would also need to be mechanisms for the operators developing new routes.

Developed countries have several ready-made templates that the region may consider. These borrowed templates may increase consumer surpluses and improve service quality as well as diversity. But these templates are also likely to reinforce the existing concentration of capital and face substantial opposition from public sector unions legitimately concerned that consumer surpluses are achieved at the expense of workers benefits and rights. If, however, Governments were to additionally provide long-term leasing arrangements to purchase buses for small driver-owned companies, it would serve to widen the spread of capital and business ownership, spread the example of entrepreneurism and facilitate the adjustment from public to private employment. And this model can be replicated for reform of other public sector activities including sanitation, highway maintenance and cleaning. It could provide a powerful opportunity for entrepreneurial empowerment through co-operative outsourcing.

Publicly Funded Education and Health with More Private Delivery

Caribbean governments spend substantial proportions of GDP on education and increasing proportions on health. In these areas strong private benefits exist. But the social externalities are also large though not uniform across all levels of education or health. There is scope for more precise targeting of public funds to improve outcomes. Today in the Caribbean, education and health services are supply driven by a state monopoly. In the case of education the state provides the buildings, teachers and curriculum. Being supply rather than demand driven has slowed innovation. Where it exists, innovation often serves the suppliers such as government departments and public sector workers rather than the users.

There is scope for Caribbean Governments to experiment, perhaps firstly through special social enterprise regimes, with private delivery of certain publicly funded education and health services to support innovation, diversity and quality. Removing the monopoly, while maintaining public funding for universal access, would allow the creation of a consumer-driven, competitive sector that could become an "exporter" and earner of foreign exchange revenues with the potential to grow beyond captured domestic markets.[9]

Education and health tourism are big business globally.[10] There is already a modest stream of parents in the Diaspora sending their children back to the Caribbean to be educated because they are concerned about indiscipline and discrimination at the schools in metropolitan centres. Already we see some regional investment in education tourism, most notably in Grenada, Antigua and Barbuda, and St Kitts and Nevis. However these schemes deliberately operate in separate regulatory regimes, thereby cutting off the potential benefits to local suppliers and consumers. Simply pulling down these regulatory walls would be a start.

The English-speaking Caribbean has the highest rates of tertiary emigration in the world with 70 per cent of graduates of The University of the West Indies going abroad to seek work. This loss of talent to the world is compounded by the fact that this education is largely funded by relatively poor taxpayers when compared to taxpayers in the importing countries. Tertiary emigration is not necessarily bad. Small states, with limited absorptive capacity, have to be in the business of exporting and importing talent. It is the financing of this export that is a problem, and yet it is one that is eminently solvable.

After a certain age, students could be granted an education account, funded by the Government, which could be spent on any approved education service. This amounts to a system of public funds providing private choice. The account could convert into a fixed-term loan if the user emigrates and leaves the local tax system. If loan repayments of educated emigrants were used to increase the size of education accounts (and expenditure) for those back home and emigration levels remained unchanged (because they reflected structural issues of economic size and opportunities). Governments could double initial education expenditures to a rank-busting 10 per cent of GDP without requiring any increase of actual Government expenditure.

Further, a mechanism where the used proportion of individual education accounts, convert into long-term, repayable loans with enforcement powers if citizens emigrate and become tax payers elsewhere, would have common elements across a number of countries. It would be wasteful, with diseconomies of small scale for each country, to develop a similar mechanism. National governments could subscribe to and pay for a regional not-for-profit service that achieves these goals.

A similar problem arises in many parts of the Caribbean where those who have worked and paid taxes abroad, return to the region to live out their lives close to their family and friends. In some countries this represents a new and increasing burden on health services. Opportunities exist for government funded health accounts that would be awarded to local taxpayers to be spent on medication and treatment for non-emergency, public health services. To encourage wise health choices, holders of these accounts could transfer part of an unused account into future years or to friends and family in need.

Unlike education, substantial private health markets already exist in the Caribbean as a result of the absence of the State and this would be a way of broadening access to this market, giving it the funding stability that could allow investments in service provision, quality of care, marketing and exports. Critically it would reduce pressure on the emergency services at public hospitals and provide resources for non-emergency care to those who cannot afford care any other way. The increased investments in medical services that this could trigger would make the islands even more attractive to those considering re-locating or just returning.[11]

Corporate Regulation: Taxes and Subsidies

Tax codes in the Caribbean are highly complex. There is much that can be done to simplify the tax code and in so doing narrowing and focusing incentives and making collection easier. There are a number of successful international examples and there are a few programmes already in existence to do this with the help of the Caribbean Regional Technical Assistance Centre (CARTAC). A simplification of the tax code will help to make incentives clearer and reduce instances where a number of tax incentives end up neutralising themselves while leaving the treasury bereft of revenues.

In the developed world, tax policy is used as an active tool of social, economic policy and environment policy. In developing countries in general and the Caribbean in particular, the use of tax as an environment or social policy is marginalised by the singled-minded focus on revenues. Taxes on new cars for example are not there to reduce congestion, but to raise revenues and so Governments sometimes turn a blind eye to the negative spill-overs of higher revenue initiatives. We will discuss the need to better align the tax and subsidy system with pressing environmental concerns, such as the use of polluting fuels, congestion, waste-management, coastal erosion and soil maintenance.

In the Caribbean, where land is generally in short supply and the environment fragile and crucial to tourism industries, shifting the incidence of taxes onto property and environmental taxes away from income taxes and import duties could incentivise efficient land use. This system also has the advantages of being easier to collect, harder to evade, and encompassing 'foreigners' in the jurisdiction. It would allow the region to become a low income and corporate tax regime. Of course, shifting the tax burden to the landed rich will not be politically easy.

Governments should be, as we have argued elsewhere, size-sensitive in creating regulatory regimes in ensure that the reporting and tax burdens fall least on those enterprises that have least impact on neighbours or the wider physical and social environment. This applies critically to tax rates and tax reporting and not just for corporate taxes, but also Value Added Tax (VAT) and other excise duties, fees and charges. There are already thresholds of income and/or employment below which there is no corporate tax or VAT payable and only modest reporting requirements in order to support emerging businesses. But these thresholds need to be raised further to limit the potential for young firms to be considered illegal and therefore unable to grow, without depriving the Treasury of significant tax revenues – something we will discuss in greater detail below.[12]

Size Intolerance: *De-Criminalising Entrepreneurship*

It is sometimes argued that where Governments are corrupt, taxpayers consider tax-raising as illegitimate and tax evasion is acceptable and endemic. Tax evasion is not about ingrained lawlessness. In these circumstances increasing the legitimacy of government is critical to reducing tax evasion. In similar vein, the plantation-legacy in the Caribbean has produced a workforce with a strong sense that the economic structure is illegitimate and with no appetite for working in large companies and a culture of distinct discomfort in providing service. This lack of enthusiasm is often incorrectly mistaken for a general unwillingness to work, a poor work ethic and various politically correct euphemisms for laziness. It is not.

Significant numbers of the population are sole traders in micro businesses. But these businesses are often not legal. The popular food stall illegally occupies its spot. The beauty salon in a converted room in the home does not have planning permission and is not VAT registered. This is largely a result of the high cost of doing business, where almost every transaction needs an expensive, busy lawyer to stamp it or a lengthy, seemingly ad hoc, approval process. But without legality there is no scope for these businesses to borrow to invest and expand or receive state support, tax credits or the like. The semi-legal status of these firms inhibits their expansion and allows for the frustration of their proprietors to fester. A vast amount of entrepreneurial economic activity in the Caribbean is being born and dies prematurely in this twilight zone.

Part of the obstacle is that the government regulatory regime is size intolerant. Local big businesses like it that way. They will argue that the same health and safety standards must apply whether a restaurant has one table or one hundred and this is true. But there is scope for the creation of regulatory fast track regimes for businesses with limited impact on others or thresholds that make micro businesses exempt from regulations and registrations where the risks the state is trying to manage are size-sensitive, allowing start ups to breathe a little and not making them stillborn. The one-on-one yoga class should not be required to submit to the same approval process as the gym with two dozen treadmills.

Where small businesses are operating outside the legal corporate structure, there are often very few assets available for security and so the risk premia they pay to borrow money or raise equity is punitive. Ownership of land and other assets is often not registered and to do so is an expensive and slow process. A programme of secured-transaction lending is required where assets are registered so that they may serve as collateral. This "property rights" agenda is far from new[13] but it is no less important for it. An added dimension in the Caribbean is that a protected legal profession obtains high, short-term, "rents" from hazy or absent property rights and this is the profession of choice for bright, middle-class, locals who, without access to capital have few other alternatives, creating a powerful incentive for the status quo.

The requirement for legal or similar representations and accounting rules must be narrowed and facilitated. I do not need a lawyer to set up and run a business in the United States or the United Kingdom so why should I need an expensive one to set up a micro-enterprise in a developing country? Online registrations and applications should be made possible. Again and again we return to this theme of high legal costs acting as a barrier to business. Ending professional monopolies in law will considerably reduce the cost of doing business in the Caribbean. A first step to breaking this monopoly is to expand the network of mutual recognition of lawyers from other jurisdictions for non-court practice. In the United Kingdom, a relatively large and competitive economy, where the gains to competitive reforms might be expected to be far more marginal, the ending of the legal profession's monopolies in 1985 on an range of activities including conveyancing, reduced the cost of transactions considerably and established a new and highly technically efficient 'conveyancing industry.'

In general, the Caribbean exhibits high barriers to business entry coupled with poor monitoring and ad hoc consequences for non-compliance. We need the exact opposite: appropriate regulations with easy application and light validation, fortified by strict monitoring and tough consequences for false or incorrect applications. We need to lower the gates but have stronger flood-lights to peer inside rather than erect high walls with dim lights shining on those who do manage to clamber over the top. In dealing with business, government must become more size-tolerant if it is to promote entrepreneurism. Given the concentration of capital and the feelings of illegitimacy towards legacy businesses, converting this entrepreneurial energy into legal activity is key for the private sector to develop, employment to grow, and most importantly, for business to be seen as a legitimate career.

Interventions to Support New Organisations of Capital

Banks are not a ready source of risk capital in the Caribbean or in other regions. In many countries in the region Governments have tried to make the public sector a source of risk capital but this is fraught with difficulty. Public sector risk-capital in the Caribbean is often administered by the national central bank, the main depository of financial expertise. But central banks are also, quite correctly, centres of risk-aversion and strict processes and so these facilities, which require bold and risky judgement, are often poorly utilised. Moreover, Government involvement in the allocation of risk capital makes the central bank vulnerable to the pressures of special pleading, vested interests and the commercial fashions of the day. Much can be done to deepen the financial sector and lower the cost of financial intermediation that is just shy of Government 'directed lending' and the litany of potential associated problems.

Governments should support the establishment of factoring agencies where invoices can be used as security for loans. It could kick start this process by offering to guarantee loans that are backed by a government contract and invoice. The cost of this measure would be minimal but its catalytic effect significant – especially where the Government in question has a procurement strategy supporting small businesses. In effect the government is taking on the risk that it will renege on its own contractual arrangements – a risk the Government should be far more willing to take on than anyone else.

Micro-leases and micro-insurance are another critical factor for micro-businesses to flourish. Governments could offer co-insurance of the risks of micro-leases and micro-insurance where there are tangible assets. In essence the government is taking on a risk that is directly correlated with the success of its own law enforcement.[14] We have already discussed the idea of Government offering leases to worker co-operatives or ownership teams to purchase vehicles to deliver public services. Where these are long-term public services, like sanitation, public transport, licensing authorities, airports, and the like, it seems appropriate for National Insurance Boards to become involved in backing some of these new businesses.

Another constraint to the deepening of the financial sector is the pursuit of narrow, national interests. There are limited cross-border mergers and acquisitions or even regional recognition of financial institutions. We need to establish, as a starting point, a regional protocol for the regulation of cross-border mergers and acquisition. An example of a regional protocol would be one where regional regulators agreed that the jurisdiction of the firm being acquired, or the smaller firm being merged, where shareholders are most vulnerable to abuse, would be the lead regulator of the transaction and all activities relating to the transaction. A regional stock market may also support the growth of a region-wide financial and capital market. This is an idea that is often booted around and it maybe that the region should first try for something less ambitious such as deepening the network of cross-listings. There could then be a race between stock markets to see who could become the place of primary listing as a result of its superior listing network, technology, cost-structure and credible regulation.

Trade and Competition Policy

In the first section we argued that trade policy is the most important policy consideration in the pursuit of increased competitiveness in the Caribbean and lies at the fulcrum of the region's problems and challenges. Consequently, we address trade policy on the economic realities, on the political economy constraints to reform and on regional initiatives. This section here merely serves to highlight some of the broader policy issues.

A cursory glance would suggest that the Caribbean's trade arrangements are clear and supportive. At the international level there are reciprocal agreements for deepening and widening market access that have asymmetrical timing arrangements, affording Caribbean producers a longer period of adjustment to imports but immediate access to large markets – the recent EPA being a case in point, as well as the soon to be negotiated FTA with Canada. At the regional level measures are being implemented toward a single Caribbean market in terms of free movement of capital and most recently in labour. CARICOM Member States have also made a commitment to the establishment of national competition authorities.

The problem is that the Caribbean has a long tradition of not implementing international trade agreements. The private sector appears at best unprepared and at worse disinterested in the hard fought concessions and appear unaware that they are only temporary. The CSME appears to be crumbling beneath the weight of political indifference. Despite all the noisy chatter about the high cost of living and price gouging by monopolistic retailers, competition authorities have yet to be established with the notable exception of Barbados.

We suggest that one way forward is for the CSME to be aggressively pursued. If free movement of labour is too much of a political hot potato in the current recessionary environment, that is not a sufficient reason to abandon the goal of free movement of capital and better regional dispersion of innovation and technology. Now is the time to pursue a regional M&A protocol and common arrangements that would facilitate the emergence of a regional stock market. Traditional trade theorists would argue that free movement of labour becomes less important where there is proper free movement of goods, capital and technology.

Governments need to implement the EPA and regional

companies need to exploit it, perhaps through greater marketing of its opportunities in the local and international press to engage the Caribbean and its Diaspora in the process. One important step in this direction is Caribbean Export.[15] More financial support is needed to strengthen the regional trade negotiating machinery and office. More investment in trade facilitation, such as overseas marketing campaigns, better information on accessing connected markets such as the Diaspora market is required. There may be little that is new in the trade facilitation and information agenda, but it remains an important area where the wider returns from investment remain high.

The Environment

A Balance Sheet Approach to Economic Policy

States with economies based around natural resources, such as Trinidad and Tobago, but also the tourism-based economies of the Caribbean need to adopt a stricter 'balance sheet approach' to economic progress rather than relying on traditional GDP or income and expenditure markers. Income derived from depleting a natural resource and then spent on temporary consumption shows up as development and GDP growth in an income–expenditure model. Yet in a real sense it represents an inflation of GDP. Countries that are growing at 2–3 per cent per year on the basis of exploiting resources in a non-renewable manner, and this can include beaches and reefs, are probably in reality shrinking. In a balance sheet model this kind of economic growth would be revealed as a deterioration of capital stock.

To move medium term economic strategies and policies towards spending out of income derived from permanent capital and reinvesting income derived from the depletion of natural resources to preserve, expand, and liquefy the capital stock, states need to design a national balance sheet. This balance sheet should assess all the natural, economic, financial, environmental, intellectual, and cultural assets against all the natural, social, economic, and demographic liabilities. Initially this will of necessity be a major, multi-disciplinary task but will only need a modest on-going investment. If successful it would change thinking towards how budgets raise the chances of a lasting prosperity rather than how they find income to spend regardless of the source of that income.

A National Economic Accounting Commission could be set up which would initially work on compiling a national balance sheet to be updated annually. It would be independent with Commissioners who are multi-disciplinary experts from the fields of auditing, environment sciences, economics, and law. The national balance sheet would serve as a touchstone in the crafting of all tax and expenditure policies. As a first step there would need to be an assessment of existing policies to ensure they are not effectively subsidising the consumption of non-renewable resources except on a temporary basis. The balance sheet approach would also encourage energy and resource conservation, though governments should be wary of putting too many eggs in one technology basket.

It would be vital to ensure that this approach was not abused by those accommodate bad financial policies on the grounds that it is supporting an intangible sense of worth. Much can be achieved in thinking of the national capital stock rather than just the flow of income without needing to rest all decisions on an assessment of intangibles. National assets need to be valued on a conservative assessment of the income they generate/save or have been shown that they can generate in a comparable situation.

Other Environmental Initiatives

One enabling approach to environmental conservation would be to adopt technical and fiscal steps to allow 'net metering' which allows consumers to earn from putting energy back into the grid as well as pay for taking it out. Governments could support electricity companies in making this offer by meeting part of the difference between the price for paying-in and the marginal cost of power generation. Net metering incentivises households and corporations alike to experiment with different technologies and methodologies. Germany showed that the problem of energy conservation is as much fiscal as technical, when for a brief period after net metering it became the largest user in the world of solar voltaic power. The process also created a lasting comparative advantage for Germany in alternative energy technologies.

International Financial Services Sector

International Financial Centres (IFCs) and the International Financial Crisis.

One of the responses to the Credit Crunch of 2007–09 was increased pressure from large countries, with large financial centres, on small countries, with international financial centres. These centres were characterised as tax and regulatory havens, detours designed to get round rules, sources of risk and generally uncooperative jurisdictions. The targets of these attacks were often large 'zero-tax-regimes' such as Liechtenstein and Switzerland. However the attack on international financial centres reverberates strongly throughout the Caribbean because it has the highest concentration of significant IFCs. Over the past 20 years, for many Caribbean countries, such as The Bahamas, Bermuda, the British Virgin Islands (BVI), the Cayman Islands and the Turks and Caicos Islands, international financial services represented the largest single source of GDP, tax revenues and employment. For others such as Anguilla, Barbados, and St Kitts and Nevis it represents the second, single, most important source of GDP, tax revenues and employment. On some measures the Caribbean is the fourth largest 'banking sector' in the world.

There is a strong historical context to these centres, many of which are British, French or Dutch overseas territories or and/or have long held preferential tax arrangements with Canada. The rise of financial sectors often mirrored the decline of the sugar industry in the 1980s and 1990s. The development of tourism and financial services in the Caribbean as an alternative to sugar, bananas and other agricultural products threatened by Latin American competition was not challenged as a development strategy for the region by the multilateral development institutions.

The Economic Role and Rationale of Caribbean IFCs

The Caribbean should defend and develop their international financial centres for a number of reasons, not least because this makes strong economic sense.[16] In the first section we argued that small and distant states should be exporting weightless professional services. The most high-valued added 'weightless' professional services are those that surround financial centres: asset managers, family offices, lawyers, accountants, asset-valuers, risk managers, financial educators and software developers. Finance can be scaled up without extra land and labour. The amount of labour and land required to manage USD$1 billion along a particular investment strategy is almost identical to the amount required to manage USD$100 billion along the same strategy, yet investment fees are not discounted for large size, indeed, they are often higher the more popular the fund is.

The same cannot be said for agriculture, manufacturing or many of the labour intensive professional services like medical diagnostics or architecture. This unusually flat supply curve of the finance industry makes it perfect for small states and, with their small public expenditures in absolute terms, allows them to charge low marginal tax rates for financial business without these taxes representing an effective subsidy.

It also makes economic sense, seemingly perversely, for large economies to let international finance migrate to specialist small states. A large financial sector has a similar effect to the Dutch disease.[17] It bids away talent from other sectors and pushes up wages across the economy to levels in which few remain internationally competitive. A large financial sector is more able to capture regulators and policy makers, to persuade Governments of the need for bank bail-outs, and for preferences or concessions. In short, a large financial sector distorts the real economy. It is therefore better located exported from places around the world where there is less 'real economy' to be distorted with the importers applying strict regulation on its consumption by vulnerable consumers or where there are systemic risk implications.

The Challenge to Caribbean IFCs

Large financial centres in large states exist today and are the source of much employment, revenues and patronage. They are not going to roll over and die. The path of international financial centres will be determined more by international politics than international economics. Blaming 'foreigners' for taking 'our' jobs or taxes always makes for good national politics. Large states will argue that IFCs beggar thy neighbours with permissive tax rates and regulation. They demand that small states harmonise tax and regulation in a way that will squeeze the breath out of them.

The attacks on IFCs are not without any justification. Some

jurisdictions are indeed more co-operative than others. But in general, these attacks amount to a non-tariff barrier against competition from small states. Evidence for this comes from the observation that the attacks are discriminatory. The largest "tax havens" such as Delaware, Nevada and Wyoming are quietly left alone. The attacks on small states ignore the use of subsidies by large states across a range of sectors that cannot be matched by small states, such as State support to the car industry.[18] Of course, these attacks are disproportionately harsh on small state IFCs given the relative lack of regulatory failure in these states. It is also a serious lapse of natural justice when conclaves of large countries, be it the G20 or OECD, appoint themselves as both judge and jury on the activities of non-members, and proceed to apply strictures to those while simultaneously resisting broad application of the same rules to themselves.

There is on the other hand, no escaping that the drivers of international financial centres 20 years ago were competitive taxes and regulation – in the same way that the UK's City of London captured the Eurobond market from New York through low taxes 40 years ago and the hedge fund and private equity market 10 years ago. (Let it not be forgotten, 'light touch regulation' was London's boast for over 10 years). Whether the attacks on IFCs are justified or not, they have been made, and will continue to be made, given the fiscal challenges in developed countries. The *realpolitik* is that low taxes and light regulation can no longer be the basis for growth or even survival of IFCs.

Critical drivers of IFCs going forward will be quality of regulation and people. To argue that quality of regulation and people will be key going forward, is like arguing for peace and love. No one will object, but the reality is more complex. The large centres will argue that the IFCs must meet their standards, notwithstanding the previous, monumental failure of these standards. This does not seem so unreasonable but the critical factor that militates against the incorporation of these standards is that they are not risk or size tolerant.

Jurisdictions where the likelihood of money laundering, for example, is slight, because of exchange controls or illiquidity, are already required to invest heavily in anti-money laundering (AML) institutions, staff and training to earn a tick in the box, without which, their banks would not have correspondent arrangements with those abroad and trade finance would be virtually impossible. The threats to support non-compliance are meaningful. There are benefits to all to eliminate money laundering from illegal activities and this is not an argument for not making efforts to do so everywhere, but we must not ignore the fact that the largest occurrences of money laundering that have been uncovered have been through the large metropolitan centres and not small state IFCs. Yet it is small state IFCs that are required to make the largest proportional investment in AML. Through these non-tariff barriers the size advantage offered by finance's scalability is neutered by the disproportionate cost small states have to pay to match the regulatory standards required by large states.

In the year before the financial crisis, the UK's Financial Services Authority (FSA) spent US$2 billion on financial regulation annually and employed over 2000 people – all to little avail, given that at one moment in 2008 the entire banking system was effectively Government guaranteed. Substantial expenditure and ticked boxes do not guarantee effective regulation, but it does represent an effective barrier to entry for small, developing countries.

The path currently being offered to small state IFCs is not a viable path. Even if an IFC had the resources to spend on the regulation of risks they are not vulnerable to, trying to imitate developed centres will always make them second best or worse in a world where customers have the ability and technology to access the best. In response to this, some Caribbean IFCs at the 2010 EU/Cariforum meeting in Antigua suggested they may have to operate, explicitly, outside the international regulatory system. This is not a viable course of action either. It most certainly does not afford any room for growth in the new world environment. But these countries need a real alternative.

A Viable Growth Strategy for Caribbean IFCs

The only viable strategy for small state IFCs is a niche strategy. IFCs should identify sectors where there is a clear and credible advantage and focus on being world class in those niches. There are more opportunities in this space for the bold than might be imagined. While trading operations of investment banks need to be located next door to the trading operations of their competitors (so they can trade staff and share technologies and practices) and as a result, are concentrated in a few financial centres in the world: New York, London and Singapore, the location of asset management firms is driven by their most important asset, their employees, and their lifestyle location choices.

It is why asset management in the US, for instance, which used to be concentrated in Manhattan, Boston, and Chicago, has now branched out to Denver, Colorado; Newport Beach, California; and Fort Lauderdale, Florida. It is why asset management is often in the 'second' less crowded, more 'liveable' city of many countries such as Edinburgh in the UK, Munich in Germany, Geneva in Switzerland and Melbourne in Australia. Arguably, many Caribbean countries could be a destination of choice for asset managers if they had appropriate regulation, especially those that as a result of tourism have extensive air connections to key markets and good broadband connectivity. The revealed preference is that many wealthy private investors already physically manage their funds from their second homes in the Caribbean.

There are important opportunities in regulatory fields as well. The primary purpose of financial regulation is to avoid systemic risk and to protect vulnerable consumers. However, in an attempt to limit regulatory arbitrage within large and complex financial systems or because regulators have been given many, legitimate, but not strictly financial-risk objectives, many of the activities which do not pose systemic or consumer risks are inappropriately regulated in the large centres.

IFCs can identify these areas and offer specialist regulation that is neither light nor heavy, but right-sized for the systemic risks involved in that activity. Bermuda is in effectively trying to do just that and is a leading innovator in the world of captive insurance. The Cayman Islands, with stiff competition from Hong Kong, is trying to be the world-class specialist regulator of hedge funds. Barbados could be a specialist regulator of wealth management by Family Offices. Trinidad and Tobago could be a world-class specialist regulator of energy investment funds since risks in the energy-related sectors are sufficiently different to warrant a different kind of risk management than provided by traditional funds. To get this right, IFCs will have to take regulation so seriously that they are not in the game of imitation, but in the game of innovation. This will require investment, especially in the field of people.

International Institute of Risk and Regulation

If the region is going to be a leader in some aspects of financial regulation it will need training capacity in financial risk that is world class; training people to a recognised standard of excellence and also being recognised as having internationally renowned thinking that can help governments and regulators articulate and advocate their specialised regulatory regimes to the Financial Stability Board, Basle Committee, International Organizations of Securities Commissions (IOSCO) and other international regulatory bodies. Bringing in senior figures from large centres looking for their retirement job after being passed over for the top job at home, is unlikely to make the region an innovator in regulation.

The training of local people will also play a critical role in deepening the developmental impact of the international financial sectors. Today, the national impact of these sectors is far more in terms of tax revenues and the services that come from servicing these businesses and their expatriate employees, than in terms of creating career-advancing opportunities for a great many local citizens. Compare that with countries such as Singapore, Hong Kong and Mumbai where locals run the subsidiaries of international firms and go on to have senior management jobs at head office.

Clearly such a research, innovation, education and training initiative, especially if it is on a scale that makes it world-class, would be best done by a regional institution. While The University of the West Indies (UWI) should therefore be the first consideration, the practitioner orientation of the work to be done, and the international credibility and standards required in a field in which the University currently has little standing, suggests that a range of options should be considered including a separate institute perhaps in a collaborative relationship with UWI or the Caribbean Centre for Money and Finance which also has a connection to UWI. After some initial help to establish itself and its reputation, such an institute is likely to quickly move to being self-financing as regulators and the industry have serious commitments to training with attendant budgets.

Regionalism and IFCs

While the training can be regional the regulation of the IFCs should not be. Each nation will be competing against others to be the best location for certain niche businesses. A regional body would only make sense if one standard set of rules are to be applied to all sectors and the enforcement costs were spread proportionately across the region. This is exactly what the large competitors want the Caribbean region to do. They feel it is a game at which they can beat the developing state IFCs given their superior ability to throw money at enforcement.

But, as we have discussed above, a successful future of IFCs in the Caribbean is as specialist regulators, where rules will be different than elsewhere in certain activities. It makes no sense for Bermuda, for instance, with a global reputation in insurance regulation that attracts international insurance business, to tie itself to a regulatory-setting body outside of Bermuda with constituents in countries that have an inferior reputation and perhaps understanding of and exposure to that industry. The same applies to the Cayman Islands' hedge fund industry.

Moreover, the governance and funding of a regional super regulator would be fraught with difficulties, in large part fuelled by important national disparities. The investment that Cayman's and Bermuda will be willing to make to the regulation of international finance given the importance of this sector to their economy, will be vastly different from what Jamaica, Trinidad and Tobago, Guyana and others will be prepared to make for a sector that is quite marginal to them.

The subsidiary of the regulation of IFCs makes sense. This is quite a different story from the regulation of domestic financial sectors and institutions with cross-border exposures and regional activities. In that space, where there are international norms and the scope for international competition in the regulation of domestic finance is less fierce, a regional regulatory body, over and above greater regional information sharing, is a worthwhile consideration.

Regionalism

There is much that Caribbean countries can do at a national level to boost competitiveness and small countries must strive for global competitiveness and the implementation of international trade agreements. Is there much role then for regional initiatives? There would appear from the foregoing discussion that there are five important areas in which regional initiatives are sought: (1) improving global competitiveness by aggressively pursuing regional competitiveness; (2) raising the quality and impartiality of governance; (3) integrating transport and other communication infrastructure; (4) convergence of the regulation of domestic and regional finance; and (5) developing regional centres of excellence in research and innovation in finance, agriculture and other areas. We have already discussed some of these and will try to limit the overlap between this section and previous sections.

The Regional Market

The way to make regional firms more competitive is not to protect them more, but to expose them more. It is possible that sudden exposure to the cold winds of global competition might do more harm than good. But the experience of trying to open the door gradually, has only served to keep it shut; temporary mitigations easily become lengthy procrastinations. An important way of sequencing greater competitiveness then, could be the gradual opening up to global competition – as negotiated under the EPA and the aggressive opening to regional competition,[19] in accordance with the Revised Treaty of Chaguaramas. It is true that not all countries will be equally aggressive in opening up to regional competition but the trade theorists would point out that the benefits to trade do not require your trading partners to be as open as you.

This is easier to say than to do. We are essentially calling for regional leaders to do what they have already agreed to do, but which, for reasons of national politics, has not happened.[20] This is not a uniquely Caribbean problem. The experience of European integration was that the enforcement of competition rules regionally could not be left only to national states. The EU achieved its goals through the full might of the European Commission's enforcement powers. The Caribbean needs the equivalent of activist Commissioners like Mario Monti and Karel Von Miert sitting in a regional Competition Authority with real teeth to enforce CARICOM treaty obligations. An effective regional Competition must be backed by legal regulations and wide enforcement powers, including fines for the most serious competition infringements. They must also be give powers to be proactive in shaping future competition policy – particularly with regard to cartels.

The sharpest teeth would be new powers to fine companies for non-compliance or attempt to distort or unfairly dominate national or regional markets. Establishing such an authority, with the requisite resources to be credible, and to attract the appropriate staff, would be easier if its initial funding was not part of the debate. This would be a more effective way of spending some of the funds allocated to improving the region's competitiveness than subsidizing inherently uncompetitive businesses.

Small states have to be in the business of importing and exporting people, experiences and skills. Of course, free movement of peoples, even within the Caribbean, remains a politically sensitive subject as it is in other regions in the world. But, as we discussed above, competitiveness will be well served if CARICOM fell short of free movement of people but achieved the free movement of goods and capital. In the case of capital, there is scope for a number of regional initiatives such as a regional stock market[21] and a regionally agreed protocol on the rules and regulations that would apply to cross border mergers and acquisitions and investing.

The Quality and Impartiality of Governance

A second important area in which regional initiatives can spur competition is in the general area of governance. In small states, like small villages, it is hard to find un-conflicted individuals. Everyone is related or connected. This undermines the perception of impartiality and predictability, and too frequently the reality of independent legal systems and confidence in impartial government permitting, licensing and planning systems.[22] This is a major inhibitor to investment and entrepreneurship. Regional co-operation through, for example, the regular swapping of senior judges and chief planners could play an important role at making the regulatory landscape more predictable and less vulnerable to partiality and, as a result, more welcoming to new business.

A true test of economic enfranchisement will be when an ordinary girl or boy from a disadvantaged background, with a brilliant new idea, could make it happen in the Caribbean and is not stymied by a closed network of Government regulations, banks, lawyers and competitors.

The Organisation of Eastern Caribbean States (OECS) have a successful programme of swapping Supreme Court judges between the nine member states and have as a result attained a level of confidence in the quality of justice legal system that exceeds what might be expected given the small size of the islands.

Communication Infrastructure

A third area for regional co-operation to deepen competitiveness is in the field of communications infrastructure, where the pooling of costs and the integration of plans could significantly help reduce the cost of doing business in the region.

The cost of transporting goods and people across the Caribbean is high, in some cases twice or three times as high as elsewhere.[23] Regional airlines have struggled to turn a commercial profit and as a result, are often starved of the investment they need to become more commercial. There are opportunities for reducing these costs through pooled investments in air and other transport solutions, but invariably the investment costs are not closely mapped onto the beneficiaries, limiting willingness to act. In a vicious cycle, small, fragile transport markets have led to state support or ownership of regional airlines that over the years have not proven conducive to investment in service innovation, further limiting market development.

Technology advances now make a high-speed ferry connection a practical option for a number of small states along the chain, but it remains too expensive for any individual country to make this investment on its own. Moreover, countries invested in the regional airlines are hesitant to fast-track this or other alternative transport projects that may undermine the fragile air transport market by fragmenting an already small market.

The physical infrastructure of a gas pipeline from Trinidad to Barbados would be prohibitively expensive, but would make economic sense if the cost was spread across a number of larger islands up the island chain, most notably, Martinique and Guadeloupe. The pipeline could also be used as a piggyback for other physical connections such as fibre optic cables. This is currently primarily a private sector initiative that is struggling with a number of public sector issues such as convincing consuming countries of the security of supply and negotiating these issues across a number of public owned utility companies. A more regional component to the governance and financing of the project may assist its progress and may be better aligned to the regional benefits.

The completion of the Takutu River Bridge, upgrading of the Lethem road connecting northern Brazil to Guyana to an all-weather surface, and the development of a deep water port near Georgetown, could be catalytic in opening up the Latin American market to the Caribbean region as a whole and reducing the cost of imports. The northern region of Brazil is the fastest growing region and the Guyanese coast is considerably closer than the Brazilian ports. The benefits to the wider regions being connected are far in excess of the narrow benefits to either Guyana or northern Brazil alone and so the risk is that there is underinvestment in this project.

The multilateral organisations are familiar with this selection of regional transport infrastructure issues. The purpose of this selection is to highlight the scope for regional integration of infrastructure plans and the need for an entity to take a regional approach to the benefits of these complex projects rather than a narrow national approach. The biggest obstacles are often not finance, but the size of social externalities and the miss-match between those benefitting and those directly footing the bill.

The fourth potential area for regional co-operation is in the regulation of domestic banking (as opposed to international financial centres). This has been discussed earlier and in particular, the necessity for regional protocols on cross-border activity. There is less scope for regional integration of the regulation of international financial centres and given that it is hard to fully separate the international from domestic financial sectors it maybe that this acts as a drag on the regional integration of domestic finance.

Regional Centres of Excellence in Research and Innovation

The fifth potential area for a regional initiative is in the area of research. We discussed earlier the importance of technology in general, and communications technology in particular, for small states often too distant from markets to be competitive. But technology in a wider sense is a key competitiveness factor. The decline of agriculture in the Caribbean was mirrored by a decline in its eminence in tropical agricultural research. Research that can spur innovation in the fields of tropical agriculture, tourism and financial services is a critical component to remaining competitive in these critical sectors.

Such research is a public good and is best carried out at a regional level and disseminated broadly across the region.[24] Instinct suggests this be housed at the regional university, UWI. But competitiveness is probably not best served by monopolies, even of the research kind. The University has a number of objectives including teaching and responding to demands from Government and other stakeholders and so occasionally it is wiser to establish these specialised research institutes independently.

It would be important to tender regional research grants in such a way that UWI and other research providers could compete. UWI is also not well served by being the repository for all (or most) research requests in the region, as being so does not allow it to develop its own focus, strategy and to build international centres of excellence. Research and education are major "industries" which can be successfully attracted to the Caribbean as St George's University in Grenada has proved. Using research grants to sharpen the competitiveness of regional research institutes and raise their international reputation for quality can serve multiple purposes.

Conclusion

The real issue is not 'what' the Caribbean should do. The economic realities leave little choice. Where overseas markets are large and local markets small, there are few alternatives to an outward orientation and a focus on services with specialty agriculture and manufactures. Where overseas markets are distant, there is little alternative to exporting 'weightless' products like professional services, like financial and creative services, or specialty products where a large proportion of the value is in the marketing and design. Where capital is tightly held and there is a plantation legacy, there is little alternative but to encourage existing businesses to expand regionally and globally, creating economic and political space to improve competitiveness at home by facilitating entrepreneurship and widening the route to capital. Where countries are physically small, it is critical to invest in preserving and enriching the natural, built and social environment.

The debate is how to enable change in this direction, because the region is showing dangerous signs of sinking under the weight of excessive introspection. The Caribbean is not globally competitive but dependent. The cost of living is high, and ratcheted up by inefficient ports, monopolistic transport markets, high fees and taxes. The appearance of 'openness' hides protectionism. Stock markets and capital markets are moribund and the recession has led to substantial crowding out of private investment.

Now that the rest of the emerging world has shaken off excessive political uncertainty and excessive liberalism, the much-vaunted stability of the Caribbean is seen as more handicap than asset. The evil twin of strong social partnerships is strong anti-growth coalitions of business, unions and government. Growth has been on a downward trajectory for over 20 years. This acts to reinforce the downtrend as the talented and bold move away to other places. Tertiary emigration rates are some of the highest in the world.

Things are the way they are because they suit enough people with enough influence. Exhortations for change and new consulting reports will be warmly received and quickly ignored. In contemplating lasting change we need to consider strategies and instruments of change that propagate change, and are 'disruptive' of existing structures, not in the sense of revolution, but creating sources of unpredictable innovation that throws up new players, new products and new opportunities. This means thinking as much about incentives as institutions and the enabling environment, not a prescriptive one.

Critical instruments of disruptive change are technology, finance, the organisation of government services and competition. Critical strategies for Governments include an aggressive stance towards regional competition, the national exploitation of technology, nudging new organisations of capital – without providing that capital – and developing new organisations of delivering public services that allows for greater competition in the delivery and more choice for the citizen. There are plenty reasons to be pessimistic, but there are also plenty reasons to be optimistic: the region boasts tremendous resilience and creativity and being small states, the scope for making impactful changes in a relatively short space of time is greater than in many large states.

Notes

* Contributed by Avinash Persaud.
* * Special thanks to Kwesi Dennis of Trinidad & Tobago, for research assistance.
1. Sir Vidya Naipaul, Derek Walcott and Sir Arthur Lewis.
2. See Regional Economic Outlook, Western Hemisphere, October 2010, IMF.
3. According to the report *Crime, Violence and Development: Trends, costs and Policy Options in the Caribbean,* murder rates in the Caribbean are higher than in any other region of the world at around 30 per 100,000 population annually.
4. See, Briguglio, Lino, Bishnodat Persaud, and Richard Stern, April 2000. *Toward an outward-orientated development strategy for small states: Issues, Opportunities, and resilience building: A review of the small states agenda proposed in the Commonwealth/*World Bank Joint Task Force Report, 2000.
5. See, Persaud, B., *Agricultural problems of small states, with special reference to Commonwealth Caribbean countries,* 1988, Agricultural Administration and Extension, Volume 29, Issue 1.
6. See, *The Product Space Conditions the Development of Nations,* C.A. Hidalgo, B. Klinger, A.L. Barabasi, R. Hausmann, *Science,* 27 July 2007, Vol. 317. No. 5837, 482–87.
7. See Horst Feldmann, 2008. 'Business regulation and labour market performance around the world', *Journal of Regulatory Economics,* Spring, vol. 33(2), 201–35, April.
8. See, Girvan, Norman, 2008, 'Cariforum-European Commission Economic Partnership Agreement: The Lessons Learned', in Winston Dookeran and Akhil Malaki (eds.) *Leadership and Governance in Small States: Getting Development Right.* Saarbrücken, Germany: 61–79.
9. See, Cable, Vincent and B. Persaud, 1987, *Developing with Foreign Investment* (Routledge).
10. See, *Health Tourism in Australia: Supply, Demand and opportunities,* C. Voigt et al.
11. See Bernal, Richard, 2007, *The globalization of the health care industry: Opportunities for the Caribbean,* CEPAL Review, 92.
12. See, Winters, A. and P. Martins. *Beautiful But Costly: Business Costs in Small Remote Economies.* Economic Paper 67. (London: Commonwealth Secretariat) 2005.

13. See, Frédéric Bastiat, 1850. *Economic Harmonies*. W. Hayden Boyers, trans.; George B. de Huszar, ed. Liberty Fund; Hernando De Soto, 1989. *The Other Path*. Harper & Row; Hernando De Soto and Francis Cheneval, 2006. *Realizing Property Rights*. Ruffer & Rub.

14. This is especially the case in small, remote, locations where effective law enforcement can be more successful. See, David, King, 2001, 'Nowhere to run; Theft of motorcycles in a remote island location.' *Caribbean Journal of Criminology and Social Policy*.

15. See 'Time is short for breathing life into the EPA', David Jessop, *Starbroek News*, November 28, 2010.

16. See DeLisle Worrell: 'The initiative of the Financial Stability Board on "non- cooperative jurisdictions" from a Caribbean perspective' and Avinash Persaud, 'Look for onshore not off-shore scapegoats,' The *Financial Times*, March 2009.

17. The Dutch Disease is an idea which links the effect of financial and goods markets of a natural resource and the decline in the rest of the economy, see 'The Dutch Disease'. The *Economist*, November 26, 1977, 82–83.

18. See, Persaud, B. (2002). 'The OECD Harmful Tax Competition Policy: A Major Issue for Small States, in International Tax Competition' (ed) Biswas, R. London: Commonwealth Secretariat.

19. See, Dookeran, Winston, 1998, *The Caribbean Quest: Directions for Structural Reform in a Global Economy* 1998 (co-editor), Stockholm University.

20. See Bernal, Richard, 2005, 'Nano-firms, Regional Integration and International Competitiveness: The Experience and Dilemma of CSME', in Denis Benn amd Kenneth Hall, eds, *Production Integration in CARICOM: From Theory to Action* (Kingston: Ian Randle Publishers) 2006.

21. A regional stock exchange was suggested by Prime Minister Michael Manley in 1989 but to date has not been established. See Dennise Williams, 'Caribbean stock exchange a pipe dream' - *Carib expert*, *Financial Gleaner*, February 3, 2006.

22. Conflicts of interest are not the only challenges of Governance in small states. For a fuller discussion, see, Dookeran, Winston, 200x, *Leadership and Governance in Small States. Getting Development Right*, Co-edited with Akhil Malaki.

23. The cost of freighting goods to the US from Guyana is 12.4% of the value of the exports compared with 4.4% for the far more distant East Asia. Despite being physically very close, the cost of freight to the US from Jamaica is 5.9%, and despite extensive shipping routes between

the US and Trinidad & Tobago as a result of Trinidad providing 75% of US, LNG imports, the cost of freighting goods to the US from Trinidad & Tobago is still higher than from East Asia at 5.4%. Source: *The Age of Productivity, Transforming Economies from the bottom up*, IDB, 2009.

24. See, Philip Cooke. *Regional Innovation Systems, Clusters and the Knowledge Economy*. Centre for Advanced Studies, University of Wales. Cardiff: University of Wales, 2001.

EPILOGUE
A New Leadership Challenge[1]

Getting the Politics of Development Right

Introduction

Getting the Politics of Development Right requires solving the alignment gap between the logic of politics and the logic of economics. International, regional and local politics may well be the most significant obstacles to development. It would appear to be also the biggest hurdle in finding solutions to the current global crisis. Getting the Politics of Development right requires cooperation and coordination of priorities, policies and action at all levels.

A new leadership with a global mindset must engage the various communities of interests to find more durable solutions in a volatile global environment. This new international leadership must find the right mix of power, politics and economics to achieve the necessary performance level for sustainable regional and global economic growth and ultimately development benefitting the citizens of all nations.

Dimensions of the Global Financial Crisis

Let us start by giving a brief synopsis of the events that we are facing globally since 2008. In the first instance the so-called financial crisis surfaced in the private sector. The bubble of the sub-prime mortgage lending had surfaced as the major indicator of things that had gone wrong and in that sense the response to the crisis was a response to the search for financial stability. Not achieving this financial stability was perceived to be the result of market failure in the private sector and in the larger global economy. In the large countries of the world it resulted from bad regulation and poor bank capitalisation.

Soon it was discovered that this was only at the surface and within the second round, the issue of financial solvency began to show its head, sovereign debt and fiscal deficits emerged. The locus of the articulation of this crisis moved from the private sector to the public sector. The issue moved from market failure to lack of having built-in market confidence that is currently engaging the entire global leadership. But even before a credible solution appeared, a third dimension of this crisis emerged – financial sustainability, which goes beyond the private and public sectors, engaging the national economies of the world. Financial sustainability goes beyond market failure and market confidence into the need for market discipline. A discussion has emerged on the exchange rate levels and regime and the phenomenon of currency realignment in response to world global imbalance. In addition, the source of exposure really comes from the imbalance between gross assets and gross liabilities.

Impact of the Global Financial Crisis

How has the global financial crisis affected the Caribbean region and the Latin American space? Clearly, the Caribbean is neither isolated nor insulated. While some have argued that the Caribbean countries are innocent bystanders in this whole phenomenon, this is not so. We live in a world that is very interconnected, and when Lehman Brothers fell in New York, so too the largest insurance company in the Caribbean, located in Trinidad and Tobago, almost collapsed. This affected over 10% of Trinidad and Tobago's GDP. In the Caribbean, it affected over 17% of GDP.[2]

The Latin American region however,has shown resilience and the recent report from the Economic Commission for Latin America and the Caribbean (ECLAC) and the development committee of the OECD had this to say about Latin America:

> Latin America's solid economic performance since 2003 has created the possibility for transformation of the state enabling the adoption of ambitious public policies that lock in the prospects of long-term development and mitigate short term risk.[3]

Trinidad and Tobago and the rest of the Caribbean remains very fragile and suspect to external shocks; the Caribbean has always lived with external shocks. Trinidad and Tobago does have immense impact on the small Caribbean economies. Trinidad and Tobago has been able to retain a solid macroeconomic performance, the debt to GDP ratio is just over 36% of our GDP. The relationship between reserves, international reserves and GDP is very high despite fiscal deficits. Substantial reserves in the stabilisation fund have allowed the country to escape some of the problems in the first round. [4]

Response to a Protracted Slowdown

In this, our part of the world that is open and does not have the benefit of large domestic demand, we have to wonder whether this will be a protracted slowdown and will we have the ability to handle it?

We cannot measure fiscal sustainability solely on the basis of arithmetic ratios in finance as practiced by many of the rating agencies. As we search for a way forward to deal with a potential protracted slowdown and a continuing deepening of the financial crisis in the global economy, our imperatives are three fold: the flexibility to adjust, the resilience to cope, and the capacity to employ buffers.

Unlike large economies who would have time and mass, small economies in the Caribbean have neither and therefore flexibility to adjust has to be a daily resolve. Whether adjustment involves revenue and expenditure, or changes in regulatory adherence, it is important to measure financial sustainability by the capacity to have flexibility to adjust.

The resilience to cope brings into play the narrow economic and the larger political issues. The best safeguard to this resilience has to do with addressing inequality of incomes in the country. In the final analysis, that is the source of resilience.

Are there enough resources put away for the rainy day? Unfortunately, many Caribbean countries are devoid of the capacity to employ buffers. However, Trinidad and Tobago, some time ago, established a heritage and stabilisation fund – a wealth fund. It represents just near to 20% of the GDP in active resources. Still, it is a visible buffer that provides a sense of security for the future.[5] More important for the Caribbean region is the issue of external buffers; buffers that are put into place by institutions like the IMF which provide lines of credit to economies facing external shocks. But such buffers are inadequate to the problems not only of the Caribbean but of many small economies worldwide.

It is for that reason that Trinidad and Tobago took the initiative recently to start a conversation with the IMF to ensure that small economies are given an active political presence in the deliberations of such bodies. We live in an interconnected world, one in which the periphery may have significant ripple effects on the centre, as Greece and Iceland have shown within recent times.[6] The core countries are at greater risk as they are holding more of the periphery countries' assets. This linkage should be a greater focal point for research.

The Missing Links in Development

The last time when there was a serious attempt by international bodies to look at the future of the global economy was in 2008. The World Bank Commission produced the *Growth Report* of 2008.[7] But the *Growth Report* did not in any way anticipate or articulate the problems of the turbulence ahead.

There were missing links in this articulation of the global paradigm. One such missing link in the search for development was the exclusion of the politics of development. We cannot exclude the politics of development from the search for that development. Secondly, the prescription for inclusive growth has been without a strategy for basic development. Inclusive development does not necessarily provide basic development in society.

A New Leadership Challenge

The time has come for a new leadership to search for a new paradigm for development; one that will identify *political logic and economic logic*; one that would construct new measures for financial sustainability; and one that will design a strategy for basic development that puts equity at the centre.

We know that we need to build a competitive world. How can we arrive at the global and regional compacts based on policy coordination in a period of market convergence? This is an issue that should bring together the public sector and the private sector in order to find the right compacts. Recent attempts by leaders in the European Union failed to produce an enforceable fiscal compact to support the monetary union. While this is happening in Europe, global leaders in South Africa[8] came together at the United Nations Framework Convention on Climate

Change to draft a global compact on climate change following the Kyoto Protocol.

The compacts have already begun to show cracks: the UK's decision not to be party to the European Union treaty and Canada's withdrawal from the Kyoto Protocol. In spite of the challenges to such regional and global compacts, in today's world, it is necessary to arrive at such compacts in order to mitigate against the risks that are globally generated.

Can we build a consensus on changing the global financial architecture and do so within a political framework like the G20? In today's interconnected world we may find that even that wider political framework is not sufficient to build consensus. To achieve consensus is to build on the politics of the situation. The technical arguments are persuasive but the political will to adhere to such solutions is critically important. Trinidad and Tobago has begun to seek that space in the global financial architectures.[9]

The most important question has emerged out of the Delhi Economic Conclave in 2011.[10] Is a financial crisis really a reflection of the deeper development crisis? Are we treating the financial stability issue? Are we treating the solvency issue? Or should we treat the sustainability issue?

This requires us to drill deeper into development. This is where the real challenge lies. This conclusion should be a turning point in the intellectual pursuit of the search for that paradigm. It is useful to think out-of-the-box and search for the space within which new solutions can be found that are sustainable and anchored in the issues of inequality in our society and jobless growth.

In the Caribbean and Latin America we look to the future; we look to the countries in the Far East and countries in Asia, like China and India. Together with the advanced countries of North America and Europe, we should articulate new thinking to ensure that smaller economies like ours do not have to be mere bystanders in this scenario.

This is a global challenge in leadership, the world is waiting for its leaders to show them the way forward.

Notes

1. Based on a speech by Winston Dookeran, delivered at the Inaugural Session of the Confederation of Indian Industry, Delhi Economic Conclave, December 10–17, 2011 New Delhi.
2. Based on the feature address by Winston Dookeran to the Caribbean Association for Audit Committee Members (CAACM) at their fifth annual general meeting and conference, July 13, 2011.
3. ECLAC, Latin American Economic Outlook 2012, Transforming the State of Development, p.7.
4. Budget Statement 2012: From Steady Foundation to Economic Transformation, presented by Minister of Finance, Winston Dookeran, October 10, 2011.
5. Ibid.
6. Based on the Statement by Winston Dookeran on the election of the new Managing Director of the IMF, June 17, 2011, addressed to Mr Paulo Nogueira Batista, Executive Director, IMF.
7. The Growth Report, Strategies for Sustained Growth and Inclusive Development, Commissioned by the International Bank for Reconstruction and Development/The World Bank (2008), Office of the Publisher, The World Bank, Washington.
8. The United Nations Climate Change Conference, Durban 2011, delivered a breakthrough on the international community's response to climate change. www.//unfcc.int/meeting/durban_nov_2011
9. See Statement by Winston Dookeran on the election of the new Managing Director of the IMF, June 17, 2011, addressed to Mr Paulo Nogueira Batista, Executive Director, IMF.
10. Inaugural Session of the Confederation of Indian Industry, Delhi Economic Conclave, December 10–17, 2011 New Delhi.

INDEX